ABRAHAM LINCOLN, CONSTITUTIONALISM, AND EQUAL RIGHTS IN THE CIVIL WAR ERA

Abraham Lincoln, Constitutionalism, and Equal Rights in the Civil War Era

by

HERMAN BELZ

Fordham University Press
New York
1998

Copyright © 1998 by FORDHAM UNIVERSITY PRESS
All rights reserved.
ISBN 0-8232-1768-X (*hardcover*)
ISBN 0-8232-1769-8 (*paperback*)
ISSN 1089-8719
LC 97-9935

The North's Civil War, No. 2

Library of Congress Cataloging-in-Publication Data

Belz, Herman
    Abraham Lincoln, constitutionalism, and equal rights in the Civil
War era / by Herman Belz.
       p.   cm.—(The North's Civil War, ISSN 1089-8719 ; no. 2)
    Includes bibliographical references and index.
    ISBN 0-8232-1768-X (hardcover).—ISBN 0-8232-1769-8
(pbk.)
      1. Lincoln, Abraham, 1809–1865—Views on the Constitution.
2. United States—Politics and government—1861–1865. 3. United
States—Constitutional history. 4. Afro-Americans—Civil
rights—History—19th century. 5. Equality before the law—United
States—History—19th century. 6. Reconstruction. I. Title.
II. Series.
E457.2.B38   1998
973.7—dc21
                                              97-9935
                                              CIP

Printed in the United States of America

CONTENTS

ACKNOWLEDGMENTS

The following permissions for republication are gratefully acknowledged:

The Louis A. Warren Lincoln Library and Museum, Fort Wayne, Indiana: *Lincoln and the Constitution: The Dictatorship Question Reconsidered* (1984).

The Abraham Lincoln Association, Springfield, Illinois, and the University of Illinois Press: "The 'Philosophical Cause' of 'Our Free Government and Consequent Prosperity': The Problem of Lincoln's Political Thought," in *Journal of the Abraham Lincoln Association*, 10 (1988–89).

The Review of Politics: "Abraham Lincoln and American Constitutionalism," 50 (1988).

The Journal of Southern History: "Protection of Personal Liberty in Republican Emancipation Legislation of 1862," 42 (1976).

Civil War History: "Race, Law, and Politics in the Struggle for Equal Pay during the Civil War," 22 (1976); and "The Freedmen's Bureau Act of 1865 and the Principle of No Discrimination According to Color," 21 (1975).

Reviews in American History: "The New Orthodoxy in Reconstruction Historiography," 1 (1973).

Benchmark: A Quarterly Review of the Constitution and the Courts: "Equality and the Fourteenth Amendment: The Original Understanding," 4 (1990).

Louisiana State University Press: "The Constitution and Reconstruction," in Eric Anderson and Alfred A. Moss, Jr., eds., *The Facts of Reconstruction: Essays in Honor of John Hope Franklin* (1991).

PREFACE

In a society responsive to momentary fads and impulses, the American people's continuing fascination with the Civil War can be taken as a sign of cultural stability. Popular interest in the war has a universal dimension, reflecting the ability of citizens in modern times to recognize and appreciate the timeless virtues of courage, honor, duty, and sacrifice. Fully to understand the place the war occupies in American memory, however, it is necessary to consider the historical context in which it occurred and its significance as a constitutive national experience. The Civil War exerts the powerful hold that it does on the public imagination because it is the central event in American history.

The Civil War resolved ambiguity about the nature of the Union that in the course of the slavery controversy became intolerably divisive. It determined the direction of national development according to the northern understanding of the principles, forms, and institutions for which the Revolution was fought and the Constitution established in 1787. The war is the pivotal event in American history in two distinct yet related senses. First, at the level of political principle and perhaps for all time, the war tested the territorial-institutional integrity of the United States as a nation. In constitutional terms, it marked a showdown between the principles of states' rights and national supremacy. Yet, titanic as the conflict was, it was not the ultimate showdown between these principles. Although the war altered the terms of the federal–state relationship, it did not eliminate competition and conflict between the states and the national government as a basic ground of American politics.

The second sense in which the Civil War is the central event in American history concerns race relations and civil rights policy. Slavery and race were involved in the making of the Constitution and the creation of the Union. The extent to which slavery and race were constitutive of the nation and defined its political character and identity was left in dispute by the Founding Fathers. The Civil War settled the question whether the existence of slavery was consistent with republican government. In doing so it gave rise, in the constitutional amendments and partisan politics of Reconstruction, to the issue of race relations and civil rights as a basic structural feature of American politics.

Although the civil rights question was subordinated from the end of Reconstruction through the New Deal, it became an issue of great urgency in American politics and society after World War Two. Similarly, the issue of states' rights *vs.* national supremacy, although at one time thought to have been conclusively settled by the New Deal, has been revived in recent years as New Deal programs have come under attack. If states' rights is to become a fully legitimate and constructive concept in national politics, however, its advocates will have to show its theoretical and practical relationship to the rights of individuals. The principle of states' rights, in other words, will have to overcome its historical association with slavery, racism, and racial discrimination.

Since 1860, when the South seceded to protect slavery, states' rights have been viewed, not without reason, as a pretext for racial subordination of black citizens by white. By the same historical token, the federal government, because it abolished slavery, has been presumed to be the ultimate protector of liberty, equality, and individual civil rights. In the post–New Deal era of disenchantment with centralized national supremacy, however, which is also the era of federally mandated affirmative action policies that confer benefits on members of protected racial groups, these assumptions may need reexamination.

This book seeks to illuminate the Civil War and Reconstruction as a constitutive national experience that in critical respects established the ground of modern American politics. Most of the essays have been previously published and appear here in revised form. The introduction and conclusion have not previously been published.

Research for this book has been generously supported by the Earhart Foundation, the Social Philosophy and Policy Center at Bowling Green State University, the American Bar Foundation, and the General Research Board of the University of Maryland. I acknowledge this support with deep gratitude. I am especially grateful for scholarly criticism and insight provided by Michael Les Benedict, Mark E. Neely, Jr., Phillip Shaw Paludan, James McClellan, and Paul Moreno. I am indebted to Dr. Paul Cimbala, editor of Fordham University Press's The North's Civil War series, for suggesting publication of this book and for his thoughtful and constructive editorial judgment. Finally I wish to thank Dr. Mary Beatrice Schulte, Executive Editor of Fordham University Press, for the expertise, energy, and good will with which she guided preparation of the manuscript.

HERMAN BELZ

Introduction: Constitution and Revolution in the Civil War Era

THE UNITED STATES IS A REVOLUTIONARY NATION that lacks a tradition of revolutionary politics. In assuming the status of an independent people, Americans created republican governments and institutionalized the principles of the American Revolution in written constitutions of liberty. The purpose of republican constitutions was to enable the people to change their government through peaceful means of political persuasion rather than the methods of force and violence traditionally associated with changes of government. American political history is the story of reform movements and political realignments, not violent revolutionary transformations.[1]

If revolutionary violence has not been part of the American political tradition, the language of American politics nevertheless makes free use of the concept of revolution. Political reform movements as diverse as Jeffersonian democracy, New Deal liberalism, and Reagan-Republican conservatism have been characterized as revolutionary in nature. One is inclined to say that Americans' success in domesticating the right of revolution in the forms and procedures of constitutionalism has given them—or pundits and professors who analyze politics on their behalf—a license to employ the vocabulary of revolution loosely and imprecisely, if not irresponsibly.

In view of the significance of the right of revolution in modern political thought, however, greater precision should be used in describing and analyzing revolution as a form of political action. Moreover, if it is a requirement of historical analysis to understand historical actors as they understood themselves, as I believe it is, then it is important to determine whether political action that is

---

[1] Richard J. Ellis, *American Political Cultures* (New York: Oxford University Press, 1993), pp. 151–75.

described as revolutionary was in fact conceived and undertaken with revolutionary intent. In the light of these considerations, it is necessary to distinguish between the definition of revolution as the deliberate overthrowing of an established political or social order, and its definition as any alteration of great magnitude in a situation or institution, irrespective of purpose and intent. Although in early modern politics the idea of revolution originally retained the meaning of revolving back or restoring things to their preordained natural order, in its accepted modern meaning revolution refers to conscious and deliberate agency aimed at establishing a new political or social order.[2]

Liberal political theory recognizes a right of revolution to alter or abolish any form of government when it becomes destructive of the ends for which it was created. Acknowledging this right, modern liberalism interprets American history in practical terms as the successful realization of a nonrevolutionary reform tradition.[3] This does not mean, as was believed a generation ago, that liberal political culture lacks significant conflict and can be understood simply as the result of consensus on fundamental principles.[4] It is nevertheless true that liberalism, both as political theory and as historical interpretation, has difficulty accounting for the single greatest conflict in American history. This was the sectional conflict over slavery, race relations, and the nature of the Union which precipitated the Civil War.

In the view of citizen and scholar alike, the Civil War has been perceived as an event of such magnitude, so exceptional to the general internal peace that has been the context of American political development, that it must in some sense be regarded as revolutionary in nature.[5] Considered from the standpoint of revolution, how-

---

[2] Hannah Arendt, *On Revolution* (New York: Viking Press, 1963), pp. 13–36.

[3] Louis Hartz, *The Liberal Tradition in America* (New York: Harcourt, Brace, 1955).

[4] See Ellis, *American Political Cultures.*

[5] A recent study of the constitutional amendment process reflects this perception. Discussing the constitutional problem of slavery and federalism, David E. Kyvig writes: "Not surprisingly, the amendment process, a mechanism whose successful functioning was predicated on shared assumptions and goals, could not resolve a conflict so deep that it would eventually lead to civil war. Amendment declined during the antebellum era because most other problems could be dealt with by the lesser means of ordinary legislation, executive determination, or judicial review; the truly monumental constitutional problem of the age could be settled only by revolution" (*Explicit and Authentic Acts: Amending the U.S. Constitution, 1776–1995* [Lawrence: University Press of Kansas, 1996], p. 134).

ever, it is unclear whether the war is to be seen as a deliberate political action by intending agents, or the result of an impersonal historical process—the equivalent in human affairs of an act of nature that indiscriminately sweeps away or transforms all that it touches. If the war was a consciously conceived revolutionary action, moreover, it is unclear whether the revolutionary agents were northern antislavery agitators seeking to destroy slavery and the social order it supported, or southern defenders of slavery seeking to establish political and constitutional guarantees for the peculiar institution.

Difficulty in determining which section, if any, was the revolutionary side in the Civil War is in considerable part owing to ambiguity about the nature of the Union in the antebellum period. This theoretical issue, debated since the ratification of the Constitution, was of the greatest practical moment since the scope and content of federal authority depended on the answer given it. Was the Union a political association of states in the nature of a compact, or a union of individuals in the nature of a sovereign nation-state? If the former, Republican and antislavery partisans who went to war to prevent the southern states from seceding were revolutionaries overthrowing the voluntary union of the founders. If the Union was the sovereign government of a unitary people, secession was a revolutionary act intended to overthrow the legitimate government of the nation.

After the war began, the question of revolutionary aims arose with respect to northern political action, in particular that of Radical Republicans referred to as "Jacobins" by their opponents. Lincoln adverted to this issue in his December 1861 annual message, expressing concern that policy disputes about how to suppress the rebellion "not degenerate into a remorseless revolutionary struggle."[6] Confederate political action, aimed at securing southern independence, was revolutionary primarily in the sense of completing the secession process by establishing an independent national government. In the thinking of the Confederates and other nineteenth-century observers, the model for this type of revolution—as a war of national liberation—existed in the secession of the American colonies from the British Empire in the Revolutionary War. The question of revolution might also arise in domestic Confederate politics, to

---

[6] Roy P. Basler, et al., eds., *The Collected Works of Abraham Lincoln*, 9 vols. (New Brunswick, N.J.: Rutgers University Press, 1953–1955), 5:49.

the extent that the war effort tended toward the establishment of a centralized government at the expense of states' rights. Furthermore, if it was true, as Lincoln stated in his December 1862 annual message, that the land that Americans occupied could not be divided, demanded union, and "would, ere long, force reunion," then a Confederate victory might bring about such a reconstruction of the American Union as would revolutionize northern political institutions.[7]

After the defeat of the Confederacy, the question of revolutionary politics concerned the program of the Republican party for reuniting the country. In this context was raised the issue of reconstructing the Union. Would Reconstruction be undertaken according to the design of the original Constitution, with reforms necessitated by the destruction of slavery, or would it involve a revolutionary transformation of the federal system and the creation of a consolidated national government?

Although perception of the Civil War as a revolutionary experience was contemporaneous with the conflict, not until the early twentieth century did serious historiographical discussion of the problem begin. In their monument to progressive history, *The Rise of American Civilization* (1927), Charles A. Beard and Mary R. Beard gave powerful expression to the idea in a chapter entitled "The Second American Revolution." Noting the unresolved controversy over the nature of the war reflected in the names given the conflict—War of the Rebellion, War Between the States, War for Southern Independence—the Beards objected that all of these descriptions used misleading symbols. What was misleading was the overemphasis on military force in determining the final outcome. According to the Beards, the armed conflict was the result of accidents of climate, soil, and geography; it was but "a transitory phase" of the cataclysm, incidental to its real nature. The "intrinsic character" of the struggle was that of a revolution: a "social war" in which capitalists, laborers, and farmers of the north and west drove the planting aristocracy from power in the national government, destroyed slavery, and directed the nation in the course of industrial development. The "so-called civil war was in reality the Second American Revolution," concluded the Beards, "and in a strict sense the First."[8]

---

[7] Ibid., 5:29.

[8] Charles A. Beard and Mary R. Beard, *The Rise of American Civilization* II (New York: Macmillan, 1930), pp. 53–54.

Although their thesis identified northern capitalists as revolutionaries, Charles and Mary Beard recognized the equivocal nature of the evidence. This appeared in their description of southern leaders' confusion about the "ethical character" of secession and the establishment of the Confederacy. While some southerners justified secession as the exercise of a constitutional right, others defended it as an act of revolution. Only later, when their cause appeared doomed, did Confederate leaders place greater emphasis on secession as a constitutional and legal right. Echoing the view of both contemporary observers and theorists of the right of revolution, the Beards wrote: "Triumphant revolution carries its own moral justification; a revolution suppressed wears another aspect."[9]

The social revolution in the North which the Beards described was the result of a transcendent historical process rather than the deliberate design of intentional political action. It was "the essential, portentous outcome" of fighting that was itself but "a fleeting incident" viewed "under the light of universal history." In the Beards' account, "the core of the vortex" lay "in the flowing substance of things"—in matters of finance, commerce, capital, industry, railways, and agriculture, as well as in provisions of constitutional law. In the crisis of the Union, "not one statesman foresaw the immediate future or read correctly the handwriting on the wall. All were caught up and whirled in a blast too powerful for their wills, too swift for their mental operations." "The physical combat that punctuated the conflict merely hastened the inevitable."[10]

To the extent that they were Marxist economic determinists, progressive historians like the Beards may have considered the Second American Revolution historically necessary. That did not mean, however, that it was a good revolution from the standpoint of social philosophy. On the contrary, the capitalist triumph marked by the Civil War threatened the existence of political and economic democracy in the United States. So strong was this implied normative judgment that, in a relative sense, the revolutionary thesis was sympathetic to the southern planter class because it resisted northern capitalism. In the perspective of Civil War historiography, the revolutionary interpretation called into question the basic nationalist judgment that

---

[9] Ibid., p. 69.
[10] Ibid., pp. 54, 62.

the war was a good war because it preserved the nation and abolished slavery.[11]

The practical implication of the Second American Revolution thesis for contemporary politics was to challenge progressive reformers to overcome the antidemocratic consequences of the triumph of big business. The Great Depression, an event as catastrophic and disruptive in its own way as the Civil War, created a situation in which a good revolution—a revolution to establish social democracy—was seen as a real possibility. The old order of laissez-faire capitalism having been swept away by the economic collapse, the New Deal was perceived in revolutionary terms as establishing a collectivist social philosophy in place of the discredited individualist public philosophy of the Second American Revolution.

As in social philosophy, so in constitutional terms, too, the New Deal Revolution rejected the legacy of the Civil War. The New Dealers' most obvious departure from the constitutional experience of the Civil War was to try to establish their revolution without formal amendment of the Constitution. Whether they considered themselves radicals or conservatives, Republican lawmakers in the Civil War era took the Constitution seriously, using the Article V amendment process to expand the powers of the federal government. In contrast, the creation of the New Deal regulatory state depended on judicial review and revisionist interpretation of constitutional law. New Deal liberalism appealed to the nationalism of Chief Justice John Marshall and the public-interest regulatory interventionism of Chief Justice Roger B. Taney. Far from a source of inspiration, the Civil War as a revolutionary experience was something to be transcended or ignored. The Civil War amendments were an unpleasant reminder of the trauma of Reconstruction, and if ever seriously enforced according to their original intent posed a threat to the power of the Democratic party in the South.

In the world of historical scholarship the meaning of the Civil War for the political culture of the New Deal was reflected in the interpretation of the war as a "needless conflict." Self-consciously identifying themselves as "revisionists," many liberal historians concluded that if modern capitalism was the result of the Second American Revolution, the Civil War served no fundamentally useful social

---

[11] Thomas J. Pressly, *Americans Interpret Their Civil War* (New York: Collier Books, 1962), pp. 242–44.

purpose. Unlike the Beards, revisionists were unwilling to view the question of Civil War causation in impersonal historicist terms. They blamed the war on a "blundering generation" of politicians whose partisanship and opportunism blinded them to the possibility of compromise. Although not overtly proslavery, the revisionists were willing to accept the continued existence of slavery that a war-avoiding compromise would have permitted. In their view, as in the Beardian interpretation, slavery was simply not a fundamental issue in the sectional conflict.

During World War II and the Cold War, the significance of slavery in American history began to appear in a different light. The progressive–revisionist evaluation of the Civil War as a revolutionary experience changed accordingly. In the struggle against Nazi and Communist tyranny, the value of capitalist industrial production and sovereign national authority for the defense of liberty was apparent. The struggle against tyranny in world politics in turn focused attention on a moral–political conflict in American politics for which the Civil War was of the utmost relevance and significance. This was the struggle of black Americans for citizenship and equal rights.[12]

In the 1950s and 1960s the civil rights movement was a political and legal effort to enforce constitutional guarantees established in Reconstruction, and for generations nullified in the South with the acquiescence of the national government. The movement could be described as revolutionary only in an expressive sense, to convey the magnitude of the goal of breaking down unlawful discriminatory barriers that only a short while before had seemed impregnable. Starting in the late 1960s, however, with the onset of affirmative action, the civil rights movement entered a more seriously revolutionary phase. This was signified in the transformation of the Reconstruction principle of individual equality of opportunity into the theory of racial and ethnic group equality of result. Furthermore, although implemented by judicial orders and administrative regulations, affirmative action was established in conditions of civil discord and social unrest more widespread than any since the Civil War. To that extent the revolutionary transformation of civil rights principles signified by affirmative action depended on force and violence.[13]

---

[12] Gunnar Myrdal's famous study of race relations, *An American Dilemma* (1944), marks the emergence of the civil rights issue in modern American politics.

[13] John David Skrentny, *The Ironies of Affirmative Action: Politics, Culture, and Justice in America* (Chicago: The University of Chicago Press, 1996), pp. 67–110.

Using the descriptive popular sense of the term, in the context of the civil rights "revolution" of the 1960s the idea of the Civil War as a revolutionary experience took on a meaning far different from progressive historians' understanding of the Second American Revolution. Simply stated: if the Civil War was a revolution, it was a good revolution because it transformed the status of the country's black population under national civil rights guarantees. The Reconstruction amendments that were intended to protect the permanent freedom of black citizens could be seen as revolutionizing the constitutional order, authorizing the federal government to exercise whatever power might be necessary to secure black liberty and equality.[14] Moreover, the Civil War could be viewed as an authentic revolutionary experience in which the slaves emancipated themselves. New interpretations of social history argued that in the upheaval caused by the war, the slaves abandoned their owners and entered Union army lines, thereby putting pressure on the Lincoln administration to adopt a policy of military emancipation and make the abolition of slavery a goal of the war.[15]

As the affirmative action phase of the civil rights revolution progressed, the Civil War came to be seen as a total war, the first such event in modern history. A people's contest requiring the full mobilization of society and economy, it was an ideological struggle revolving around slavery which fulfilled the abolitionist goal of a human rights revolution. In the Reconstruction amendments and civil rights laws, the war established, on behalf of black citizens, claims on American society for social justice that remained unfulfilled in the late twentieth century.[16] The war as a revolutionary experience was seen as giving the country a new constitution.[17] The corollary of this development was that the original Constitution, because it sanctioned slavery as a form of property, was judged to be corrupt. And corrupt also because associated with slavery were the founders' ideas

---

[14] Robert J. Kaczorowski, "To Begin the Nation Anew: Congress, Citizenship, and Civil Rights After the Civil War," *American Historical Review*, 92 (1987), 45–68.

[15] Ira Berlin et al., *Slaves No More: Three Essays on Emancipation and the Civil War* (Cambridge: Cambridge University Press, 1992).

[16] Eric T. Dean, Jr., "Rethinking the Civil War: Beyond 'Revolutions,' 'Reconstructions,' and the 'New Social History,'" *Southern Historian*, 15 (1994), 28–50.

[17] David A. J. Richards, *Conscience and the Constitution: History, Theory, and Law of the Reconstruction Amendments* (Princeton, N.J.: Princeton University Press, 1993); Bruce Ackerman, *We the People: Foundations* (Cambridge, Mass.: The Belknap Press of Harvard University Press, 1991).

of liberty and property. These concepts required revolutionary transformation, not merely resynthesis or reconstruction.[18]

As traditionally understood, the basic principles of American constitutionalism are the natural rights of individuals, property rights and free enterprise, limited government, the rule of law, and a federal division of sovereignty between the general government and the states. This constitutionalism can be described as revolutionary in the sense that its principles and values emerged and were given institutional expression in the era of the American Revolution. In the historiography inspired by the affirmative action revolution, by contrast, the constitutionalism of the Civil War and Reconstruction is revolutionary in a substantive sense. It authorizes the exercise of unlimited national power to achieve unlimited, open-ended goals of liberty and equality.

Civil War revolutionary constitutionalism, as the accounts of its recent historiographical expounders recognize, did not announce itself as such in explicit and unequivocal terms. On their face, the Civil War amendments appeared to modify the federal system by extending citizenship and civil rights on nonracial terms to a class of persons—the black population—who in practical terms had previously been excluded from American citizenship. The real meaning of Civil War constitutionalism, according to the civil rights version of the Second American Revolution thesis, was revealed in the concept of racial identity.

In affirmative action constitutionalism, and in the Civil War revolutionary constitutionalism that is adduced as its historical foundation, race is a reasonable classification for public-policy purposes. The key to its significance is that it provides a dispensation or exemption from constitutional limitations which the Reconstruction amendments otherwise appear to recognize. Not apparent in the text of the amendments, this racial dispensation is conferred by history. It exists as the obvious inference to be drawn from knowledge of the historical situation—the fact that slavery was the cause of the Civil War, emancipation was the aim of the war and a higher goal than preserving the Union, and the abolition of slavery and guaran-

---

[18] Raymond T. Diamond, "No Call to Glory: Thurgood Marshall's Thesis on the Intent of a Pro-Slavery Constitution," *Vanderbilt Law Review*, 42 (1989), 93–131; Vincent Gordon Harding, "Wrestling Toward the Dawn: The Afro-American Freedom Movement and the Changing Constitution," *Journal of American History*, 74 (1987), 718–39.

tee of the permanent freedom and equality of black Americans was the purpose of the Reconstruction amendments. In civil rights revolutionary constitutionalism the assumption is implicit—until the point is reached where it must be made explicit—that *black* civil rights are the object and rationale of the new constitution. The authority of the national government can accordingly be exercised to any extent necessary to secure black claims to liberty and equality. This racial dispensation transforms the limited-government, rule-of-law constitutionalism of the Founding into a constitutionalism of unlimited national power in pursuit of open-ended revolutionary goals.[19]

The essays in this book address three issues of fundamental importance in the interpretation of the Civil War and Reconstruction as a revolution.[20] First is the question of Lincoln's statesmanship, which I consider in relation to his exercise of the executive power, his political thought, and his construction of the Constitution. The rev-

---

[19] The constitutional significance of the Civil War is now routinely explained in revolutionary terms as the removal of limitations on the power of the national government. David E. Kyvig illustrates when he writes of the Civil War: "Thereafter it [the Constitution] no longer would be thought of as a confining set of specific authorizations but as a grant of authority adequate to sanction a broad range of reasonable government actions" (*Explicit and Authentic Acts*, p. 478). Even more potent national authority results when the affirmative action dispensation is introduced into constitutional law, making race a reasonable classification for legislation and public policy.

[20] The revolutionary nature of the Civil War and Reconstruction has been dealt with in numerous articles and essays, though not in a comprehensive and systematic historical account. Among the more useful discussions of the problem are Barrington Moore, Jr., "The American Civil War: The Last Capitalist Revolution," a chapter in his *Social Origins of Dictatorship and Democracy* (Boston: Beacon, 1966); Raimondo Luraghi, "The Civil War and the Modernization of American Society: Social Structure and Industrial Revolution in the Old South Before and During the Civil War," *Civil War History*, 18 (1972), 230–50; Eric Foner, "The Causes of the American Civil War: Recent Interpretations and New Directions," ibid., 20 (1974), 197–214; Joseph A. Stromberg, "The War for Southern Independence: A Radical Libertarian Perspective," *Journal of Libertarian Studies*, 3 (1979), 31–54; Peyton McCrary, "The Party of Revolution: Republican Ideas About Politics and Social Change, 1862–1867," *Civil War History*, 30 (1984), 330–50; James M. McPherson, *Abraham Lincoln and the Second American Revolution* (New York: Oxford University Press, 1991), which contains two essays arguing the revolutionary thesis. In contrast to this body of writing, it is worth noting that Phillip Shaw Paludan, *"A People's Contest": The Union and Civil War, 1861-1865* (New York: Harper & Row, 1988), makes no reference to the Civil War as a revolution. He employs the concept of the "Second American System" in describing social and economic changes during the Civil War.

olutionary interpretation of the Civil War does not necessarily require that Lincoln be viewed as a revolutionist. In the Beards' account, for example, Lincoln was "no dictator standing for a triumphant majority," but a man of moderate temperament, a practical and astute politician who was made an emancipator by circumstances and expediency rather than by his own initiative.[21] The thesis of a Second American Revolution is nevertheless more cogently argued when Lincoln is cast in the role of revolutionary leader, as he is in several recent interpretations.[22] My understanding of Lincoln questions this interpretation. A principal ground on which I do so is the fact that Lincoln conceived of his political thought and actions in constitutionalist rather than revolutionary terms.

Discussing the Civil War as a revolution, James M. McPherson observes that imprecision in defining the word 'revolution' has been the source of historiographical confusion in interpreting the conflict. McPherson proposes a common-sense definition of revolution as "the overthrow of the existing social and political order by internal violence."[23] In analyzing revolution historically as a type of political action, however, and in the light of political theory, it seems to me equally important to take into account the element of deliberate design and conscious intent. Is there, to take McPherson's definition, the purpose and intent to overthrow existing institutions? If the distinction between intentions and results is important in moral philosophy, it needs to be recognized also in historical evaluation of events where it forms an essential element in the political situation.[24] Considered in this light, Lincoln does not meet the test of revolutionary political action, surely not with respect to northern

---

[21] Beard and Beard, *Rise of American Civilization* II, pp. 63, 93.

[22] Otto H. Olson, "Abraham Lincoln as Revolutionary," *Civil War History*, 24 (1978), 213–24; James M. McPherson, *Abraham Lincoln and the Second American Revolution*, pp. 23–42; Garry Wills, *Lincoln at Gettysburg: The Words That Remade America* (New York: Simon & Schuster, 1992), pp. 20–39.

[23] McPherson, *Abraham Lincoln and the Second American Revolution*, pp. 14–16.

[24] A natural disaster that causes destruction might be said to have a 'revolutionary' impact, but is not understood as a revolution. So war, while it can have devastating effects that alter social conditions and institutions, has been distinguished from revolution both in history and in political theory. According to Hannah Arendt (*On Revolution*, pp. 2–9), war and revolution both involve violence, but are distinguished in theory and practice by different motives and purposes. Wars have traditionally been fought for conquest, expansion, defense of vested interests, and other considerations of power politics. Revolution, in contrast, is a modern concept that aims at the establishment of freedom by creating a new social and political order.

institutions and perhaps not even where southern institutions are concerned.

McPherson's interpretation of Lincoln as a revolutionary, when examined in relation to the element of self-understanding and conscious intent, takes on a curiously impersonal and historicist aspect. He concedes that Lincoln was no ideological revolutionary, like Robespierre or Lenin proposing a blueprint for a new society. The war itself, McPherson says, not the ideas of Lincoln, generated the radical momentum that caused it to become the Second American Revolution. The war—not Lincoln or other political leaders—determined the thrust and direction of the revolution. Lincoln was a "pragmatic revolutionary" whose strategy and sense of timing determined the pace of the revolution and ensured its success. As an historical event, the revolution occurred because "the Civil War snowballed into huge and unanticipated dimensions and took on a life and purpose of its own far beyond the causes that had started it." In this view, as the war became "a remorseless revolutionary conflict," Lincoln became a revolutionary leader.[25] I question the value of this revolutionary interpretation both as a contribution to historical understanding of Lincoln's statesmanship and constitutionalism and as a teaching concerning the nature of the American political tradition.

A second issue relevant to the war as a revolutionary experience is the nature and tendency of civil rights policy in the Civil War era. The revolutionary thesis argues that wartime emancipation, the abolition of slavery, and the conferral of citizenship upon blacks in the Reconstruction amendments fundamentally altered American society and revolutionized the constitutional order. In my view this thesis erroneously accepts the proslavery interpretation of the Constitution as the correct understanding of the disputed points concerning the constitutional status of slavery and the nature of the Union. The implication that proslavery constitutionalism was correct applies not merely at the level of empirical description of the actions of proslavery decision makers in the antebellum period, but also to the question of constitutional theory and principle. If the Civil War was a constitutional revolution, the Constitution before the war was in essence, form, and substance a proslavery document. This conclusion seems to me unfounded. I argue that wartime eman-

---

[25] McPherson, *Abraham Lincoln and the Second American Revolution*, pp. 32, 41–42.

cipation and the postwar prohibition of slavery did not revolutionize the constitutional system. Civil rights law and policy that emerged during the Civil War, and was given permanent shape during Reconstruction, signified a nonrevolutionary extension to black persons of guarantees of liberty and equality contained in the original Constitution. The establishment of national civil rights policy involved the extension of concepts of liberty and equality in the original Constitution that were in principle racially neutral, although limited in their practical application by prudential considerations and competition for power between the states in the federal system.

Reconstruction is the third basic component of the Second American Revolution thesis examined in this book. If the war was a revolution, then Reconstruction as a confirmation of the results of the war was by definition a revolutionary process. Although northern war aims were not revolutionary, it is true that at the end of the war conditions were sufficiently unsettled to constitute a potentially revolutionary situation. Under the circumstances, Reconstruction might have been projected with revolutionary purpose and intent. So unrevolutionary was the thinking of the Republican authors of Reconstruction policy, however—or so inconclusive and unformed any revolutionary aspirations they may have harbored—that they forced the defeated Confederates to exercise the right of consent and participate in the reconstruction of their own state governments. However inconsistent this policy may have been, after a decade of political turmoil a Reconstruction settlement was reached through legitimate, if controversial, political action that reflected more of constitutional continuity than revolutionary innovation.

To view the Civil War as a successful revolution, with Lincoln cast in the role of revolutionary leader, is to accept the southern interpretation of the conflict. Convinced that the Republican party was committed to destroying slavery in violation of the constitutional compact, southerners withdrew from the Union. Given the ambiguities of the antebellum constitutional order, secession could be justified as the exercise of a reserved or preconstitutional right of the states as sovereign political communities to defend themselves. In practical terms this was indistinguishable from the right of revolution that southerners also claimed. Under Lincoln's leadership, the Republican party resisted this claim of revolutionary right. Appealing to the principles of constitutionalism and the rule of law, Republicans were willing to use force to preserve the Union of the states, the federal government, existing private property relations and market structures, and the established social order, including slavery in the states where it existed. When it became clear that the prewar Union could not be fully restored and refounding would be necessary, Lincoln's purpose and intent were to reconstruct the Union more consistently and securely on the principles of the Founding. The War of the Rebellion, the name given the conflict by the Union government, was in reality a war against a belligerent people and government. It was not a revolution to transform the existing political and constitutional order or create a new one.

Americans take pride in their Revolution, a unique event that became the foundation and source of a nonrevolutionary political tradition. They take pride as well in the constitutions—the Articles of Confederation and the Constitution of 1787—by which they organized their national existence in peaceable political competition on the basis of Revolution principles. Americans might therefore be excused a tendency, in their political rhetoric, to join the concepts of revolution and constitution in the symbolic language of 'constitutional revolution' or revolutionary constitutionalism. Such language may serve the psychological function of permitting those who use it to bear witness to their revolutionary origins, while professing fidelity to the value of constitutionalism. For purposes of historical analysis, however, the idea of revolutionary constitutionalism obscures more than it illuminates about the American political tradition.

A revolution may issue in a new constitutional order, as the American Revolution did. The idea of a constitutional revolution, however, if it is more than a literary device for describing significant change according to prescribed forms and procedures, is a contradiction in terms. It obscures the fact that written constitutions in America were intended and have historically served as an effective substitute for revolutionary violence.

There was political controversy at the time, and there has been historical controversy since, over the revolutionary character of the Civil War as a political event. In part this is because war and revolution are historically related phenomena in which force and violence are both present. In the United States the relationship between war and revolution is complicated by the fact that, in the conflict between North and South, each section believed the other harbored a revolutionary purpose toward its institutions and was willing to go to war to defend itself.

The United States Constitution made provision for the conduct of war and anticipated cases of rebellion, insurrection, and domestic violence.[26] It neither anticipated nor provided for revolution, however, a political event that the framers considered beyond "any ordinary rules of calculation" and antithetical to the nature and purpose of constitutionalism.[27]

Considered in political terms, if the Civil War and Reconstruction were revolutionary, they were not constitutional. If they were constitutional, they were not revolutionary. It is impossible to know what would have happened to the United States and the U.S. Constitution if the Confederacy had won the Civil War. From the point of view of the Union government and public opinion, however, the historical evidence supports the conclusion that the Civil War, and its settlement in the events of Reconstruction, confirmed rather than revolutionized the American political tradition and the U.S. Constitution.

---

[26] U.S. Constitution, Art. I, section 8, section 9; Art. IV, section 4.

[27] *The Federalist Papers*, Introduction by Clinton Rossiter (New York: New American Library, 1961), pp. 118, 277.

1

Lincoln and the Constitution: The Dictatorship Question Reconsidered

A CONVENTION HAS GAINED ACCEPTANCE in American historiography which, in this Orwellian year that has come to symbolize totalitarian rule, it is fitting for us to consider. I refer to the convention that regards Abraham Lincoln not simply as a forceful war leader who demonstrated the vast power inherent in the presidency, but as a dictator, albeit in many accounts a benevolent and constitutional dictator. Lincoln, it is said, took the law into his own hands in meeting the attack on Fort Sumter and subsequently in dealing with the problems of internal security, emancipation, and Reconstruction. The author of a well-known treatise on emergency government in the Western political tradition states that "it was in the person of Abraham Lincoln that the constitutional dictatorship was almost completely reposed. . . ."[1] To be sure, some writers use the dictatorship convention in an expressive rather than analytical way to describe the growth of executive power during the Civil War. Moreover, although the characterization derives from contemporary attacks on Lincoln by the Confederate foe and the Democratic political opposition, it has not on the whole been applied with hostility. Yet it is fair to ask whether any description of Lincoln as a dictator—whether constitutional or otherwise—is accurate. As one who himself has employed the convention, I claim the privilege of reconsidering it. I do so not only with a view toward providing a more historically sound description of Lincoln's exercise of presidential power, but also in order to arrive at a clearer understanding of

---

An earlier version of this chapter was delivered on May 10, 1984, as the Seventh Annual R. Gerald McMurtry Lecture.

[1] Clinton Rossiter, *Constitutional Dictatorship: Crisis Government in the Modern Democracies* (Princeton, N.J.: Princeton University Press, 1948), p. 238.

the conception of constitutionalism that sustained his wartime leadership.

I

The dictatorship charge was directed at Lincoln at the start of the Civil War by both Confederates and northern Democrats who objected to the swift and decisive manner in which he placed the country on a war footing to resist secession. Some of Lincoln's actions, such as his calling up of the militia, were clearly covered by existing law. Other actions, such as his suspending the writ of habeas corpus, ordering an increase in the size of the regular army and navy, and directing that money be paid out of the treasury for war materials, were taken without authority of any existing national statute. Were these actions illegal, unconstitutional, and lawless? This became a bitterly disputed question in the early months of the war, and it aroused even more passionate controversy when Lincoln subsequently, under what he claimed was the war power of the government, imposed martial law in parts of the North, declared military emancipation in rebellious areas, and reorganized loyal state governments in the occupied South. Northern Democrats condemned these measures as the acts of a ruthless military dictator which undermined the Constitution and the rule of law. Southerners joined in the condemnation, and after the war clung to the view of Lincoln as a despot.[2]

Although in a much modified form, the dictatorship theme appears first to have found serious scholarly expression in the writing of William Archibald Dunning. In his pioneering *Essays on the Civil War and Reconstruction* (1897), Dunning described the emergence in 1861 of a revolutionary brand of constitutionalism that substituted popular demand for express legal mandate as the basis of executive action. Reviewing Lincoln's actions after the attack on Sumter, he wrote: "In the interval between April 12 and July 4, 1861, a new principle thus appeared in the constitutional system of the United States, namely, that of a temporary dictatorship. All the powers of government were virtually concentrated in a single department, and

---

[2] Michael Davis, *The Image of Lincoln in the South* (Knoxville: University of Tennessee Press, 1971), pp. 80, 130–33.

that the department whose energies were directed by the will of a single man." Dunning interpreted Lincoln's presidential dictatorship, approved by lawmakers and the electorate, as evidence that the idea of a government limited by "the written instructions of a past generation had already begun to grow dim in the smoke of battle." For Dunning and his followers the gravest departures from the old constitutional law and morality were perpetrated by Congress during Reconstruction, but the decline began with Lincoln's abrogation of constitutional limits in the name of military necessity and popular demand.[3]

Dunning's astringent analysis established the dictatorship question as a theme in historical writing on the Civil War. Historians' interest in the question in part represented an attempt to penetrate myths surrounding Lincoln's political career which had prevented it from being studied in a spirit of critical realism. The appeal of the dictatorship thesis also reflected the interest in strong executive leadership evinced by scholars and reformers in the progressive era. Whatever the reasons, scholarly opinion on Lincoln's exercise of power during the Civil War assumed points of view that have persisted to the present.

Three basic positions may be distinguished in the literature. The first, represented in the work of Dunning, adopted a critical if not openly hostile attitude toward the idea of presidential dictatorship. A second point of view, seen in the account of James Ford Rhodes, expressed critical approval of Lincoln's purportedly dictatorial actions. A third position viewed Lincoln's wartime dictatorship with unqualified approval, and was illustrated in the robust writing of John W. Burgess.

Whereas Dunning drew basically negative conclusions about constitutional dictatorship, James Ford Rhodes described Lincoln's exercise of war powers with qualified approval. In the third volume of his history, Rhodes said executive measures taken at the start of the war were "the acts of a Tudor rather than those of a constitutional ruler." Yet, while attributing despotic powers to Lincoln, he observed that "never had the power of dictator fallen into safer and nobler hands."[4] In his fourth volume Rhodes was more critical.

[3] William Archibald Dunning, *Essays on the Civil War and Reconstruction* (New York: Macmillan, 1904; repr. Harper & Row, 1965), pp. 20–21, 56–59.

[4] James Ford Rhodes, *History of the United States from the Compromise of 1850 to the Final Restoration of Home Rule at the South in 1877*, 7 vols. (New York: Macmillan, 1893–1900), 3:441–42.

Quoting at length from two of Lincoln's keenest critics, former Supreme Court Justice Benjamin R. Curtis and conservative legalist Joel Parker, he expressed disapproval of the arbitrary arrests and interference with freedom of the press for which Lincoln was responsible. The respect for the Constitution commonly ascribed to Lincoln, Rhodes suggested, had prevented the post-Civil War generation from appreciating "the enormity of the acts done under his authority." The historian also faulted Lincoln's defense of the government's policy in the famous Vallandigham affair as the argument of a clever attorney and politician, not that of a statesman. Nevertheless, Rhodes concluded on a favorable note, declaring that Lincoln was "no Caesar or Napoleon . . . sought no self-aggrandizement, . . . [and] had in his own loyal and unselfish nature a check to the excessive use of absolute power. . . ."[5]

Archnationalist John W. Burgess, not only acknowledging presidential dictatorship during the Civil War but also praising it as both wise and constitutional, represented a third point of view on the dictatorship question. Burgess agreed that certain of Lincoln's actions, such as his directing an increase in the size of the army and navy, contradicted express constitutional provisions. Yet, may not the President, he asked, "in accordance with the spirit of the Constitution, in time of invasion or rebellion . . . ask his fellow-countrymen to come to the armed support of the Government and the country"? Burgess regarded congressional approval of Lincoln's actions in 1861 as placing the President "practically in the position of a military dictator." And in his opinion this was "good political science and good public policy." A constitution that did not permit the exercise of extraordinary dictatorial power, he reasoned, invited violation in times of national crisis.[6] Burgess conceded, however, that the question of the President's temporary dictatorial powers was an unresolved constitutional problem.[7]

World War I stimulated further consideration of the dictatorship problem and reinforced the tendency to examine Lincoln in this

---

[5] Ibid., 4:169, 171, 234–35, 250.

[6] The same point was made by Sydney George Fisher in "The Suspension of Habeas Corpus During the War of the Rebellion," *Political Science Quarterly*, 3 (September 1888), 454–85. Fisher, thoroughly approving of Lincoln's actions, did not describe them as in any way dictatorial.

[7] John W. Burgess, *The Civil War and the Constitution*, 2 vols. (New York: Scribner's, 1901), 1:228, 232, 236.

light.[8] For some historians, critical realism demanded acknowledgment of Lincoln's successful exercise of dictatorial powers, tempered by doubts about the wisdom of such a course if attempted by less-gifted leaders. Nathaniel W. Stephenson, for example, examining the contradiction during the Civil War between the exercise of war powers and individual liberty, attributed to Lincoln the belief that in time of emergency the only recourse was to follow the Roman precedent and permit the use of extraordinary power. Lincoln's view, he concluded, was that democracy must learn to use the dictator as a necessary war tool. Yet it remained to be seen, Stephenson wrote in 1918, whether Lincoln's approach ought to become the model for democratic governments to follow.[9] In his *Constitutional Problems Under Lincoln* (1926), James G. Randall similarly recounted emergency executive actions during the war that went far beyond the normal sphere of presidential power. In Randall's view, Lincoln acted with notable restraint and leniency, and a high regard for individual liberty. Reflecting the growing acceptance of the despotism theme, he wrote apologetically: "If Lincoln was a dictator, it must be admitted that he was a benevolent dictator." Yet it was questionable, Randall concluded, whether in a democracy even a benevolent dictator ought to be encouraged.[10]

Randall explored the dictatorship problem more fully in a subsequent essay. Although accepting the analytical usefulness of the concept, he was concerned to draw distinctions between Lincoln's exercise of power and dictatorship as a phenomenon of twentieth-century politics. Randall conceded that in seeking legislative approval for emergency measures at the start of the war, Lincoln acted

---

[8] See Lindsay Rogers, "Presidential Dictatorship in the United States," *Quarterly Review*, 131 (1919); Henry Jones Ford, "The Growth of Dictatorship," *Atlantic Monthly*, 121 (1918), 632–40; Charles Warren, "Lincoln's 'Despotism' as Critics Saw It in 1861," *The New York Times*, May 12, 1918, section 5, p. 2. In 1923 John W. Burgess wrote a bitter lamentation concerning the growth of democratic Caesarism and the demise of limited government. Not surprisingly considering his Unionist background, yet perhaps significantly, he attributed none of this development to Lincoln, but rather saw Theodore Roosevelt as its source. See his *Recent Changes in American Constitutional Theory* (New York: Columbia University Press, 1923).

[9] Nathaniel W. Stephenson, *Abraham Lincoln and the Union* (New Haven, Conn.: Yale University Press, 1918), pp. 160–61. Reflecting the anti–Radical outlook of most historians at this time, Stephenson believed that the Radical Republicans in Congress presented a far more serious threat of dictatorship than Lincoln. See his *Lincoln* (Indianapolis and New York: Bobbs-Merrill, 1922).

[10] James G. Randall, *Constitutional Problems Under Lincoln*, rev. ed. (Urbana: University of Illinois Press, 1951), pp. 30–47.

in the manner of a dictator, and departed significantly from previous constitutional practice in the United States. Lincoln's exercise of power was tempered by humane liberal instincts, however, so that compared to contemporary examples his governing methods fell far short of genuine dictatorship. The principal difference between Lincoln and modern dictators, Randall pointed out, was that Lincoln used his extraordinary powers to save democracy, not to subvert it. Randall's judicious assessment, critical from the standpoint of traditional limited government yet ultimately approving of Lincoln, was echoed in other works of the 1930s and 1940s.[11]

In 1948 Clinton Rossiter, a political scientist, gave powerful reinforcement to the dictatorship theme in a comparative study of crisis government in England, France, Germany, and the United States. Reflecting the faith in executive power shared by many political scientists in the New Deal era, he argued that temporary conferral of absolute power on a single ruler was an essential feature of constitutional government. Rossiter recognized that federalism, the separation of powers, and civil liberties guarantees were major obstacles to the creation of constitutional dictatorship in the United States. The existence of a strong executive made it possible, however, and Lincoln's actions during the Civil War first demonstrated this truth. Acting "on no precedent and under no restraint," Lincoln, in Rossiter's view, "was the government of the United States" from the attack on Sumter until the convening of Congress three months later. Thereafter the President shared power with the legislature on many issues, but acted unilaterally as necessity demanded. "Lincoln's actions," Rossiter concluded, "form history's most illustrious precedent for constitutional dictatorship." Although Rossiter admitted that this precedent could be used for bad as well as good purposes, his endorsement of constitutional dictatorship was as enthusiastic and unapologetic as Burgess's fifty years earlier.[12]

Outside the "lost cause" tradition carried on by unrepentant Con-

---

[11] James G. Randall, "Lincoln in the Role of Dictator," *South Atlantic Quarterly*, 28 (July 1929), 236–52. Cf. Carl Russell Fish, *The American Civil War*, ed. William E. Smith (New York: Longmans, Green, 1937), p. 464; Homer C. Hockett, *The Constitutional History of the United States, 1826–1876* (New York: Macmillan, 1939), pp. 273–75, 287; George Fort Milton, *The Use of Presidential Power, 1789–1943* (Boston: Little, Brown, 1944), pp. 109–11.

[12] Rossiter, *Constitutional Dictatorship*, pp. 212, 224. See also Rossiter's "Constitutional Dictatorship in the Atomic Age," *The Review of Politics*, 11 (October 1949), 395–418.

federate sympathizers, few if any writers of serious history in the period from 1900 to 1950 applied the dictatorship idea to Lincoln in an outright condemnatory manner.[13] But this changed in the 1960s as the liberal consensus in American historical writing collapsed, and presidential government—now called the "imperial presidency"—came under attack in the aftermath of the Vietnam War. A harbinger of the overtly anti-Lincoln point of view was Edmund Wilson's essay on the Civil War President in *Patriotic Gore* (1962). Wilson argued that in the Lyceum Address of 1838, Lincoln identified with the tyrant against whom his appeal for law and order was ostensibly directed. "In the poem that Lincoln lived," Wilson wrote, "it was morally and dramatically inevitable that this prophet who had crushed opposition and sent thousands of men to their deaths should finally attest his good faith by laying down his own life with theirs."[14]

Subsequently a number of scholars followed the direction pointed by Wilson. Reviving the view expressed earlier by Dunning, the political scientist Gottfried Dietze described Lincoln's exercise of power as a "constitutional tragedy." Dietze said that at the start of the war Lincoln believed in limited government and was committed to preserving the constitutional order. He did not act with revolutionary intent or ambition, and was not guilty of contempt of the Constitution. Nevertheless, Dietze argued, wartime exigencies drove Lincoln to construe the war clauses of the Constitution in a revolutionary manner that produced dictatorship. The critical element was the vagueness of the concept of emergency power and the discretion of the executive in defining it. Dietze concluded that despite his intentions and aspirations as a constitutionalist, "Lincoln's administration thus opened the way for the development of an omnipotent, national executive who as spokesman for the people might consider himself entitled to do whatever he felt was good for the Nation."[15]

---

[13] On the neo-Confederate view of Lincoln, see Don E. Fehrenbacher, "The Anti-Lincoln Tradition," *Papers of the Abraham Lincoln Association*, 4 (1982), 17–22. Edgar Lee Masters attacked Lincoln as a tyrant in *Lincoln the Man* (New York: Dodd, Mead, 1931), but while his work was not in the neo-Confederate tradition, neither ought it to be regarded as a serious scholarly contribution.

[14] Edmund Wilson, *Patriotic Gore: Studies in the Literature of the American Civil War* (New York: Oxford University Press, 1962), p. 130. Wilson's essay was first published in 1953.

[15] Gottfried Dietze, *America's Political Dilemma: From Limited to Unlimited Democracy* (Baltimore: The John Hopkins University Press, 1968), pp. 17–62.

Willmoore Kendall, viewing Lincoln as the precursor of liberal activist Presidents in the twentieth century, went beyond the dictatorship charge to accuse him of derailing the American political tradition. According to Kendall, Lincoln placed the United States on the road to centralized egalitarianism by making equality a supreme commitment and standard of judgment in American politics. Lincoln did this by assigning the Declaration of Independence constitutional status, undermining the tradition of community self-government under majority rule and legislative supremacy.[16] In an essay comparing Lincoln and Chief Justice Roger B. Taney, Robert M. Spector asserted that Lincoln's example of unilateral executive action formed a dangerous precedent because it could allow a demagogic leader to determine the meaning of the Constitution. Insisting on the law of necessity in contrast to Taney's attempt to maintain the rule of law, Lincoln in Spector's judgment left a destructive constitutional legacy.[17]

More recently, M. E. Bradford, writing with a passion worthy of preeminent Lincoln-hater Lyon Gardiner Tyler, has condemned Lincoln's wartime dictatorship. Bradford sees Lincoln's actions as the start of the imperial presidency and the point in our history where republican government began to degenerate into egalitarian democracy.[18] In a breathtaking psychohistorical interpretation that demonstrates the convergence of ideological extremes, radical political scientist Dwight G. Anderson contended that Lincoln "arrogated to himself virtually dictatorial power" and transformed the presidency into an elective kingship. Driven by his desire for fame and distinction, Lincoln is described as having repudiated the constitutional order of the framers and founded a new Union which he made the basis of a political religion. Anderson concluded that Lincoln thus provided a revolutionary model of executive leadership that has

---

[16] Willmoore Kendall and George W. Carey, *The Basic Symbols of the American Political Tradition* (Baton Rouge: Louisiana State University Press, 1970), pp. 85–94.

[17] Robert E. Spector, "Lincoln and Taney: A Study in Constitutional Polarization," *American Journal of Legal History*, 15 (July 1971), 199–214.

[18] M. E. Bradford, "The Lincoln Legacy: A Long View," *Modern Age*, 24 (Fall 1980), 355–63. A little-noticed irony occurred in 1981 when Bradford, author of notorious anti-Lincoln diatribes, was considered for the position of director of the National Endowment for the Humanities by the newly elected Republican administration of President Ronald Reagan. More than any President in recent memory, Reagan invoked the principles and rhetoric of Lincoln. The appointment was not made, evidence that the southern strategy of the Republican party did not go so far as to tolerate a passionate criticism of Lincoln.

driven twentieth-century presidents to project the United States into a world imperialist role.[19]

In 1979 Don E. Fehrenbacher stated that more historians have described Lincoln as a dictator or constitutional dictator than any other President.[20] Fehrenbacher did not do so himself, however, thereby implicitly aligning himself with those historians who have rejected the dictatorship theme in relation to Lincoln.[21] Lord Charnwood, for example, with notable simplicity, stated in his biography that Lincoln was neither a dictator nor an English prime minister, but an elected officer whose powers and duties were prescribed by a fixed constitution.[22] Andrew C. McLaughlin, in a memorable essay of 1936, viewed Lincoln as "an archconstitutionalist" whose "dominating impulse was to protect the very nature of the republic."[23] More recently, the English scholar K. C. Wheare and the American constitutional historian Harold M. Hyman have criticized the interpretation of Lincoln as a dictator.[24] Nevertheless, the convention persists. Thus, Arthur M. Schlesinger, Jr., in his account of the impe-

---

[19] Dwight G. Anderson, *Abraham Lincoln: The Quest for Immortality* (New York: Alfred A. Knopf, 1982), pp. 8, 10–11, 166, 219. Anderson's critique, written from a leftist point of view, strikingly resembles the Kendall–Bradford conservative attack. What both points of view have in common of course is hostility toward bourgeois capitalism and liberal democracy, with which Lincoln identified himself.

[20] Don E. Fehrenbacher, "Lincoln and the Constitution," in *The Public and the Private Lincoln: Contemporary Perspectives*, ed. Cullom Davis (Carbondale: Southern Illinois University Press, 1979), p. 127.

[21] In describing the dictatorship convention I do not imply that virtually every book on Lincoln presents him in this light. Most works in the Lincoln field, general biographical accounts and specialized studies, are not concerned with governmental problems and do not take up the dictatorship question. In referring to historians who have rejected the dictatorship thesis, I refer to those few who have expressly considered it and found it persuasive.

[22] Lord Charnwood [Godfrey Rathbone Benson], *Abraham Lincoln* (New York: Henry Holt, 1917; repr. New York: Garden City Publishing, 1938), p. 266.

[23] Andrew C. McLaughlin, "Lincoln, the Constitution, and Democracy," *International Journal of Ethics*, 47 (October 1936), 1–24.

[24] K. C. Wheare, *Abraham Lincoln and the United States* (London: English Universities Press, 1948), p. 165; Harold M. Hyman, *A More Perfect Union: The Impact of the Civil War and Reconstruction on the Constitution* (New York: Alfred A. Knopf, 1973), p. 75. Also to be noted are two accounts of the civil liberties question during the Civil War which refute the dictatorship argument: A. C. Cole, "Lincoln and the American Tradition of Civil Liberty," *Illinois State Historical Society Journal*, 19 (October 1926–January 1927), pp. 102–14, and Kenneth A. Bernard, "Lincoln and Civil Liberties," *Abraham Lincoln Quarterly*, 6 (September 1951), 375–99. Richard N. Current, in "The Lincoln Presidents," *Presidential Studies Quarterly*, 9 (Winter 1979), 32, aptly observes that political scientists and politicians invoking Lincoln's example have exaggerated his usurpations as President. "Neither by word nor by deed,"

rial presidency, states that "Lincoln successfully demonstrated that, under indisputable crisis, temporary despotism was compatible with abiding democracy," while political scientist Richard M. Pious in a new study of the presidency describes Lincoln's exercise of power as a constitutional dictatorship.[25]

II

In assessing the validity of the dictator theme in the study of Lincoln's presidency the historian may properly turn to the political scientist for analytical assistance. The essence of dictatorship is unlimited absolute power or domination of the state by an individual or a small group. According to the classic work of Alfred Cobban, the political power of the dictator must emanate from his will, it must be exercised frequently in an arbitrary manner, it must not be limited in duration to a specific term of office, and the dictator must not be responsible to any other authority.[26] Arbitrary and unpredictable in its effects, dictatorial power has the connotation of transgressing legal limitations and the boundaries of political legitimacy. The concept of constitutional dictatorship is apparently intended to remove the stigma of illegality or nonlegitimacy, and refers to the temporary investing of absolute power in a single ruler.[27]

Although dictatorship existed in ancient times, it appears in modern form under the aspect of the executive power, of which it is a distortion and exaggeration. Almost all writers on government have

---

Current concludes, "did Lincoln give any real justification for the idea of 'executive privilege' or of an 'imperial presidency.' "

[25] Arthur M. Schlesinger, Jr., *The Imperial Presidency* (Boston: Houghton Mifflin, 1973), p. 74; Richard M. Pious, *The American Presidency* (New York: Basic Books, 1979), p. 57.

[26] Otto Stammler, "Dictatorship," *International Encyclopedia of the Social Sciences*, 17 vols. (New York: Macmillan, 1968), 4:161–68; Alfred Cobban, *Dictatorship: Its History and Theory* (New York: Scribner's, 1939), p. 26.

[27] Henry R. Spencer, "Dictatorship," *Encyclopedia of the Social Sciences* (New York: Macmillan, 1931), 5:133. The concept of *constitutional* dictatorship appears to have been an attempt to retain the original meaning of dictatorship as the voluntary adoption of one-man rule by a republic or democracy, in the face of the establishment in the twentieth century of permanent dictatorships by totalitarian states. In earlier times the idea of a permanent dictatorship would have been regarded as a contradiction in terms, and would have been described as despotism. Cf. Robert C. Brooks, *Deliver Us From Dictators!* (Philadelphia: University of Pennsylvania Press, 1935), p. 22.

recognized that there are times when the values of the rule of law are best served by departing temporarily from the law, in actions unrestricted by the need to deliberate or consult. In the political theory of John Locke this is referred to as the prerogative, or the power of doing "public good without a rule." Subject only to the rule of prudence, this discretionary power constitutes an important part—but only a part—of the ambiguity of the executive power. For the principal meaning of the modern executive is that of executing or administering the will of another, namely, the people or the people's representatives in the legislative branch of government. In the separation of powers, the organizing principle of limited government in the modern era, and in the requirement of popular elections, institutions exist which republicanize and constitutionalize the executive power.[28]

Notwithstanding the pedigree of the notion of constitutional dictatorship, there is merit in the suggestion that the existence of institutions of accountability and responsibility marks the critical and essential difference between dictatorship and constitutional government. Where such institutions exist, the idea of constitutional dictatorship becomes meaningless.[29] Those who have subscribed to the dictatorship thesis in analyzing Lincoln have generally acknowledged that emergency government in the United States bears little resemblance to the methods of crisis government in other countries. Rossiter, the most systematic exponent of the dictatorship idea, himself said that it was stretching the point considerably to describe any American government as a constitutional dictatorship. He conceded that his use of the concept was "little more than a convenient hyperbole." The most obvious characteristic of American government in periods of crisis, he observed, was the extent to which a "tenacious" adherence to the pattern of peacetime continued.[30]

How, then, to account for the persistence of the dictatorship convention? For those who are hostile to Lincoln it is of course an effective term of condemnation. Among those whose historical judgment of Lincoln is favorable, reliance on the dictatorship theme is more puzzling. It may have appeal as a way of understanding and dealing

---

[28] Harvey C. Mansfield, Jr., *Taming the Prince: The Ambivalence of Modern Executive Power* (New York: Free Press, 1989), pp. 189, 247–78.

[29] Karl Loewenstein, review of *Constitutional Dictatorship*, by Clinton Rossiter, *American Political Science Review*, 42 (October 1949), 1008.

[30] Rossiter, *Constitutional Dictatorship*, pp. 209, 286.

with situations which require the application of force, without abandoning the idea of limitations on power. In the context of the first half of the twentieth century, the dictatorship convention appears to be related to the progressive belief that in the conditions of modern industrialized society centralized executive and bureaucratic power is a necessity of good government. All the more is this so in time of war and in periods of economic crisis that are considered the equivalent of war. For those who would innovate in the use of executive power, it is helpful to point to radical innovation by a previous chief executive, especially one of Lincoln's stature.

Whatever reasons may have made the dictatorship idea analytically appealing in the past, it is my contention that its use distorts our constitutional history in general, and that it is especially misleading and inaccurate as a description of Lincoln's presidency. Where real and distinct limitations on the exercise of governmental power exist, in the form of counterbalancing authority and institutions of accountability, there dictatorship—be it called constitutional or otherwise—does not exist.[31] The dictatorship theme is particularly inapposite, moreover, with reference to Lincoln's exercise of power during the Civil War, which was constantly subjected to the restraints of congressional initiative and reaction, political party competition, and the correcting pressures of public opinion. But in rejecting the dictatorship convention we have more to rely on than the fact that politics—and the freedom that it necessarily implies—

---

[31] Henry Jones Ford, a prominent advocate of executive power in the early twentieth century, provides a good example of the scholarly attraction to the dictatorship idea despite its apparent incompatibility with basic democratic values. Ford emphasized the distinction between responsible and irresponsible government, rather than limitations on executive power, as the essential difference between constitutional government and despotism. Strangely, however, Ford did not regard the enforcing of accountability as a limitation on power. It is difficult to see in Ford's analysis, and in the writings of other proponents of the constitutional dictatorship thesis, the existence in the United States of the absolute and unlimited power which in their view characterizes this institutional condition. Cf. Ford's, "Growth of Dictatorship."

Pertinent in this connection is the assertion of Karl Dietrich Bracher, that crisis government results when "the system of limitation and balance of power typical of a constitutional government" is abandoned in favor of enlarged executive or military power. Bracher does not cite the United States as an example of crisis government in this sense. He states that in the United States constitutional theory agrees on implied or inherent powers for the President as a way of dealing with emergencies. He notes, however, that controls by courts and the legislature are not curtailed in emergencies by the exercise of executive power. Bracher, "Crisis Government," *International Encyclopedia of the Social Sciences*, 3:514.

ontinued during the war. We are afforded unique insight into the problem of wartime government by Lincoln's own analysis of the dictatorship question and by the constitutional justification that sustained his exercise of power between Sumter and Appomattox.

III

A critic of the Democratic doctrine of broad executive power early in his political career, Lincoln throughout his presidency was conscious of and respected the legal limits which circumscribed the office of chief magistrate. In part seeking to allay southern apprehension, in part expressing his considered constitutional judgment, he saw fit, upon taking office in 1861, to comment on the generally restricted scope of the federal government's field of action. The Constitution, he said in his First Inaugural Address, gave government officials "but little power for mischief." No single administration, he asserted, as long as the people to whom it was accountable remained virtuous and vigilant, could seriously injure the government within a four-year term. As chief executive, Lincoln conceived it his duty to administer the government as it came to him and transmit it to his successor unimpaired. Addressing the issue of secession, he emphasized in his inaugural address that he had no discretionary authority to fix terms for the separation of the states, a thing that only the people could do if they so desired.[32]

Lincoln's respect for the legal limits on executive power was evident in his dealing both with pedestrian administrative questions and with larger matters of state. In March 1861, for example, he drafted an order establishing a central bureau to supervise the organization, drill, and equipment of the militia. Inquiring as to his legal authority to do so, he was informed by the Attorney General that none existed, and the order was not given.[33] On numerous other issues Lincoln routinely sought opinions concerning his legal authority to perform executive acts.[34] And consistent with the narrow view

---

[32] Roy P. Basler et al., eds., *The Collected Works of Abraham Lincoln*, 9 vols. (New Brunswick, N.J.: Rutgers University Press, 1953–1955), 4:270–71.

[33] Ibid., 4:291.

[34] For example, to appoint an officer whose assignment would be temperance work among the troops, or to remit a fine imposed on a restaurateur for selling spirits to a soldier (ibid., 4:451, 5:270).

of executive power which he had expressed in the 1840s, he denied that he could veto legislation merely on the basis of subjective disagreement with the policy contained in legislation.[35]

From time to time Lincoln specifically commented on the dictatorship question, which was a controversial subject throughout the war. He did so for the first time in the Browning letter of September 22, 1861, dealing with his revocation of the emancipation order issued by General John C. Frémont in Missouri. Writing to Republican Senator Orville H. Browning of Illinois, Lincoln expressed the opinion that slaves, like other property, could be seized and temporarily used for military purposes. But their permanent status could not be determined by a military decree, such as Frémont's, that was based on "purely political" reasons "not within the range of *military* law, or necessity." To do that, said Lincoln, would be "simply 'dictatorship,'" for it would assume that a military commander "may do *anything* he pleases," such as, in the present instance, confiscating the lands and freeing the slaves of loyal as well as disloyal people. Lincoln believed that Congress might by legislation permanently fix the status of slaves employed for military purposes. "What I object to," he explained, "is that I as President, shall expressly or impliedly seize and exercise the permanent legislative functions of the government."[36]

The usual view of Lincoln's presidency is that he abandoned this narrow conception of executive power in favor of a more plenary one which allowed him to do what he had prohibited Frémont from doing.[37] In May 1862, for example, he revoked another emancipation order, issued by General David Hunter in South Carolina. In doing so he announced: ". . . whether it be competent for me, as Commander-in-Chief of the Army and Navy, to declare the Slaves of any state or states, free, and whether at any time, in any case, it shall have become a necessity indispensable to the maintenance of the government, to exercise such supposed power, are questions which, under my responsibility, I reserve to myself. . . ."[38] Of apparently similar import is Lincoln's statement of September 1862 that he had

---

[35] Ibid., 7:414. This veto concerned a bill reducing the fees paid to the marshal of the District of Columbia.

[36] Ibid., 4:531–32.

[37] Edward S. Corwin, *The President: Office and Powers*, 4th rev. ed. (New York: New York University Press, 1957), pp. 450–51.

[38] Basler et al., eds., *Collected Works*, 5:222.

no objection to a proclamation of emancipation, since his power as commander in chief gave him "a right to take any measure which may best subdue the enemy."[39] It was of course on this military basis that the Emancipation Proclamation rested—a basis succinctly described by Lincoln in the Conkling letter of August 1863 when he wrote: "I think the constitution invests its commander-in-chief, with the law of war, in time of war."[40]

This apparent progression toward a concept of plenary executive power is cited in support of the constitutional dictatorship thesis.[41] Yet the position attributed to Lincoln in 1862–63 does not necessarily contradict the position he assumed in 1861, as expressed in the Browning letter. At that time Lincoln said that military power could not be used for purely *political* reasons to emancipate slaves and determine their future status. He did not, in the Browning letter, disclaim power as commander in chief to free and fix the status of slaves for *military* reasons essential to the preservation of the government. In 1863 he deemed it necessary to exercise such power, which may properly be regarded as having been reserved in the revocation of the Frémont order.

In explaining his view of dictatorship, Lincoln in the Browning letter also disavowed the ability of the executive to exercise "the permanent legislative function of the government," as in determining the permanent status of slaves used for military purposes. This position, too, he maintained later in the war.

Here it is important to note the controversy in 1863 over the validity and legal effect of the Emancipation Proclamation. Democrats called the proclamation an unconstitutional and illegal nullity; conservative Unionists thought it was temporarily effective where military authority might make it so; and the main body of Republicans said it conferred a right of personal liberty.[42] Lincoln believed the Emancipation Proclamation constitutional, though acknowledg-

---

[39] Ibid., 5:421. This statement was made in reply to a memorial supporting emancipation adopted by a public meeting of Christians of all denominations in Chicago in September 1862.

[40] Ibid., 6:408. Lincoln described the Emancipation Proclamation "as a fit and necessary war measure" for suppressing the rebellion, authorized under the power vested in him as commander-in-chief of the army and navy "in time of actual armed rebellion against authority and government of the United States . . ." (ibid., 6:29).

[41] Rossiter, *Constitutional Dictatorship*, p. 233.

[42] Herman Belz, *A New Birth of Freedom: The Republican Party and Freedmen's Rights, 1861–1866* (Westport, Conn.: Greenwood, 1976), pp. 36–40.

ing it might be found to be otherwise, and pledged to maintain the freedom of emancipated slaves.[43] Yet he claimed no authority to fix the legal status of freed slaves or to abolish slavery in state laws and constitutions. It soon became clear that a constitutional amendment prohibiting slavery and permanently guaranteeing the freedom of the emancipated blacks was necessary. Lincoln of course lent his political support to this undertaking, but in a constitutional sense the framing and adoption of the Thirteenth Amendment were none of his affair as chief executive.[44] This ultimate exercise of the legislative power, as Lincoln noted in the Browning letter of 1861, belonged to the people and their elected representatives in the lawmaking branch.

Lincoln remained conscious of the restriction on military power which he considered the essential safeguard against dictatorship. Urged by Secretary of the Treasury Salmon P. Chase in 1863 to extend the Emancipation Proclamation to parts of Virginia and Louisiana that had been exempted, he refused on the ground that the order "has no constitutional or legal justification, except as a military measure." To apply it in the absence of military necessity, he told Chase, "without any argument, except the one that I think the measure politically expedient, and morally right," would be to give up "all footing upon the constitution or law. . . ." In the language used in his 1861 comment upon dictatorship, it would be acting for "purely political" reasons. Lincoln asked: "Would I not thus be in the boundless field of absolutism?" And would not such a course provoke fears that "without any further stretch, I might do the same in Delaware, Maryland, Kentucky, Tennessee, and Missouri; and even change any law in any state?"[45]

---

[43] Lincoln wrote in August 1863: "During my continuance here, the government will return no person to slavery who is free according to the proclamation or to any of the acts of congress, unless such return shall be held to be a legal duty, by the proper court of final resort, in which case I will promptly act as may then appear to be my personal duty" (Basler et al., eds., *Collected Works*, 6:411; see also 6:408).

[44] For obvious political reasons, Lincoln signed the resolution submitting the Thirteenth Amendment to the states. This action, however, was constitutionally anomalous, as the Senate pointed out in a resolution of February 7, 1865, stating that presidential approval of resolutions proposing constitutional amendments was unnecessary (ibid., 8:253–54).

[45] Ibid., 6:428–29. See also Lincoln's letter to Albert G. Hodges, April 4, 1864, in which he stated his belief that the presidency did not confer "an unrestricted right to act officially" upon the basis of his antislavery feelings, or "in ordinary civil administration . . . to practically indulge my primary abstract judgment on the moral question of slavery" (ibid., 7:281).

LINCOLN AND THE CONSTITUTION

It is possible of course to dismiss these professions of concern for constitutional limitations and determination to avoid dictatorial solutions as mere rhetoric. It is virtually impossible, however, to deny the most impressive evidence weighing against the dictatorship thesis—the continuation of party competition in the election of 1864.

As Mark E. Neely, Jr., has recently observed, historians have generally failed to appreciate the critical nature of this election, in which the Democrats demanded the cessation of hostilities and refrained from opposition to slavery. Although one cannot know what would have happened had McClellan won, the possibility of a negotiated settlement recognizing the Confederacy and the greater likelihood of the continuation of slavery ought to be acknowledged.[46] Historians have also, it should be noted, failed to appreciate the significance for American constitutionalism in the very fact that the election was held. In part this failure stems from the tendency common in stable democratic societies to take for granted institutions and procedures that most other countries must still struggle to achieve. It also reflects the peculiar American attitude toward politics, which at times seems to regard elections as more to be regretted and endured than applauded as a vital part of constitutional government. In any case, in facing the Democratic challenge in 1864, Lincoln accepted a risk and permitted his power to be threatened in a way that no dictator, constitutional or not, would have tolerated.

Lincoln was aware of the critical nature of the election and of its importance for republican constitutionalism. Although Democratic victory might lead to disunion and the preservation of slavery, he never wavered in his willingness to accept the possibility of a change in administration. In August 1864 he recorded privately his determination, should he lose the election, to cooperate with the Democratic President-elect in a final effort to save the Union.[47] When the

---

[46] Mark E. Neely, Jr., "The Lincoln Theme Since Randall's Call: The Promises and Perils of Professionalism," *Abraham Lincoln Association Papers*, 1 (1979), 18–21.

[47] Lincoln wrote this memorandum on August 23, a few days before the Democratic convention. He believed that should the Democratic candidate win, "he will have secured his election on such ground that he cannot possibly save [the Union] afterwards." The final effort to save the Union must therefore come between the election and the inauguration of the next president in March 1865. Lincoln evidently anticipated a "peace plank" such as the Democrats included in their platform. The platform called for "a cessation of hostilities, with a view to an ultimate convention of the States, or other peaceable means, to the end that, at the earliest

election was over, Lincoln told his cabinet of this resolve, explaining that both duty and conscience required it.[48] As Charles A. Beard wrote, "This is not the language of a despot, a Caesar or a wrecker. It is the language of a man remarkably loyal to constitutional methods, ready to abide by the decision of the people lawfully made. . . ."[49]

During the campaign there were rumors that, if defeated, Lincoln would try to "ruin the government," as a dictator might contemplate doing.[50] In October 1864 Lincoln addressed these rumors. Stating that he was trying to save the government, not destroy it, he publicly pledged that he would serve as President until March 4, 1865, and that whoever was constitutionally elected would at that time be installed as chief magistrate. Lincoln also intended this statement to allay apprehension that if the Democratic party won, it would try to seize the government.[51]

After the election, Lincoln summed up its significance before a public gathering at the White House. If the rebellion tested the people when they were united, he suggested, "must they not fail when *divided*, and partially paralyzed by a political war among themselves?" But the election was a necessity. "We can not have free government without elections," he declared, "and if the rebellion could force us to forego, or postpone a national election, it might fairly claim to have already conquered and ruined us." Returning to the question that he had posed at the start of the war, namely, whether a democratic government could defend itself, he said the election demonstrated "that a people's government can sustain a national election, in the midst of a great civil war."[52]

Lincoln's well-reasoned and persuasive analysis of the dictatorship question ought not to strike us as remarkable. What is remarkable, in view of the evidence that so plainly refutes it, is the persistence

---

practical moment, peace may be restored on the basis of the federal Union of the States."

[48] Basler et al, eds., *Collected Works*, 7:514.

[49] Charles A. Beard, *The Republic* (New York: Viking Press, 1944), p. 68.

[50] Basler et al., eds., *Collected Works*, 8:52. Lincoln acknowledged the rumors in response to a serenade, October 19, 1864.

[51] Lincoln noted that the Democratic convention did not adjourn *sine die*, but to meet again if called to do so. This fact, he said, had led to speculation that, if elected, the Democratic candidate would try to seize the government immediately (ibid., 8:52).

[52] Ibid., 8:100–101.

of the dictatorship convention. Surely there is a more accurate way to describe the exercise of presidential power during the Civil War and its constitutional justification than by invoking this dubious notion. Nor will the concept of a "constitutional" dictatorship, as I have suggested, answer our needs. In either version the dictatorship argument is flawed because it requires the conclusion that the existing Constitution was inadequate.

An alternative interpretation of Civil War government, noting its substantial continuity with prewar practices, would hold that the Constitution, limitations and all, was adequate to the needs of the Union in this its severest crisis. The nation's organic law was not set aside for an unlimited, dictatorial concentration of power. On the contrary, the Constitution continued to serve both as symbol and source of governmental legitimacy and as a normative standard for the conduct of politics. To assist in understanding this alternative constitutional outlook we can consult no more perceptive or authoritative explanation than the rationale that Lincoln himself offered for wartime executive action.

IV

Lincoln employed a two-track constitutional justification in explaining the legitimacy of controversial measures adopted under executive authority. The first and more familiar track involved legalistic arguments from the text of the Constitution. The second involved more broadly political arguments concerning the relationship between the Union, the Constitution, and the nature of republican government.[53]

An able lawyer familiar with constitutional analysis, Lincoln frequently advanced legalistic arguments in which the Constitution was conceived of as a form of positive law.[54] Perhaps his best-known

---

[53] In positing this concept of constitutional reasoning and justification I follow the views expressed by Charles L. Black, Jr., *Structure and Relationship in Constitutional Law* (Baton Rouge: Louisiana State University Press, 1969).

[54] Lincoln's effective use of this conceptual outlook can be seen in the First Inaugural Address, in the contention that no right "plainly written in the Constitution" had ever been denied. In lawyer-like fashion, he cleverly sought to disarm the secessionists by arguing that only if a "plainly written" constitutional right were denied by an electoral majority would revolutionary action by a minority (in this instance, secession) be morally justified. Happily, he continued, "All the vital rights

argument in this mode concerned executive suspension of the privilege of the writ of habeas corpus. In his July 4, 1861, message to Congress, he cited Article I, Section 9 of the Constitution, which confers power to suspend the writ of habeas corpus in cases of rebellion or invasion when the public safety requires it. Since the Constitution does not specify who may exercise this power, Lincoln reasoned that the President could do so, in time of emergency when Congress was not in session.[55]

Lincoln offered additional constitutional justification of habeas corpus suspension in the Corning letter of June 1863. Democratic critics contended that the government could make no arbitrary arrests or suspend the habeas corpus privilege outside the area of rebellion and lines of military occupation. Lincoln argued in contrast that since the Constitution "makes no such distinction, I am unable to believe that there is any such constitutional distinction." The writ could be suspended and arrests made *whenever* the public safety required it, he insisted, and *wherever* this might occur.[56] Lincoln was similarly legalistic in responding to a Democratic argument that rested on the hypothetical assumption that the Constitution be read without the habeas corpus suspension clause. To this Lincoln countered: "Doubless [*sic*] if this clause of the constitution . . . were expunged, the other guarranties would remain the same; but the question is, not how those guarranties would stand, with that clause out of the constitution, but how they stand with that clause remaining in it. . . ."[57]

Couched in the usual idiom of constitutional politics, Lincoln's arguments were appropriate expressions of the legalistic side of American constitutionalism.[58] Yet, ironically, it is possible to interpret some of Lincoln's statements in this idiom in a way that sup-

---

of minorities, and of individuals, are so plainly assured to them, by affirmations and negations, guarranties and prohibitions, in the Constitution, that controversies never arise concerning them." In fact, he explained, controversies arise over rights and powers that are not "plainly written," such as the fugitive slave law and slavery in the territories (Basler et al., eds., *Collected Works*, 4:267).

[55] Ibid., 4:430–31.

[56] Ibid., 6:265.

[57] Ibid., 6:302.

[58] I refer to the fact that while the American constitution in the broadest sense is the complex of principles, institutions, laws, practices, and traditions by which political life is carried on, its minimal and irreducible basis is a form of positive law—the written documentary Constitution. This circumstance gives American constitutionalism a highly legalistic character.

ports the dictatorship thesis. In his message to the special session of Congress in 1861, referring to habeas corpus suspension, Lincoln asked: ". . . are all the laws *but one*, to go unexecuted, and the government itself to go to pieces, lest that one be violated?"[59] In a message to Congress of May 1862, he described some of the measures taken at the start of the war as "without any authority of law. . . ."[60] And in a statement of 1864 he seemed to imply that the Constitution might be broken to save the Union. "By general law life *and* limb must be protected;" he observed, "yet often a limb must be amputated to save a life; but a life is never wisely given to save a limb."[61] In this metaphor the nation is the life to be saved; the Constitution, the limb that might need amputation. The inference can be drawn that emergency action to save the government is expedient, yet also unconstitutional and lawless.

Lincoln of course denied that emergency measures to save the government were unlawful, adducing the legalistic arguments noted above. In addition, and more persuasively, he offered a political-philosophical defense of executive actions that dwelt on the relationship between the Union and the Constitution.

The perspective from which Lincoln offered this more systemic constitutional justification appears in the fragment on the Constitution and the Union presumably written in January 1861. Reiterating the theme that absorbed him as the struggle over slavery reached its climax, Lincoln stated that beyond the Constitution and the Union lay the principle of liberty expressed in the Declaration of Independence. The assertion of this principle, he wrote, "was the word, 'fitly spoken' which has proved an 'apple of gold' to us." "The *Union*, and the *Constitution*," he continued, "are *the picture* of *silver*, subsequently framed around it." Observing that the picture was made for the apple and not the other way around, he urged actions to ensure "that neither *picture*, or *apple* shall ever be blurred, or bruised or broken."[62]

In this passage Lincoln was primarily concerned to define republican liberty as the fundamental purpose of national existence. For our purposes what is of interest is the equivalence or identity assumed to exist between the nation (the Union) and the Constitution. De-

---

[59] Basler et al., eds., *Collected Works*, 4:430. See Corwin's interpretation of this statement in *President: Office and Powers*, p. 230.

[60] Basler et al., eds., *Collected Works*, 5:242.

[61] Ibid., 7:281.

[62] Ibid., 4:168–69.

stroy liberty—or allow this sacred principle to be eroded by the spread of slavery—and both the nation and the Constitution would be lost.

Justifying emergency actions taken at the start of the war, Lincoln in his message to Congress of July 4, 1861, reaffirmed liberty as the purpose of national existence. The war, he declared, was "a People's contest . . . a struggle for maintaining in the world, that form, and substance of government, whose leading object is, to elevate the condition of men. . . ."[63] But an equally important issue was also involved: "whether a constitutional republic, or a democracy . . . can, or cannot, maintain its territorial integrity, against its own domestic foes." " 'Is there, in all republics,' " Lincoln asked, " 'this inherent, and fatal weakness?' 'Must a government, of necessity, be too *strong* for the liberties of its own people, or too weak to maintain its own existence?' " Seeking to avoid both extremes, Lincoln announced: ". . . no choice was left but to call out the war power of the Government; and so to resist force, employed for its own destruction, by force, for its preservation."[64]

Was it, then, lawful and constitutional to defend the Union and the Constitution? And was it possible to do so without resort to dictatorial power? Plainly, Lincoln believed it was, and this not mainly in consequence of any construction of positive law or constitutional text, but rather on the self-evident truth that the Constitution justifies extraordinary action to preserve the substance of political liberty that constitutes both its own end and the purpose of the nation. In the Hodges letter of April 1864, Lincoln expressly equated Union and Constitution in justifying executive actions. He wrote: "I felt that measures, otherwise unconstitutional, might become lawful, by becoming indispensable to the preservation of the constitution, through the preservation of the nation."[65] To preserve the nation, in other words, was to preserve the Constitution. "I could not feel that, to the best of my ability, I had even tried to preserve the constitution," he added, "if, to save slavery, or any minor matter, I should permit the wreck of government, country, and Constitution all together."[66]

In this sentence Lincoln twice uses the word "constitution,"

---

[63] Ibid., 4:438.
[64] Ibid., 4:426.
[65] Ibid., 7:281.
[66] Ibid.

spelling it with a lower-case and then an upper-case "C." Does this mean he has in mind two different conceptions of the term? One may perhaps draw that inference, considering the two-track constitutional justification he employed to explain the lawfulness of emergency war measures. The Constitution was not only the written instrument of government adopted at the nation's Founding and intended to function as a supreme legal code. It was also the principles, ideals, institutions, laws, and procedures tending toward the maintenance of republican liberty by which the American people agreed to order their political existence. The Constitution, in other words, was not merely positive law, derivative or reflective of national life, as in the life-and-limb metaphor noted above that is typically used to illustrate Lincoln's approach to constitutional justification. Rather, the Constitution was the nation, or—to put it the other way around in a way that is perhaps more meaningful and revealing—the nation was the Constitution: America was the system of political liberty created by the founders and now defended against an internal enemy.[67] In the Hodges letter Lincoln asked whether it was "possible to lose the nation, and yet preserve the constitution."[68] If the Constitution was simply a legal code, the possibility existed. But under Lincoln's political-philosophical view of the Constitution it was not possible to lose the nation while preserving the Constitution. To lose one was to lose the other.

This nonlegalistic, nonjuridical conception of the Constitution was not nearly so uncommon in the nineteenth century as it has become today. Indeed, it was vigorously expressed in an influential treatise by Lincoln's legal advisor in the War Department, William Whiting, in his widely circulated *War Powers Under the Constitution of the United States*. Strict constructionists, Whiting noted, insisted on the letter of the Constitution and were unable to see that the Constitution was "only a frame of government, a plan in outline for regulating" national life. Strict constructionists saw the Constitution as "incapable of adaptation to our changing conditions, as if it were . . .

---

[67] Compare the recent analysis of Lincoln's constitutional theory by political scientist Gary Jacobsohn: "Lincoln saw the Constitution as both a legal code and a statement of the ideals which we as a people chose 'in the end to live by' " (Gary J. Jacobsohn, "Abraham Lincoln 'On This Question of Judicial Authority': The Theory of Constitutional Aspiration," *Western Political Quarterly*, 36 [March 1983], 52–70, at 66.

[68] Basler et al., eds., *Collected Works*, 7:281.

an iron chain, girdling a living tree, which could have no further growth unless by bursting its rigid ligature." Whiting rejected this narrow legalism. The Constitution, he wrote, "more resembles the tree itself, native to the soil that bore it, waxing strong in sunshine and in storm, putting forth branches, leaves, and roots, according to the laws of its own growth. . . ." Foregoing metaphor, Whiting then offered an historical analogy: "Our Constitution, like that of England, contains all that is required to adapt itself to the present and future changes and wants of a free and advancing people."[69] Whiting's commentary seems to express a tendency in Lincoln's constitutionalism.

It is of course the nature of Lincoln's constitutionalism that is placed in dispute by the dictatorship convention. Advocates of that interpretation ultimately see Lincoln as disregarding or transcending constitutional limitations. Their position is implicitly reinforced by those who describe Lincoln as a pragmatic instrumentalist who subscribed to the theory of the "living Constitution" and regarded it as a social document capable of organic growth.[70] This is perhaps a plausible conclusion which the quotation from Whiting, and Lincoln's own equating of the Constitution and the nation, might appear to support. The trouble with the pragmatic-instrumentalist approach to the Constitution, however, is that it tends to negate the idea of constitutional limitations. It encourages an "anything goes" mentality that justifies purposes and objects remote from those envisioned by the framers of the Constitution, and presumably excluded by them except through the process of constitutional amendment. It rejects original intention as a guide to constitutional interpretation. And, I believe, it gravely misunderstands Lincoln and the Civil War generation, who were closer in outlook to the fixed constitutionalism of the Founding Fathers than to the pragmatic liberalism of the twentieth century.

We may take Chief Justice John Marshall as illustrative of the constitutional outlook of the Founding generation and the early national period, which informed Lincoln's statesmanship. In his most famous admonition, in *McCulloch* v. *Maryland*, Marshall declared:

---

[69] William Whiting, *War Powers Under the Constitution of the United States*, 43rd ed. (Boston: Lee & Shepard, 1871), pp. 8–9.

[70] Cf. Morgan D. Dowd, "Lincoln, the Rule of Law, and Crisis Government: A Study of his Constitutional Law Theories," *University of Detroit Law Journal*, 39 (June 1962), 633–49.

"We must never forget that it is a *constitution* we are expounding . . . intended to endure for ages to come, and consequently, to be adapted to the various *crises* of human affairs."[71] Marshall did not mean that the Constitution was infinitely flexible or that new powers and purposes of government could be fashioned out of whole cloth, as advocates of the "living constitution" seem to assume. He meant that the purposes and objects set forth by the framers in the fundamental law must always be the touchstone and test of constitutional legitimacy, the criterion to be employed in constitutional adaptation and adjudication. May we not consider defense of the Union and the Constitution a legitimate object assigned to the federal government by the framers? And may we not conclude that Lincoln's exercise of power to this end was compatible with the concept of a fixed Constitution?

Ultimately, Lincoln appealed to a kind of constitutional common sense that, while respecting the requirements of procedural regularity and formal legality, was concerned above all with preserving the substance of republican liberty—the purpose both of American nationality and of the constitutional order.

Criticism of Lincoln as a dictator and revolutionary constitutional innovator rests, to a considerable extent, on the assumption that his wartime actions not only permitted, but in some vaguely defined historical sense also caused, twentieth-century presidents to exceed the limits of the executive office. But for Lincoln's example, the argument implicitly runs, the imperial presidency could never have developed. In analyzing the historical relationship between Lincoln's actions and future patterns of executive governance, however, it is necessary to distinguish between a constitutional precedent and a political model.

In the United States, whose government is based on a written constitution that has a definable meaning and is not completely flexible, measures that depart from existing constitutional rules in the face of necessity do not establish precedents for future departures, regrettable though they may be. Such measures do not prove, or require, that future actions cannot be made to conform to the constitution. This is not to deny that, at a later date and in a different political context, a controversial action or measure can be cited

---

[71] 4 *Wheaton* 316 (1819), at 407.

and used as a model for political action.[72] It is obvious, however, that the individual whose action is subsequently taken as a political model has no control over this process of historical appropriation and cannot reasonably be held responsible for measures predicated on his example. To be specific, whether the historical appropriation of Lincoln's wartime measures as a model for subsequent presidential action is politically successful in conferring legitimacy depends on the nature, circumstances, and effect of the subsequent action.

A proper understanding of the meaning of constitutional precedent provides the basis for a defense of Lincoln against interpretations that present him as a revolutionary constitutional innovator. Harry V. Jaffa, for example, observes that expansions of federal authority attributed to Lincoln stemmed from his construction of his constitutional duty faithfully to execute the laws and his authority as commander in chief in cases of rebellion and invasion. These were crisis powers, not expansions of the commerce and general welfare powers of Congress, or other enumerated powers the delegation of which by the legislature to the executive vastly enlarged the scope of presidential authority in the twentieth century. Jaffa argues that Lincoln's actions under the crisis or war powers did not establish precedents for an expanded peacetime role of the presidency in particular or of the federal government in general. In the exercise of crisis powers Lincoln adopted measures, to be sure, that dealt with persons and property, the evaluation of which is relevant to the dictatorship problem. As long as such measures were incidental to the exercise of the war powers, however, as was true of Lincoln, they did not constitute a permanent expansion of federal authority.[73]

Unfortunately, a chief executive may assume to exercise power over persons and property not as a genuine incident of the war powers, but under a pretext thereof that is rhetorically justified by an appeal to national security. It is difficult to believe, however, that but for Lincoln's conduct of the executive office during the Civil War such a claim could never be made.

When Lincoln took emergency action based on his prudential judgment of what was necessary under the circumstances, he acted not in his own name but in the name of the Constitution. The deci-

---

[72] Sotirios A. Barber, *On What the Constitution Means* (Baltimore: The Johns Hopkins University Press, 1984), p. 191.

[73] Harry V. Jaffa, *How to Think About the American Revolution: A Bicentennial Celebration* (Durham, N.C.: Carolina Academic Press, 1978), p. 26.

sion to adopt military emancipation, although superficially it can be viewed as revolutionary, was constitutional in the deeper sense signified in this understanding of the executive power. Lincoln's suspension of the writ of habeas corpus and defense of the nation through internal security measures were similarly constitutional. Of course the executive power can be used in ways that do injury to the public good. Under the Constitution, however, as Lincoln said in response to criticism of his suspension of the writ of habeas corpus, if the executive "uses the power justly, the people will probably justify him; if he abuses it, he is in their hands, to be dealt with by all the modes they have reserved to themselves in the constitution."[74] We may conclude, therefore, that Lincoln was neither a revolutionary nor a dictator, but a constitutionalist who used the executive power to preserve and extend the liberty of the American Founding.

---

[74] Basler et al., eds., *Collected Works*, 6:303.

2

The "Philosophical Cause" of Free Government: The Problem of Lincoln's Political Thought

WERE WE TO JUDGE FROM PERSONAL EXPERIENCE, most of us would probably assent to the proposition that reason and intellect—manifested in conscious, deliberate, and rational thought—form an important part of our nature and that they are essential in guiding our actions. Extending our horizon to the world at large, we might agree that reason, intellect, and conscious thought are essential to the conduct of affairs, including political matters. When we enter the world of scholarship, however, and seek an explanation of historical events, we discover a different view. We find that thought and reason are little recognized as the basis of political action. We find instead that actions and events are explained with reference to social, economic, cultural, or ideological forces beyond the rational comprehension and control of individual actors.

As an example of this point of view, let us consider historical accounts of the statesmanship of Abraham Lincoln. In a recent anthology, *Abraham Lincoln and the American Political Tradition*, Lincoln is viewed in several guises: an ambitious member of a political fraternity, a political tactician and party leader, an embattled executive, a revolutionary, and a master of political discourse.[1] Nowhere in the volume is Lincoln regarded as a political thinker. Even such a distinguished scholar as Don E. Fehrenbacher refrains from any consideration of Lincoln as a thinking, rational political actor. In his essay,

An earlier version of this essay appeared in the *Journal of the Abraham Lincoln Association*, 10 (1988), 47–71.

[1] John L. Thomas, ed., *Abraham Lincoln and the American Political Tradition* (Amherst: University of Massachusetts Press, 1986), p. 10.

"The Words of Lincoln," Fehrenbacher observes that in the words of statesmen one finds the substance of their principal deeds and the clearest traces of their character.[2] To know what Lincoln said, he adds, is the firmest foundation for an understanding of what his life meant.[3] But are not words, spoken and written, more specific and fundamental evidence of conscious rational thought? In the words of statesmen, do we not find the substance of their reason, intellect, knowledge, and understanding? I am sure that Fehrenbacher would agree with this suggestion. Yet, is it not symptomatic of much contemporary scholarship that his discussion of the words of Lincoln and the analyses of Lincoln and the American political tradition by his fellow historians fail to consider their subject from the point of view of a rational, thinking statesman, taking thought about political reality and expressing that thought in speech, writing, and action?[4]

It has been suggested that contemporary historiography is premised on the disintegration of the belief that conscious, rational thought, the highest form of human activity, defines us as a species.[5] Despite this widespread view, there is reason to doubt that history can be described and analyzed accurately without recognition of the decisive importance of reason and rational thought in human affairs. Rather than assume this to be the case, however, I should like to approach the issue with a limited inquiry into the extent that historical accounts recognize the role of rational thought. I propose to

---

[2] Don E. Fehrenbacher, "The Words of Lincoln, " in ibid., p. 31.

[3] Ibid., p. 42.

[4] To some extent Fehrenbacher recognizes Lincoln's reason when he writes of the First Inaugural: "Here, then, was an occasion calling for eloquence; here was an ear keenly tuned to the music of the English language; here was intellectual grasp and moral urgency; here was great emotional power under firm artistic control. Here, in short, was the mastery that we associate with genius" (ibid., p. 46). More characteristic of contemporary historical scholarship is Thomas's editorial comment on Fehrenbacher's analysis: "An appreciation of Lincoln's political language . . . involves a certainty as to its provenance, a clear sense of the relevant audience, an understanding of political strategy, but above all, a susceptibility to the sheer power of language" (ibid., p. 5). This seems to mean that Lincoln's success in political speech and writing was owing not to the power of his reason and intellect but to his "susceptibility" to a power outside himself, namely, language. This view, associated with the linguistic interpretation of political thought, comes close to regarding language as the causal agent in history. See the discussion at note 62 below. A useful survey on the question is John E. Toews, "Intellectual History after the Linguistic Turn: The Autonomy of Meaning and the Irreducibility of Experience," *American Historical Review*, 92 (October 1987), 879–907.

[5] Toews, "Intellectual History After the Linguistic Turn," 879.

conduct this inquiry by examining the problem of Abraham Lincoln's political thought.

This problem refers to the specific content of Lincoln's ideas on a variety of questions, including nationalism, equality, democracy, constitutionalism, and economic freedom. Each topic has been the subject of scholarly dispute and warrants careful investigation. I shall approach the question of Lincoln's thought at its more problematic level: whether or in what sense Lincoln engaged in political thinking, the nature of his thoughts on politics, and how such thinking, if it existed, related to his actions as a statesman.

I

Political thought has not been a principal category of analysis employed by Lincoln scholars. Nor have Lincoln's ideas been discussed prominently by students of American political thought.[6] Lincoln was preeminently a lawyer, politician, and statesman—not a writer, intellectual, or philosopher. Political leaders of more abstract and doctrinaire bent, such as Thomas Jefferson and John C. Calhoun, have received far more attention than Lincoln. In modern historical accounts Lincoln is typically described as a practical politician of non-philosophical tendency. Many years ago, Lord Charnwood observed that no political theory stands out from Lincoln's words or actions and if he reflected much on forms of government, it was with a dominant interest in something beyond them.[7] According to Allan Nevins, Lincoln "took [democracy] on faith, without analysis." Instead of discoursing on the theory of democracy, he dealt with the practical problems attending its course.[8] Richard N. Current writes that Lincoln was a flexible pragmatist whose principles happened to coincide with his ambitions. No political theorist or philosopher, Lincoln mastered the classic statements of the American political

---

[6] Cf. Max J. Skidmore, *American Political Thought* (New York: St. Martin's, 1978); David W. Minar, *Ideas and Politics: The American Experience* (Homewood, Ill.: Dorsey, 1964); Alan P. Grimes, *American Political Thought* (New York: Henry Holt, 1955).

[7] Lord Charnwood [Godfrey Rathbone Benson], *Abraham Lincoln* (New York: Henry Holt, 1917; repr. New York: Garden City Publishing, 1938), p. 455.

[8] Allan Nevins, *The Statesmanship of the Civil War*, 2d ed. (New York: Macmillan/Collier Books, 1962), pp. 99–100.

faith and applied them through practical politics.[9] This view, which might be described as the principled but nonphilosophical interpretation, characterized the writings of leading Lincoln scholars of the mid-twentieth century.[10]

More recently, Mark E. Neely, Jr., has expressed the same view in cautioning against overintellectualized interpretations of Lincoln. Discussing constitutional issues, Neely says that Lincoln's "impulse almost always was toward the practical" and that thinking in constitutional ways did not come naturally to him. Though conceding that Lincoln's thought was "not nakedly opportunistic or embarrassingly shallow," Neely asserts: "Lincoln was not an intellectual, certainly not a systematic political thinker: he was a politician and one slights the instrumental side of Lincoln's statements only at great peril."[11] Robert W. Johannsen has presented the nonphilosophical view with more explicit emphasis on its contextual dimension. He criticizes interpretations that inaccurately and unhistorically regard Lincoln "as somehow divorced from time and place, as a spirit hovering over us all, mouthing timeless phrases and wonderful-sounding ideas." Johannsen would have us understand, however, that Lincoln was influenced by his political, social, cultural, and intellectual context and that "his ideas are very much attuned to his particular historical period." Nor does it rob Lincoln of any of his importance to say that he reflects his time.[12]

---

[9] Richard N. Current, *The Lincoln Nobody Knows* (New York: Hill & Wang, 1958), p. 196; Richard N. Current, ed., *The Political Thought of Abraham Lincoln* (Indianapolis: Bobbs-Merrill, 1967), pp. xxix–xxx.

[10] See Stanley Pargellis, "Lincoln's Political Philosophy," *Abraham Lincoln Quarterly*, 3 (June 1945), 275–90; James G. Randall, *Lincoln the Liberal Statesman* (New York: Dodd, Mead, 1947); T. Harry Williams, "Abraham Lincoln—Principle and Pragmatism in Politics: A Review Article," *Mississippi Valley Historical Review*, 40 (June 1953): 89–106; David Donald, "Abraham Lincoln and the American Pragmatic Tradition," *Lincoln Reconsidered: Essays on the Civil War Era* (New York: Alfred A. Knopf, 1956), pp. 187–208; Norman A. Graebner, "Abraham Lincoln: Conservative Statesman," in *The Enduring Lincoln: Lincoln Sesquicentennial Lectures at the University of Illinois*, ed. Norman A. Graebner (Urbana: University of Illinois Press, 1959), pp. 67–94; Don E. Fehrenbacher, ed., *Abraham Lincoln: A Documentary Portrait Through His Speeches and Writings* (Stanford: Stanford University Press, 1964); Fehrenbacher, *Prelude to Greatness: Lincoln in the 1850s* (Stanford: Stanford University Press, 1962).

[11] Mark E. Neely, Jr., "Lincoln and the Constitution: An Overview," *Lincoln Lore*, No. 1777 (March 1987), 2–4; No. 1778 (April 1987), 1–2.

[12] Robert W. Johannsen, "Lincoln, Liberty, and Equality," in *Liberty and Equality Under the Constitution*, ed. John Agresto (Washington, D.C.: American Historical Association and American Political Science Association, 1983), p. 63.

Johannsen points to a different perspective, however, when he states that in the sectional conflict of the 1850s, Lincoln's ideas on liberty and equality "assumed their final transcendent meaning."[13] It is not clear whether this development was a result of the conditions and circumstances of the time or whether Lincoln was responsible for it through his power of reason and intellect.[14] To describe political ideas as having transcendent meaning is to raise the question of a rational-philosophical approach to the study of political thought.

The point of view of rational-philosophical analysis rests on certain epistemological assumptions. Foremost is the correspondence theory of truth, whereby statements made about present or past reality should be taken to describe, represent, or correspond to something that has an independent existence.[15] Within that perspective the rational-philosophical approach regards reason, intellect, and ideas as independent variables in history, rather than mere reflections of social and material interests or unconscious psychological drives. Ideas shape events in the sense that individuals act on them.[16] Through reason, individuals are capable of apprehending true ideas that are authoritative in the sense of determining action by virtue of obligating it.[17]

An example of the rational-philosophical approach to the study of Lincoln is Herbert Croly's 1909 essay "Lincoln as More Than an American." Croly described Lincoln as a man of "vision," using the word in a rational-empirical sense that contrasts markedly with the connotation of ideological aspiration and progressive imagination attached to the term today. Referring to the political crisis of the

---

[13] Ibid., p. 53.

[14] Professor Johannsen's account is ambiguous. He states that in responding to the challenge posed by Stephen Douglas, "Lincoln strengthened his commitment to liberty and equality, sharpened their meanings and raised them to new heights of moral expression." This implies that Lincoln did this through thoughtful reflection. Yet, Johannsen also says that "Lincoln's views were not unusual. . . . they revealed a commitment to a free labor ideology that was shared by most Americans . . . [and] was ultimately shaped in the crucible of the antislavery movement" (ibid.).

[15] David Boucher, "Language, Politics, and Paradigms: Pocock and the Study of Political Thought," *Polity*, 17 (Summer 1985), 769.

[16] Ralph Lerner, *The Thinking Revolutionary: Principle and Practice in the New Republic* (Ithaca, N.Y.: Cornell University Press, 1987), pp. ix–x, 2–14.

[17] John R. Diggins, *The Lost Soul of American Politics: Virtue, Self-Interest, and the Foundations of Liberalism* (New York: Basic Books, 1984), p. 351.

1850s, Croly said that "Lincoln's vision placed every aspect of the situation in its proper relations. . . . Lincoln's peculiar service to his countrymen before the war was that of seeing straighter and thinking harder than did his contemporaries." Croly believed that the key to Lincoln's statesmanship was his ability to harmonize the faculties of reason and will. His participation in legal practice and political affairs kept his will firm and vigorous, as if he were really no more than a man of action. Yet Lincoln's "luminous and disciplined intelligence" served to enlighten his will, and his will established the mature decisions of his intelligence. Lincoln's life was distinguished by the fact that his energy and powers were not devoted exclusively to practical ends. He "preferred the satisfaction of his own intellectual and social instincts, and so qualified himself for achievements beyond the power of a Douglas." Croly judged that Lincoln was an example of "high and disinterested intellectual culture"; he "rarely, if ever, proclaimed an idea which he had not mastered, and he never abandoned a truth which he had once thoroughly achieved."[18]

Croly, of course, wrote before Marxist and Freudian assumptions revolutionized American intellectual life, undermining belief in conscious, rational thought as the end and highest attribute of human nature, and as a decisive influence on history. Historiography in particular was influenced by the theory of the sociology of knowledge, according to which ideas and thought were defined as ideology that reflected class interests. Historians were also affected by the concept of rationalization in psychology, which taught them to discount formal, conscious expressions of thought and rationality and to look for unconscious drives and motivations as the real source of human conduct. The introduction of these new concepts of human action challenged, without necessarily invalidating, the older rational-philosophical approach. As profound as it was, however, the effect was gradual, and many historians continued to adhere to the traditional assumptions of rational idealism, at least in the case of Lincoln.

Summarizing an account of changing views on the Lincoln legend, Roy P. Basler wrote in 1935 that the basic issue in assessing Lincoln was whether he was an opportunist or a principled statesman. Basler was impressed by the timeliness of Lincoln's political actions, as well as their permanence or timelessness, and he rejected the notion

---

[18] Herbert Croly, *The Promise of American Life* (New York: Macmillan, 1909), pp. 87, 89, 91–92.

that Lincoln was an opportunist. Quoting Lord Charnwood, he stated that the only alternative to the opportunist interpretation was the opposite view, "which ascribes to him an originality, an undeviating consistency, and a philosophic grasp of facts in relation to a deeply thought-out principle, such as few others, if any, of the world's great statesmen have shown."[19]

Basler relied on Lord Charnwood, whom we have identified with the principled but nonphilosophical interpretation of Lincoln. Other historians who advanced that view appear to have shared Basler's judgment. Such scholars as James G. Randall, T. Harry Williams, and Richard N. Current might dismiss the rhetoric of radical Republicans as a mask of capitalist-class interests, but they did not apply the same analysis to Lincoln, or deny the rational-philosophic ground of the settled convictions and principles that they believed guided his statecraft. Fehrenbacher, for example, describes Lincoln's writings as strictly functional and directed toward practical results rather than ultimate truth, but he attributes to Lincoln a political philosophy based on the belief in ethical purposes not subject to the daily barter of politics.[20]

Marxist economic interpretation premised on the critique of political thought as class-based ideology began to affect the field of Civil War scholarship significantly in the writings of revisionist historians of the 1930s. Its introduction into the Lincoln field occurred later with the publication of Richard Hofstadter's 1948 essay "Abraham Lincoln and the Self-Made Myth." The impact was considerable. Earlier progressive historians had lamented the triumph of middle-class capitalism in the Civil War era without implicating Lincoln. Thus, Charles A. Beard called Lincoln "the great mystic in the White House," wrote of his "uncanny genius for practical affairs," and praised his "words of wisdom" and the "deathless music of his spirit."[21] Vernon Louis Parrington, in describing Lincoln's "spontaneous liberalism" and "deep-rooted equalitarianism," said that Lincoln held other rights more sacred than property rights and was able to amalgamate idealism and economics.[22]

---

[19] Roy P. Basler, *The Lincoln Legend: A Study in Changing Convictions* (Boston: Houghton Mifflin, 1935), pp. 29–30.

[20] Fehrenbacher, ed., *Abraham Lincoln: A Documentary Portrait*, p. xxix; Fehrenbacher, *Prelude to Greatness*, p. 95.

[21] Charles A. Beard and Mary R. Beard, *The Rise of American Civilization* II (New York: Macmillan, 1930), pp. 32, 97.

[22] Vernon Louis Parrington, *Main Currents in American Thought*. 2 vols. (New York: Harvest Books, 1954), 2:145–53.

In contrast, Hofstadter offered an unflattering, sharply critical view of Lincoln. He reduced Lincoln's political ideas and the American political tradition in general to "the ideology of self-help, free enterprise, competition, and beneficent cupidity." Lincoln, to be sure, believed in equalitarian democracy, but Hofstadter derogatorily judged this to be "a democracy in cupidity rather than democracy of fraternity."

Lincoln's historical significance was to serve as the preeminent example of the self-help idea at the core of the American ideology. Thus, his political thought was guided by his understanding of the impulse "to rise in life, to make something of himself through his own honest efforts." In Hofstadter's view, however, a political philosophy grounded in narrow self-interest was not a sound basis for political action because it led Lincoln into contradiction and inconsistency. For example, Hofstadter acknowledged the penetrating character of Lincoln's attack on slavery but noted his circumspectness in practical politics wherever blacks were concerned. Lincoln's attack carried "the conviction of a man of far greater moral force than the pre-presidential Lincoln ever revealed in action." Of Lincoln's assertion that "Republicans are for both the man and the dollar, but in case of conflict the man before the dollar," Hofstadter commented that "One sees the moral idealism of the man; it is there, unquestionably, but he hopes that the world will never force it to obtrude itself."[23]

Lincoln's most glaring contradiction, according to Hofstadter, appeared in his professions of fidelity to the Declaration of Independence as an instrument of democracy. The revisionist roots of Hofstadter's liberal interpretation are evident in his discussion. The Declaration of Independence was the primary article in Lincoln's political creed and provided his most formidable political ammunition. Yet, in the end, "it was the Declaration that he could not make a consistent part of his living work." The principal reason for this conclusion is that "Lincoln suppressed secession and refused to acknowledge that the right of revolution he had so boldly accepted belonged to the South." In Hofstadter's opinion, the North was fighting the war to deny southern self-determination. Lincoln, however, in his Special Message to Congress in July 1861, "skillfully . . .

---

[23] Richard Hofstadter, *The American Political Tradition* (New York: Alfred A. Knopf, 1948), pp. vii, viii, 99–102.

inverted the main issue of the war to suit his purpose." Assisted "by the blessed fact that the Confederates had struck the first blow," Lincoln "presented it as a war to defend not only the Union but the sacred principles of popular rule and opportunity for the common man." Unwilling to apply the democratic principle to the southern white majority, Lincoln was also grossly inconsistent where slavery and blacks were concerned, Hofstadter argued. Always thinking primarily about free white labor, Lincoln was never much troubled about blacks. His attitude toward slavery, Hofstadter tells us, was "expediency tempered by justice." Only under pressure from the radicals did he "conduct . . . a brilliant strategic retreat toward a policy of freedom." Finally, when "things had gone from bad to worse," Lincoln issued the Emancipation Proclamation, expressing, in Hofstadter's well-known characterization, "all the moral grandeur of a bill of lading."[24]

In the early phases of the civil rights movement, Hofstadter's astringent view of Lincoln and the Republican party on the question of black equality was drawn too sharply to gain historiographical endorsement. Purged of revisionist sympathies, however, Hofstadter's general interpretation of the class basis of American political thought was adapted into a more benign ideological interpretation of the Republican party in the Civil War era. In this view, the ideology of Lincoln's party was more than the convenient rationalization of material interests: It was the system of beliefs, values, fears, prejudices, reflexes, and commitments that constituted the social consciousness of the free-soil and antislavery forces.[25] For purposes of the present analysis, we note that this revision of the concept of ideology avoids some of the egregious reductionism of earlier studies inspired by the more simplistic sociology of knowledge. Nevertheless, it basically denies the importance of individual thought by treating ideas as an expression of social strain and anxiety, as well as economic class interest. It has had little effect, therefore, in illuminating Lincoln's political thought. At most, a few neo-Hofstadterites have placed Lincoln in the context of Beard's Second American Revolution, variously depicting him as a reluctant, unconscious, conservative, and pragmatic revolutionary.[26]

---

[24] Ibid., pp. 102–103, 108, 125, 132.

[25] Eric Foner, *Free Soil, Free Labor, Free Men: The Ideology of the Republican Party Before the Civil War* (New York: Oxford University Press, 1970), pp. 4–6.

[26] Otto H. Olson, "Abraham Lincoln as Revolutionary," *Civil War History*, 24 (September 1978), 213–24; Stephen B. Oates, "Abraham Lincoln: Republican in the

Not long after Hofstadter offered his acerb account from a Marxist perspective, Edmund Wilson wrote an essay that approached Lincoln from a literary-psychological point of view. Paralleling Hofstadter's thesis of the self-made economic man, Wilson described Lincoln as the product of psychodramatic self-fabrication. The general interpretive scheme of Wilson's *Patriotic Gore* dismisses political leaders' statements of rational moral purpose as propaganda designed to conceal the power instinct, zoological and biological in nature, that Wilson posits as the true source of acts of state. Like Hofstadter expressing revisionist proclivities, Wilson more specifically dismisses antislavery and pro-Union rhetoric as rabble-rousing, "pseudo-moral" issues intended to justify the suppression of southern self-determination. Within this perspective Wilson sees Lincoln, in company with Lenin and Bismarck, as a leader who became a ruthless dictator in the service of his own kind of idealism.[27]

The most novel feature of Wilson's interpretation that attracted the attention of later historians was his argument that in the Springfield Lyceum Address, in which Lincoln warned the people against tyrants who would seek to overthrow the institutions of the Founding Fathers, Lincoln "has projected himself into the role against which he is warning them." Pursuing this theme, Wilson shows Lincoln's involvement in the slavery struggle, his talk about right and wrong, and his role in turning the conflict between North and South into "a Holy War led by God." In sum, Wilson states that Lincoln "created himself as a poetic figure, and . . . thus imposed himself on the nation." In all this, Lincoln's powerful intellect and literary ability, which Wilson fully appreciates, are subordinated to the psychological drive that leads him to seek the heroic role. In ever more mystical and religiously prophetic ways, Lincoln fashioned the drama in which he crushed the opposition, sent thousands of men to their deaths, and finally laid down his own life with theirs. This end, Wilson writes, "was morally and dramatically inevitable."[28]

Years later, when Wilson's cynical view of power politics and national ideals was more widespread, his dramatic analysis became the

---

White House," in *Abraham Lincoln and the American Political Tradition*, ed. John L. Thomas (Amherst: University of Massachusetts Press, 1986), pp. 98–110; James M. McPherson, "Abraham Lincoln and the Second American Revolution," in *Abraham Lincoln and the American Political Tradition*, ed. Thomas, pp. 142–60.

[27] Edmund Wilson, *Patriotic Gore: Studies in the Literature of the American Civil War* (New York: Oxford University Press, 1962), pp. xvii–xviii.

[28] Ibid., pp. 108, 114–15, 123, 130.

basis of several psychohistorical accounts of Lincoln's political career. In these works no conscious rational thought of individuals controls the action. Psychological processes and mechanisms generally
defined by intergenerational conflict are in control. While they may
be viewed as either conscious or unconscious, they are in any event
beyond reason.[29] The most satisfactory of these accounts from a biographical perspective is Charles B. Strozier's *Lincoln's Quest for Union*,
which is nevertheless unilluminating on the relationship between
ideas and events. Strozier employs an updated revisionism when attributing to Lincoln and his antislavery friends a collective paranoia
and rage that divided the "group self" of the nation and was "inherently irrational." The rage could be absorbed only by war—"the collective version of the temper tantrum."[30] In analyzing Lincoln,
Strozier uses a "self-cohesiveness" model that regards humor, empa-
thy, creativeness, and wisdom as the criteria of sound personality
development. He offers evidence to illustrate each of these criteria
except wisdom. The closest we get to wisdom or to a rational explanation of Lincoln's achievements is the assertion that Lincoln possessed a facility for language. He had "power with words," and he
used it creatively and productively until, by 1861, he "could turn a
phrase that mobilized a nation."[31] In this version of the Lincoln
story, rational political thought counts for little, if indeed it exists at
all.

A combination of the ideological and psychological approaches to
Lincoln appears in Daniel Walker Howe's essay "Abraham Lincoln
and the Transformation of Northern Whiggery." Howe states that
Lincoln's political ideas were influenced by cultural antecedents and

---

[29] George B. Forgie, *Patricide in the House Divided: A Psychological Interpretation of
Lincoln and His Age* (New York: W. W. Norton, 1979); Michael Paul Rogin, "The
King's Two Bodies: Abraham Lincoln, Richard Nixon, and Presidential Self-Sacrifice," *Massachusetts Review*, 20 (Autumn 1979), 553–73; Dwight G. Anderson, *Abra-
ham Lincoln: The Quest for Immortality* (New York: Alfred A. Knopf, 1982); Charles B.
Strozier, *Lincoln's Quest for Union: Public and Private Meanings* (New York: Basic Books,
1982); James Chowning Davis, "Lincoln: The Saint and the Man," *Presidential Studies Quarterly*, 17 (Winter 1987), 71–94. For a critique of this writing, see Richard N.
Current, "Lincoln After 175 Years: The Myth of the Jealous Son," *Papers of the
Abraham Lincoln Association*, 6 (1984), 15–24.

[30] Strozier, *Lincoln's Quest for Union*, p. 201.

[31] Ibid., p. 227. Strozier notes, with no sense of contradiction, that Lincoln was
influenced by the Ciceronian ideal in the oratorical tradition "of rational man reaching his noblest attainment in the expression of an eloquent wisdom" (ibid.,
pp. 226–27).

by personal experience. "Lincoln's public philosophy was of one piece with his personal character." It was a manifestation of the Whig personality type of bourgeois compulsiveness and an expansion of "a dedication to human self-development." Following Wilson, Howe emphasizes Lincoln's ambition, his conflict with the Founding Fathers, and the dramatic conceit by which he created himself as a poetic figure and imposed himself on the nation. In Howe's view it is not Lincoln's rational understanding that leads him to involvement in the slavery issue but his "dramatic insight" into the effect of the Kansas–Nebraska Act on national policy. According to Howe, Lincoln formulated a distinctive Republican political philosophy in his debates with Douglas. And during the Civil War he enlisted religious sentiment on behalf of Enlightenment reason, "creating a 'tradition of modernity'" and offering "a Burkean justification for the rights of man."[32] These "philosophical" changes, however, appear to be the result of psychological-religious developments rather than rational thought.

II

The appeal of the economic-ideological and the psychological approaches to the study of human action directed attention away from the history of ideas as a major scholarly concern. In the past generation, however, the history of political thought has enjoyed a revival. Two methods have recommended themselves for this enterprise. The first is the rational-philosophical approach, which formed the framework for historical analysis before the advent of the ideological and psychological critiques of conscious rationality. The second approach to political thought is that of linguistic-ideological analysis.[33] Both methods have been employed in the study of Lincoln's political thought.

An important though little-known work by Richard M. Weaver pointed the direction that Lincoln scholarship would take in the

---

[32] Daniel Walker Howe, *The Political Culture of the American Whigs* (Chicago: The University of Chicago Press, 1979), pp. 267–70, 285, 296.

[33] See J. G. A. Pocock, *Politics, Language, and Time: Essays on Political Thought and History* (New York: Atheneum, 1973); Anthony Pagden, ed., *The Languages of Political Theory in Early-Modern Europe* (Cambridge: Cambridge University Press, 1987), pp. 1–38.

civil rights era of the 1950s and 1960s. Weaver was a student of rhetoric who approached Lincoln from the perspective of a body of thought which, almost uniquely in modern times, sustained the classical philosophical tradition against the claims of scientific positivism. Weaver viewed Lincoln as a statesman whose grasp of fundamental moral principles enabled him successfully to resist proslavery secessionism and Democratic popular sovereignty, doctrines based on moral relativism that were advocated by his political opponents.

According to Weaver, Lincoln was a conservative Whig who saw that conservatism in order to be politically effective needed to be grounded in an "ideal objective." The moral idea of freedom and the political idea of Union were ideal objectives which Lincoln made central to the program of the Republican party in the 1850s. Though he was a gifted politician, Lincoln's political success ultimately was attributable to his philosophical and rhetorical stance. Throughout his life, and increasingly as the sectional conflict reached a climax, Lincoln argued and acted from first principles and definitions concerning the nature of things, including human nature.[34] Comparing Lincoln's philosophical-rhetorical posture to that of the Founding Fathers, Weaver said it prepared him to deal with the problem of slavery at the deepest level involving the nature of man rather than as a matter of history, law, and political expediency.[35]

Weaver declared: "All the arguments that the proslavery group was able to muster broke against the stubborn fact, which Lincoln persistently thrust in their way, that the Negro was somehow and in some degree a man." Equally important, Lincoln was able to demonstrate that Douglas's argument for popular sovereignty, by straddling the slavery question, broke down the essential definition of man, just as the argument for slavery did. Lincoln realized that "the price of honesty, as well as of success in the long run, is to stay out of the excluded middle." Weaver denied the revisionist historians' view that Lincoln's advantage as a statesman lay in his flexible-minded pragmatism, unhampered by metaphysical abstractions. As firmly as anyone in practical politics could, Lincoln, faithful to the established principles of American government, repudiated the relativistic interpretations and sophistries used by his opponents to evade the force

---

[34] Richard M. Weaver, *The Ethics of Rhetoric* (Chicago: Henry Regnery, 1953), pp. 56, 112–13.
[35] Ibid., p. 91.

of basic principles. Weaver concluded that at the height of his powers, in his great wartime speeches, Lincoln adopted a transcendent perspective that enabled him to see things from an ultimate point in space and time.[36]

The preeminent Lincoln scholar writing in the rational-philosophical tradition is Harry V. Jaffa, author of *Crisis of the House Divided*. A student of the political philosopher Leo Strauss, Jaffa has answered economic-ideological-revisionist interpretations of Lincoln in a series of works that advance a comprehensive theory of American politics based on the idea of classical natural right. In Jaffa's view, the founding of the republic on the principles of natural right set forth in the Declaration of Independence and Lincoln's preservation of the republic during the Civil War in accordance with natural right ideas are the central events in American history.

The doctrine of classical natural right, according to Jaffa, holds that unchanging principles of right are inherent in the universe, standards of justice that are true everywhere and always. As human beings are distinguished by reason, it is also their nature and highest goal to pursue philosophic wisdom and understanding and to try to live in accordance with the truth they have discovered. This is the meaning of virtue and moral excellence. In politics the doctrine of natural right teaches the establishment of the best regime in accordance with nature. Since it is not always possible to establish the best regime, classical natural right also teaches the virtue of prudence—the practical wisdom to choose courses of action that will attain the greater good or the lesser evil. In the modern world, according to Jaffa, the doctrine of natural right was transformed and restated in the natural rights philosophy of Hobbes and Locke. The natural rights doctrine holds that individuals should pursue their personal happiness and self-interest and that the purpose of government is to protect the civil rights of individuals so that they may do so. This philosophy differed radically from the teaching of classical natural right. Against the conventional Lockean interpretation of American politics, Jaffa advanced the challenging argument that the American Founding signified a conflation of classical natural right and modern natural rights.[37]

---

[36] Ibid., pp. 91, 94, 105, 108–109.

[37] Jaffa sets out these themes in the following works: *Crisis of the House Divided: An Interpretation of the Issues in the Lincoln–Douglas Debates* (New York: Doubleday, 1959; repr. Chicago: The University of Chicago Press, 1982); *Equality and Liberty:*

Jaffa's analysis of Lincoln's political thought centered on his understanding of the tension between the principles of equality and consent in the Declaration of Independence. Slavery denied equality and consent, yet it existed in the American republic and was supported in varying degrees by the approval or toleration of public opinion. How to resolve the conflict between slavery and the principles of the American regime became the central issue in politics of the 1850s. The problem from the standpoint of political theory was: How wrong could popular opinion be and still constitute the legitimate foundation for government? In Jaffa's view, the South had long since abandoned the principle of equality, and the question was whether the North would also abandon that principle by following Douglas's doctrine of popular sovereignty.

Contrary to the accepted historical view at the time, Jaffa said that a profound gulf separated the political thought of Lincoln and Douglas. Douglas confined the principle of equality to those citizens of the existing political community, and he held that under the principle of consent the people could rightfully decide all matters pertinent to their self-interest, including the slavery question. Jaffa argued, however, that Lincoln applied the equality principle to all men, including slaves, and insisted that self-government based on consent was limited by its dependence on the principle of equality. Thus, if the nation was consistent with the principles on which it was founded, slavery could not be rightfully recognized.[38] The extension of slavery into the territories must therefore be opposed. Jaffa contended that it was not simply sound political instinct which led Lincoln to adopt this position. He did so in accordance with the requirements of practical wisdom, in light of the political philosophy grounded in natural right and asserting natural rights that he had formulated years earlier. In the Springfield Lyceum Address, for example, Lincoln analyzed the problem of popular government in relation to the eternal antagonism between reason and passion, and he proposed to preserve republican institutions by a reverence for the Constitution and the laws, which he referred to as a "political reli-

---

Theory and Practice in American Politics (New York: Oxford University Press, 1965); *How to Think About the American Revolution: A Bicentennial Cerebration* (Durham, N.C.: Carolina Academic Press, 1978); and *American Conservatism and the American Founding* (Durham, N.C.: Carolina Academic Press, 1984). See also Thomas S. Engeman, "Assessing Jaffa's Contribution," *The Review of Politics*, 49 (Winter 1987), 127–30.
[38] Jaffa, *Crisis of the House Divided*, pp. 330–62.

gion." The essence of Lincoln's teaching, termed "political salva-
tion" by Jaffa, was that "the people . . . must be made subject to a
discipline in virtue of which they will demand only those things in
the name of their own supreme authority that are reasonable; i.e.,
consistent with the implications of their own equal rights."[39]

Perhaps the most controversial part of Jaffa's interpretation of
Lincoln was his analysis of the nature of equality in the American
political tradition. Jaffa argued that at the beginning of the republic,
as conceived by Jefferson in the Declaration of Independence,
equality was a self-evident truth. It was the effective basis of political right and the necessary and sufficient condition of the legitimacy
of government authority over the people. In his Gettysburg Address,
however, Lincoln stated that equality was not a self-evident truth
but a proposition to be proved. Jaffa asserted that equality in Lincoln's thought now became "a transcendental goal." Where Jefferson
saw civil society as moving away from the condition of actual equality
presumed to exist in the state of nature, Lincoln saw civil society
moving *toward* a condition of actual equality for all men. Thus, Lincoln "transforms and transcends" the original meaning of equality in
preparation for the new birth of freedom signified by the abolition
of slavery.[40]

In a political climate marked by changing race relations and
heightened civil rights consciousness, *Crisis of the House Divided* was
recognized as a persuasive refutation of the needless war thesis of
revisionist historiography and as a convincing statement of the cen-
trality of slavery as a moral issue in the coming of the Civil War.
Historians sympathized with Jaffa's "liberal" position on the slavery
question, without necessarily appreciating the conservative philosophical framework within which he presented his account.[41] Jaffa
later observed that his work was intended as a new type of political

---

[39] Ibid., p. 226.

[40] Ibid., pp. 318–21. Jaffa's argument provoked the conservative political philosopher Willmoore Kendall to advance a vigorously anti-Lincoln interpretation of the
problem of equality and the American political tradition. Kendall argued that Lincoln, pursuing equality in the way Jaffa described, derailed the political tradition
from the path of community control under legislative sovereignty and turned it in
the direction of modern egalitarianism. See Willmoore Kendall and George W.
Carey, *The Basic Symbols of the American Political Tradition* (Baton Rouge: Louisiana
State University Press, 1970).

[41] See, for example, the reviews by Edwin C. Rozwenc in *Political Science Quarterly*,
75 (December 1960), 604–606, and by Don E. Fehrenbacher in *American Historical
Review*, 65 (January 1960), 390.

science, critical of positivism and grounded on natural right, rather than as a book about American history.[42] *Crisis of the House Divided* was nevertheless historiographically significant, not only as an answer to revisionism but also for its reassertion of the rational-philosophical approach to the study of Lincoln's thought.

Several works subsequently appeared that shared the intellectual perspective of *Crisis of the House Divided.* The political scientist Glen E. Thurow, for example, analyzed Lincoln's political philosophy in a study that complements Jaffa's and similarly rests on a natural-right foundation. Thurow examined the Lyceum Address, the Gettysburg Address, and the Second Inaugural as expressions of Lincoln's "political religion," a body of ideas that Thurow saw as the result of Lincoln's lifelong reflections on American politics, which were "meant in some way to stand independent of the immediate circumstances."[43] He argued that the Gettysburg Address changed the meaning of equality from a self-evident principle that serves as a starting point for politics to a proposition that needs to be proved and thus becomes an end or goal. Universalistic and impelling to action, the Gettysburg Address suggests that there are no limits to politics. In contrast, the Second Inaugural emphasizes God's purposes rather than man's, suggesting that there are limits to politics. Taking the religious statements seriously, Thurow concludes that Lincoln assumed a theological perspective, transcended an exclusively nationalist outlook, and taught the people that they must temper their sovereignty by seeing events under God's judgment.[44] Lincoln resolved the crisis of the Union through actions based on natural-right understanding and prudence, the horizons of which lay beyond mere obedience to the laws or the American political tradition.[45]

George Anastaplo has similarly analyzed the Emancipation Proclamation from the perspective of natural right, finding Lincoln's state paper to be a model of prudential judgment and practical reason. He shows, for example, how Lincoln's preliminary proclamation shifted attention to the expected measure of January 1, 1863, away from the extraordinary pronouncement of the radical measure. Anastaplo

---

[42] Jaffa, *Crisis of the House Divided*, pp. 2–3.

[43] Glen E. Thurow, *Abraham Lincoln and American Political Religion* (Albany: State University of New York Press, 1976), p. 18.

[44] Ibid., pp. 87–116.

[45] Glen E. Thurow, "Reply to Corlett," *Political Theory*, 10 (November 1982), 543.

comments that the statesman must adjust his action to the prejudices and limitations of the community and often settle for less than
the best. "But the most useful adjustment is not possible," he
writes, "unless one *does* know what the very best would be." In Anastaplo's view, Lincoln knew what was best because he "thought as
deeply as any American statesman has about the character, aspirations and deficiencies of our regime."[46]

Thomas S. Engeman has contributed further to the natural-right
interpretation of Lincoln's political thought. His broad analysis of
the nature of American politics follows Jaffa in stating that the American regime was based partly on self-interest and individual rights,
partly on virtue and wisdom, but most distinctly on the "permanently radical" principles of the Declaration of Independence. A
sign of its inevitable modernity, this fact introduced into American
politics a messianic, utopian element that could threaten the stability of the regime unless it was engrafted onto the Constitution. According to Engeman, political parties became the vehicle by which
utopian democratic passions could be accommodated to the regime.
Lincoln understood this fact. When the Democratic party rejected
the revolutionary tradition in the crisis of the 1850s he helped found
the Republican party based on the principles of the Declaration of
Independence. Lincoln balanced recognition of the necessity of
party conflict as an expression of the utopian element in all modern
politics against fidelity to the Constitution as the source of order
and prudence in the exercise of power. Engeman concluded that
Lincoln knew that the passion for equality and liberty—
fundamental to American political experience—made the prudence
and moderation that the Constitution was designed to elicit all the
more necessary.[47]

Jeffrey Tulis has illuminated the field of presidential studies with
penetrating observations on Lincoln that are similarly grounded in
rational-philosophical analysis. Concerned with the selection of presidential candidates, Tulis questions the typology of presidential

---

[46] George Anastaplo, "Abraham Lincoln's Emancipation Proclamation," in *Constitutional Government in America*, ed. Ronald L. K. Collins (Durham, N.C.: Carolina
Academic Press, 1980), pp. 421–46.

[47] Thomas S. Engeman, "Utopianism and Preservation: The Rhetorical Dimension of American Statesmanship," in *The American Founding: Politics, Statesmanship,
and the Constitution*, ed. Gary L. McDowell and Ralph A. Rossum (Port Washington,
N.Y.: Kennikat, 1981), pp. 143–56.

character that places high value on the "active-positive" and denigrates the "active-negative" leader. On the basis of this schema, Tulis considers Lincoln an active-negative president. How, then, could he have been so successful and served the needs of the nation so well?[48] Tulis's answer is that Lincoln possessed "uncommon perspicacity," a trait the contemporary model of presidential character does not take into account. Great Presidents like Lincoln pose difficulties for modern analysis because they are thought to have minds incapable of description according to criteria simple and formal enough to be applied to most people. Tulis contends that whereas modern theory discounts understanding and insight, in Lincoln's time people approached political choice on the basis of issues. His point, illustrated by Lincoln, is that reason and understanding, more than personality characteristics and style, shape political action and should be the focus of presidential selection.[49]

An analysis of Lincoln as master politician, by political scientist William H. Riker, similarly rests on rational-philosophical explanation. Riker focuses on the Freeport question, wherein Lincoln forced Douglas to reassert the doctrine of popular sovereignty against the *Dred Scott* decision, as the capstone of the Republican strategy of splitting the Democratic majority, thus preparing the way for the electoral triumph of 1860. Lincoln's strategy is the most important illustration in American history of the "heresthetical art," a term invented by Riker to describe the ability of a politician, through language, reasoning, and argument, to alter the dimensions of a political situation and manipulate the outcome to achieve a desired end.[50] Lincoln's question, which was recognized at the time as "a work of genius," trapped Douglas intellectually so that no matter

---

[48] According to the criteria in James David Barber's analytical model, Lincoln was an active-negative President because he was heavily involved in political details, had negative feelings about himself, was inflexible on basic issues, and did not enjoy being President. Stephen A. Douglas, by contrast, can be seen as an active-positive leader.

[49] Jeffrey Tulis, "On Presidential Character," in *The Presidency in the Constitutional Order*, ed. Joseph M. Bessette and Jeffrey Tulis (Baton Rouge: Louisiana State University Press, 1981), pp. 283–311.

[50] William H. Riker, *The Art of Political Manipulation* (New Haven, Conn.: Yale University Press, 1986), pp. ix–xi, 1–9. Riker proposes "heresthetic" as a parallel term to logic, rhetoric, and grammar, the traditional liberal arts of language. He defines heresthetic as concerned with the strategy-value of language, as distinguished from the concern of logic for its truth-value, rhetoric its persuasion-value, and grammar its communications-value.

how he answered, the response would give Lincoln and his party a future victory. According to Riker, "there is no more elegant example of the heresthetical device of splitting the majority, and it displays Lincoln the politician at his grandest."[51]

Although political scientists led the way, historians have also approached Lincoln's political thought from the perspective of rational-philosophical analysis. In a stimulating account of American political thought, John P. Diggins has forcefully reasserted the rational-philosophic defense of ideas as the basis of action, against the linguistic-ideological view that treats language of discourse as the active, determining agent in history.[52] Combining theological and philosophical perspectives, Diggins states that Lincoln reconceptualized the republic on the basis of the Declaration of Independence and the Christian concept of virtue. Lincoln's political course was guided by the profession of political religion contained in the Lyceum Address, when he exhorted Americans to overcome passion and self-interest and be governed by the pure spirit of political ideas. Diggins emphasizes the religious dimension of Lincoln's thought.[53] Especially significant is the conclusion that Lincoln assumed the existence of "universal, transcendent ideas." Diggins writes that Lincoln "believed . . . that certain ideas were absolute because they involved fundamental principles." He held that ideas had an essential meaning not dependent upon circumstances, that ideas owed their truth to the meaning of their constituent terms, and that individuals act on the basis of universal ideas. Diggins states further that Lincoln believed that "ultimate moral questions did not admit of relativistic interpretations." Lincoln's significance in the American political tradition is that he undertook to restore the authority of political ideas.[54]

Students of Lincoln's constitutional thought have also discerned

---

[51] Ibid., p. 6.

[52] Diggins, *Lost Soul of American Politics*, pp. 347–65. While Diggins does not adopt a final position on the question of whether ideas cause actions or are only a reflection or rationalization of social interests, he argues that the rational-philosophical approach should be employed as the appropriate mode of analysis when studying people in the past who thought in that way (ibid., pp. 357–58).

[53] He writes that Lincoln's idea of a return to first principles was more Christian than classical and "was based on the conviction that republican regeneration could only occur through the rites of blood sacrifice, a theology of suffering, death, atonement, and redemption" (ibid., pp. 306–307).

[54] Ibid., pp. 314–18.

rational-philosophical premises for his actions. According to Phillip S. Paludan, Lincoln's insight into the meaning of the American Revolution led him to emphasize the rule of law and the preservation of revolutionary ideas as a solution to the problem of maintaining order in a democratic society.[55] George M. Fredrickson places Lincoln within a legal community attached to the natural law foundations of the republic that countered the passions and irrationality of militant democracy. Fredrickson sees a rationalistic concern for order as central to Lincoln's thought in the 1850s, which during the Civil War he combined with the ideal of majoritarian democracy and a religious sense of American destiny to form a transcendent synthesis.[56] In an analysis of the Lyceum Address, Major L. Wilson interprets Lincoln's call for a political religion as an attempt to create a moral community based on absolute concepts of right and wrong. Comparing Lincoln to Van Buren, he sees Lincoln as a prophet of political religion, who sought moral improvement of the nation as well as preservation of its basic principles, and Van Buren as a priest who opposed any fundamental change. Following Jaffa, Wilson emphasizes Lincoln's insistence on the idea of equality as a substantive limitation on democratic government.[57]

It might almost be said that consideration of Lincoln and the Constitution requires the perspective of rational-philosophical analysis. While this would no doubt be disputed by the legal realists, it forms the premise of Gary J. Jacobsohn's study of Lincoln's legal philosophy, which he characterizes as a theory of constitutional aspiration. Reflecting the influence of Jaffa, Jacobsohn asserts that Lincoln was deeply committed to the natural rights philosophy of the Declaration of Independence and saw its principles as providing the core meaning of the Constitution. Furthermore, as a proponent of natural right, Lincoln believed the Constitution embodied timeless principles and rejected the marketplace test of the truth of political ideas espoused by legal positivism.[58] An analysis of Lincolnian constitu-

---

[55] Phillip S. Paludan, "Lincoln, the Rule of Law, and the American Revolution," *Journal of the Illinois State Historical Society*, 70 (February 1977), 10–17.

[56] George Fredrickson, "The Search for Order and Community," in *The Public and Private Lincoln: Contemporary Perspectives*, ed. Collum Davis (Carbondale: University of Southern Illinois Press, 1979), pp. 86–100.

[57] Major L. Wilson, "Lincoln and Van Buren in the Steps of the Fathers: Another Look at the Lyceum Address," *Civil War History*, 29 (September 1983), 197–211.

[58] Gary J. Jacobsohn, "Abraham Lincoln 'On This Question of Judicial Authority': The Theory of Constitutional Aspiration," *Western Political Quarterly*, 36 (March 1983), 52–70.

tionalism by the present writer similarly underscores Lincoln's fidelity to the written Constitution of the framers as a guide to political action aimed at upholding the principles of the Declaration of Independence.[59]

A study of Lincoln's ideas on the right of revolution adds to our understanding of the rational-philosophical dimension in his political thought. Thomas J. Pressly shows that before the Civil War Lincoln supported the right of revolution for democratic ends, while opposing revolution in the domestic context of mob violence and the slavery controversy. In 1861 he said that the right of revolution was not a legal right, but that a majority had a moral right to overthrow their government when they grew weary of it and that a minority had a moral right of revolution when deprived of a vital constitutional right. A right to oppose unjustified revolution also existed. According to Pressly, Lincoln concluded that revolution was no better than counterrevolution and that evaluation of any particular attempt to exercise the right depended on the issues involved. Pressly said it might be concluded that Lincoln's views changed as his political and social interest changed, depending on the historical situation. Pressly also suggested "that Lincoln's synthesis of his ideas concerning the 'right of revolution' is distinguishable from the thought of a number of other individuals because of its comprehensiveness and depth," and that "he was led to his opinions . . . partly through a mind that probed deeper and had a wider vision than most." Lincoln provided "insight and standards for the evaluation of any particular exercise of the 'right of revolution.' "[60]

Still another analysis of Lincoln's political thought from a rational-philosophical perspective has been offered by Hans J. Morgenthau. A distinguished student of international politics, Morgenthau sees Lincoln as a statesman of unique greatness, whose significance, at once historical and philosophical, was "to teach men what it means to be a man and how to act as one." Morgenthau says that Lincoln's political philosophy was the result of innate qualities of mind and character rather than theoretical reflection, study, or even experience. Lincoln's intelligence revealed itself above all in "a philosophic understanding of public issues" and a mastery of political

---

[59] See Herman Belz, "Abraham Lincoln and American Constitutionalism," *The Review of Politics*, 50 (Spring 1988), 169–97; reprinted below as Chapter 3.

[60] Thomas J. Pressly, "Bullets and Ballots: Lincoln and the 'Right of Revolution,'" *American Historical Review*, 67 (April 1962), 661–62.

manipulation in military judgment. Evincing practical wisdom, Lincoln was prepared to subordinate political morality and right and wrong to higher purposes, including the preservation of the Union. Morgenthau describes the content of Lincoln's political thought as constitutional democracy—the uniqueness of republican America—and the ultimate value of the Union. What distinguished Lincoln's ideas, Morgenthau concludes, was that he formulated them "in philosophic terms of universal applicability."[61]

The rational-philosophical approach to Lincoln's thought finds prominent expression in recent writings. Indeed, it has been more influential in this area than in the study of earlier American political thought, where the linguistic-ideological method of analysis has dominated. The latter approach holds that political ideas can be understood only with reference to the linguistic-rhetorical context in which they appear. Rejecting both idealism (rational-philosophical inquiry) and materialism (economic-ideological analysis), the linguistic method regards thinking as an activity of communicating and distributing power by linguistic means. It views the activity of language—the vocabularies, structures, and rules by which it operates—as an historical agent. In this approach the historian of political thought seeks to identify the language or vocabulary within which an author operated and to show how language functioned to prescribe what he or she might say.[62]

In actual practice the language that proponents of this approach have found most historically significant is civic humanism, also known as classical republicanism. It is represented in the Lincoln field mainly by William S. Corlett's essay "The Availability of Lincoln's Political Religion." Corlett argues that Lincoln was a civic humanist concerned above all with the problem of democratic "lethargy," rather than the danger of democratic passions, as in the Jaffa natural-right interpretation. Lincoln's principal enterprise, therefore, was to revitalize political participation. Denying any theological dimension in Lincoln's thought, Corlett sees his political religion as strictly secular. He dismisses Lincoln's religious language as a rhetorical strategy dictated by family background and political circumstances. The gravamen of Corlett's argument is that Lincoln was not

---

[61] Hans J. Morgenthau and David Hein, *Essays on Lincoln's Faith and Politics*, ed. Kenneth W. Thompson (Lanham, Md.: University Press of America, 1983), pp. 5, 59, 67, 99.

[62] Pocock, *Politics, Language, and Time*, pp. 11–12, 14, 25.

a godlike figure of transcendent virtue but a humanist who believed that the "people need to be saved not from themselves but from their lethargy." He regards Lincoln as a leader for whom "politics became an endless opportunity to create new orders of things."[63]

The linguistic-ideological approach is modified in historical accounts that focus on political culture. John L. Thomas illustrates this approach. He asserts that Lincoln was shaped by the democratic forces of the age in which he lived, and was thus concerned with the problem of how to relate to the legacy of the Founding Fathers and spread democracy across the world. Observing that Lincoln appropriated other themes from "the edges of the popular mind"—the advantages of a humble origin and the rise from obscurity in a land of opportunity, for example—Thomas states: "The search for the political culture from which Lincoln emerged leads out of the halls of state into the American heartland of popular assumptions and aspirations where programs give way to persuasions, platforms to preferences, ideology to *mentalité*." From these materials Lincoln in turn fashioned a national liberal tradition and a doctrine of liberal nationalism. Initially bound by the expectations and constraints of Jacksonian society, Lincoln finally transcended them. And he did so, Thomas implies, not through reason and intellect but apparently through his words and language, which at their most eloquent became "forms of moral action." In his political language, Lincoln demonstrated, "above all, a susceptibility to the sheer power of language." Presumably it was this "susceptibility" that enabled Lincoln, in all the "guises" and "postures" that he assumed, to collect the raw materials afforded by an emergent national culture and forge from them "his own vision of liberty and union."[64]

III

My purpose has been the modest one of investigating, through a consideration of the problem of Lincoln's political thought, the extent to which historical accounts recognize insight and understand-

---

[63] William S. Corlett, Jr., "The Availability of Lincoln's Political Religion," *Political Theory*, 10 (November 1982), 537.

[64] John L. Thomas, Introduction, *Abraham Lincoln and the American Political Tradition*, ed. John L. Thomas (Amherst: The University of Massachusetts Press, 1986), pp. 4, 5, 10.

ing as an influence upon actions and events. Writers employing ideological and psychological interpretation tend to discount or dismiss rational thought as dependent on forces outside the individual or outside the faculty of conscious reason. A number of studies of Lincoln advance this view. At the same time many scholars have seen Lincoln as a thinking, deliberative statesman who, through rational insight and understanding, adopted wise courses of action. The evidence is obviously limited, and if Lincoln was the unique figure some students believe him to have been, the finding may be even more restrictive. Nevertheless, even if we confine our attention to statesmen, the conclusion seems warranted that thought, reason, and intellect—at least some of the time—influence events.

The presentation of changing views of Lincoln's political thought raises the question of which is the most historically sound and accurate analysis. One response would be that the three basic interpretations—the Hofstadter economic-ideological, the Wilson psychodramatic, and the Jaffa rational-philosophical analysis—rest on different assumptions and are all equally valid. This does not appear to be a satisfactory response, however, for if one interpretation were as good as another, no one would bother to study the problem. The question persists, and students of Lincoln continue to try to provide a true account of what he did and why he did it. They continue to seek the causes of his actions.

Each interpretation posits a different view of the causes of human action or the nature of thought and its relation to action. The economic-ideological view holds that class interests and social conditions determine action in the sense that thought, on which action appears to be based, is really ideology, which is a reflection of social forces and interests. The psychological view holds that thought is a function of unconscious or perhaps even irrational drives and urges, which are the real causes of action. The rational-philosophical view holds that action is based on knowledge, insight, and understanding acquired through the use of critical reason. In judging the truth or validity of these competing explanations of action, we might begin with our own experience of trying to act on the basis of reason and understanding. More broadly, we might note that in ordinary language we explain the cause of an action by talking about the reasons for it, implying that thought is involved in the effort to do something. Broader still, we consult the record of history in order to understand the causes of human action. That extremely broad and varied record contains written and unwritten materials and artifacts. A most important part, however, consists of the speeches and writings of individual actors. Certainly this is true in the study of political events.

We are then forced to consider how political speech and writing are to be read, interpreted, and understood. How is their meaning to be apprehended? This is, of course, a wide-open scholarly question today, as semioticians, anthropologists, philosophers, literary critics, political scientists, and historians argue about text and context, linguistic paradigms and deconstruction, reader-response theory, and many other recondite questions. In the face of scholarly uncertainty, it may be helpful to consult experience and ask how historians read the texts on which they base their accounts. Do they approach speech and writing with the assumption that statesmen and political actors say what they mean and mean what they say? Generally I believe the answer is yes, although they do not do so uncritically. The scholar looks for contradictions and inconsistencies, implications, and omissions that might clarify or illuminate the context of the explicit statements in the text. He considers the context in which political speech or writing appears and evaluates it in relation to other evidence. Nevertheless, within the framework of these qualifications, historians rely on political speech and writing as the best kind of evidence for understanding the reasons why statesmen acted as they did. And it seems to me that this is the method of rational-philosophical analysis.

The rational-philosophical approach to the problem of thought and action may be intrinsic to the way we lead our lives. It may be our nature as human beings. If so, it is reasonable to think that people throughout history have acted the same way. Whether or not we accept this proposition, perhaps we can agree that in order to understand and evaluate political statements it is necessary to understand them as their authors understood and intended them. Moreover, if people in an earlier time acted politically on the basis of a rational-philosophical perspective not because it was part of their nature but simply because they happened to do so, the method of objective historical analysis, which insists on seeing things in context and from the standpoint of the participants, would seem to require that we approach their political statements from that point of view.[65] On the basis of these considerations we may say that the method of rational-philosophical analysis provides the most reliable and historically sound approach to the study of Lincoln's political thought.

There is abundant evidence that Lincoln's statesmanship was grounded in rational-philosophical analysis. Reflecting on the nature and sources of the American experiment in the weeks before his inauguration in 1861, Lincoln wrote: "All this is not the result of accident. It has a philosophical cause." The Constitution and the Union were necessary elements, but they were not the primary reason for the nation's success. Behind these, "entwining itself more closely about the human heart," was "the principle of Liberty to all." This was the "philosophical cause" of "our free government and consequent prosperity." Lincoln described liberty as the word " 'fitly spoken' " which has proved "an 'apple of gold,' " and the Constitution and the Union as the "picture of silver" framed around it. He urged his fellow citizens to act so that "neither *picture*, or *apple* shall ever be blurred, or bruised or broken." And "That we may so act," he admonished, "we must study, and understand the points of danger."[66]

As President, Lincoln studied and understood and acted on the basis of practical reason. Lord Charnwood's assessment of his statesmanship is apt. When the war was over, Charnwood wrote, "It seemed to the people that he had all along been thinking their real thoughts for them; but they knew that this was because he had fearlessly thought for himself."[67]

It is necessary in studying Lincoln to account for the esteem with which he is regarded in the opinion of mankind.[68] The word "transcendent" appears in many descriptions of Lincoln by historians of varying outlook.[69] Fehrenbacher states that through his virtues and deeds Lincoln has acquired "symbolic and universal meaning."[70] His

---

[65] Leo Strauss, *Natural Right and History* (Chicago: The University of Chicago Press, 1953), pp. 56–62.

[66] Roy P. Basler et al., eds., *The Collected Works of Abraham Lincoln*, 9 vols. (New Brunswick, N.J.: Rutgers University Press, 1953–1955), 4:168–69.

[67] Charnwood, *Abraham Lincoln*, p. 454. I am indebted to Walter Berns for calling this statement to my attention.

[68] Fehrenbacher, ed., *Abraham Lincoln: A Documentary Portrait*, p. xvi.

[69] For example, Johannsen, Thomas, Fredrickson, and Stanley Pargellis, among other historians, refer to Lincoln in this way.

[70] Fehrenbacher, ed., *Abraham Lincoln: A Documentary Portrait*, p. xvii.

words are memorialized, and in them, as Fehrenbacher says, we see an expression of his character. More significantly, however, it is Lincoln's thought, expressing an understanding of democratic principles, that is memorialized and that accounts for his preeminent status. In remembering and studying Lincoln's words, we do not acknowledge the creative influence of the social conditions and climate of opinion of his time. The very notion is preposterous. On the contrary, in studying Lincoln's words we recognize the range, depth, and power of his insight and understanding. We honor his ability to think beyond the horizons of his time and the limits of the American experience.

3

Abraham Lincoln and American Constitutionalism

As THE NATURE OF THE AMERICAN POLITICAL TRADITION in its formative period may be said to depend on the relationship between the Constitution and the Declaration of Independence, so the nature of twentieth-century American government may be said to depend on the relationship between the Civil War and the American Founding. Lest we lose sight of this fact in undue celebration of the Founding Fathers, we have been urged to turn our attention to the constitution makers of the 1860s, who are said to have improved on the work of the framers by refusing "to acquiesce in outdated notions of 'liberty,' 'justice,' and 'equality.'" The source of this advice, Mr. Justice Thurgood Marshall of the United States Supreme Court, goes so far as to say that while "the Union survived the Civil War, the Constitution did not." "In its place," writes Justice Marshall, "arose a new, more promising basis for justice and equality, the 14th Amendment."[1] The nation, we are led to infer, was thus given a new fundamental law by the constitution makers of the Civil War era.

Coming as it does from a custodian of the Constitution, who reflects the views of many contemporary scholars, this provocative thesis commands our attention. The purpose of the present essay accordingly is to evaluate it through analysis of the thought and action of the figure who stands at the center of any serious consideration of Civil War constitutionalism—Abraham Lincoln. Lincoln of course did not live to take part in the events leading to the adoption of the Fourteenth Amendment. He did, however, play a decisive role in determining the outcome of the issue that forms the premise of Justice Marshall's argument, namely, whether the Constitution survived the Civil War.

An earlier version of this essay appeared in *The Review of Politics*, 50 (Spring 1988), 169–92.

[1] Remarks of Thurgood Marshall at the Annual Seminar of the San Francisco Patent and Trademark Law Association in Maui, Hawaii, May 6, 1987, pp. 7–8.

Like the Founding Fathers, Lincoln acted as statesman and president in a time of crisis when the meaning of the nation's fundamental law was called into question. The framers intended the Constitution as a permanent instrument of government for the American people. Lincoln's historic responsibility, as he believed, was to perpetuate the institutions of the Founding as expressed in the organic law. It is important to ask, therefore, whether his conception of the Constitution and theory of constitutionalism were essentially those of the framers. The question gains pertinence from the fact that in recent years Lincoln's relation to the Founding has been challenged. He has been described as tearing down the inherited structure of government and building by dictatorial means a new Union based on the dogma of equality, or, less threateningly, as rejecting the limited-government, natural-rights Unionism of the Founders in favor of an organic nationalism that anticipated twentieth-century statism.[2] Moreover, in view of recent controversy over the nature of constitutional jurisprudence in the United States, it is pertinent to ask whether Lincoln practiced a text-based constitutionalism restrained by the forms and purposes of the Founding, or a pragmatic instrumentalism that in effect created an organic, unwritten constitution.[3]

In the analysis that follows I shall argue that the attempt to divorce Lincoln from the American Founding, like Justice Marshall's positing of a new constitution in consequence of the Civil War, is contradicted by the historical record. Lincoln adhered to the written Constitution of the framers—its forms, procedures, principles, and spirit—and was guided by it in political action aimed at achieving the ideals asserted in the Declaration of Independence. Prudent and

---

[2] See Edmund Wilson, *Patriotic Gore: Studies in the Literature of the American Civil War* (New York: Oxford University Press, 1962), pp. 99–130; Willmoore Kendall and George W. Carey, *The Basic Symbols of the American Political Tradition* (Baton Rouge: Louisiana State University Press, 1970), pp. 84–95, 137–38; M. E. Bradford, "The Lincoln Legacy: A Long View," *Modern Age*, 24 (Fall 1980), 355–63; Richard J. Bishirjian, ed., *A Public Philosophy Reader* (New Rochelle, N.Y.: Arlington House, 1978), pp. 47–70; Michael Paul Rogin, "The King's Two Bodies: Abraham Lincoln, Richard Nixon, and Presidential Self-Sacrifice," *Massachusetts Review*, 20 (Autumn 1979), 553–73; Dwight G. Anderson, *Abraham Lincoln: The Quest for Immortality* (New York: Alfred A. Knopf, 1982), passim; James A. Rawley, "The Nationalism of Abraham Lincoln," *Civil War History*, 9 (September 1963), 283–98.

[3] For a discussion of the varieties of constitutional jurisprudence, see Walter E Murphy, James E. Fleming, and William F. Harris, II, *American Constitutional Interpretation* (Mineola, N.Y.: Foundation Press, 1986), pp. 1–18, 81–85, passim.

practical in his statesmanship, Lincoln possessed in himself and in-culcated in the people constitutionalist conviction that regarded preservation of republican self-government as the nation's defining and paramount purpose.

I

Although constitutions are usually thought of as dealing with proce-dural and organizational matters, in reality they are equally if not more concerned with substantive matters of political purpose. It is success in resolving the basic question of the ends of government, placing it beyond ordinary political dispute, that causes a constitu-tion to be perceived as mainly formal and organizational. Accord-ingly, making a constitution, as the framers did, should be viewed as a form of political action within the mainstream of Western political thought. By the same token running a constitution, especially in a time of crisis when first principles are at stake, raises fundamental issues relevant to the concerns of political philosophy.[4] It is in this perspective that Lincoln's constitutionalism warrants consideration.

Philosophers are at liberty to formulate ideas of political right from whatever source reason leads them to consult. Whether those who run a constitutional regime are equally free to choose among available political theories is debatable. The question is especially pertinent in the United States, where from the beginning of the government political actors and public officials to a significant extent have been under an obligation to maintain the ends and purposes of the Founding. This issue has special relevance for the study of Lin-coln, who has been described as repudiating the Union of the fram-ers even as he professed to save it. Our general inquiry, then, concerns the relation of Lincoln's constitutional thought and action to that of the authors of the Constitution. We shall approach the problem by asking a more manageable preliminary question: namely, what was the Constitution, as Lincoln understood it?

---

[4] There is of course an extensive literature on the relationship between political philosophy and constitutionalism. For illuminating nontechnical discussion of the problem, see Martin E. Spencer, "Plato and the Anatomy of Constitutions," *Social Theory and Practice*, 5 (Fall 1978), 95–130; and Edward S. Corwin, "Constitution v. Constitutional Theory," in *American Constitutional History: Essays by Edward S. Cor-win*, ed. A. T. Mason and G. Garvey (New York: Harper & Row, 1964), pp. 99–108.

It is doubtful that anyone in Lincoln's generation would know the meaning of terms now used in constitutional analysis, such as "interpretivists" and "noninterpretivists" or "preservationists" and "pragmatic instrumentalists."[5] As had become habitual in political practice from ratification on, when people in the nineteenth century referred to the Constitution they meant the written document of the Founding Fathers. With the outbreak of civil war, opportunity existed for a new kind of constitutionalism to emerge, and while it is true that in a formal sense federal authorities did not set the Constitution aside, the question persists as to whether they did not change the ends and objects of government under the façade of maintaining old constitutional forms. Did they in reality substitute an unwritten constitution, consisting of laws, policies, and actions of government officials, in place of the written document?[6] Lincoln has been depicted in these terms by writers both sympathetic and critical. Evaluation of the claim involves not only Lincoln's place in the constitutional tradition, but also the nature of that tradition. If it could be shown that an organic, unwritten constitution became the basis of American government during the Civil War, the fact would go far toward justifying further rejection of the framers' constitutionalism.

Lincoln's analysis of the right of revolution in the First Inaugural, the occasion for what political scientist Walter F. Murphy has described as "the most important single act of American constitutional interpretation," expressed the view of the Constitution that he maintained throughout his political career.[7] "If, by the mere force of numbers, a majority should deprive a minority of any clearly written constitutional right," Lincoln reasoned, "it might, in a moral point of view, justify revolution." Denying that this was the case in regard to the South, he said all the vital rights of minorities and of individu-

---

[5] See Lief H. Carter, *Contemporary Constitutional Lawmaking: The Supreme Court and the Art of Politics* (New York: Pergamon, 1985).

[6] Contrary to constitutional orthodoxy, there was occasional discussion of an unwritten constitution in this period. See "The Constitution: Written and Unwritten," *The American Review: A Whig Journal of Politics, Literature, Art, and Science*, 6 (July 1847), 1–3; Sidney George Fisher, *The Trial of the Constitution* (Philadelphia: J. P. Lippincott, 1862), pp. 41, 56.

[7] Walter F. Murphy, "Who Shall Interpret? The Quest for the Ultimate Constitutional Interpreter," *The Review of Politics*, 48 (Summer 1986), 405. The act of interpretation to which Murphy refers is contained in Lincoln's statement that "in contemplation of universal law, and of the Constitution, the Union of these States is perpetual."

als were plainly assured to them "by affirmations and negations, guaranties and prohibitions, in the Constitution." However, no organic law could anticipate every question that might arise in the course of administering the government. And it was from "questions of this class," Lincoln said—for example, the failure of the Constitution to say expressly whether Congress *may* prohibit slavery or *must* protect it in the territories—that "all our constitutional controversies" came.[8]

"I hold," Lincoln declared upon taking the oath of office, "that in contemplation of universal law, and the Constitution, the Union of these States is perpetual."[9] Whether, in referring to universal law, he was expressing a belief in philosophical natural right is not clear, but whatever authority was signified it was separate from the Constitution. "I take the official oath to-day," he announced, "with no mental reservations, and with no purpose to construe the Constitution or laws, by any hypercritical rules."[10] In these statements Lincoln makes clear his adherence to the orthodox conception of the Constitution as a written instrument. Although he was not, as we shall see, a pure positivist in his view of the Constitution, his approach to constitutional interpretation remained firmly text-bound. A review of his constitutional arguments and reasoning shows Lincoln's fidelity to the constitutionalism of the Founding.

When Lincoln referred to the Constitution he meant the framers' document, which he knew well and quoted with telling effect. In his speech on the Sub-Treasury in December 1839, Lincoln defended a national bank as constitutional on the basis of previous interpretation of the text by the framers, Congress, and the Supreme Court, and on his own construction of the organic laws (the necessary and proper clause in conjunction with the clause authorizing Congress to lay and collect taxes). Turning Democratic strict construction against his Democratic opponents, he made the professedly novel argument that the lack of express authority in the Constitution for a national bank applied with equal force to the Sub-Treasury plan. If the bank proposal was unconstitutional because not necessary in the sense of being indispensable to the exercise of the taxing power, so too was the Sub-Treasury idea unconstitutional for the same rea-

---

[8] Roy P. Basler et al., eds., *The Collected Works of Abraham Lincoln*, 9 vols. (New Brunswick, N.J.: Rutgers University Press, 1953–55), 4:267.

[9] Ibid., 4:264.

[10] Ibid.

son. "Upon the phrase '*necessary and proper*,' in the Constitution," he stated, "it seems to me more reasonable to say, that *some* fiscal agent is *indispensably necessary*; but, inasmuch as no *particular sort* of agent is thus *indispensable*, because some *other* sort might be adopted, we are left to choose that sort of agent, which may be most '*proper*' on grounds of expediency."[11]

Lincoln was similarly precise and document-bound in constitutional argument throughout his career. Moreover he took it for granted that the original intent of the framers was relevant in determining the meaning of the Constitution. Objecting to Polk's action in the outbreak of war with Mexico, Lincoln said that to allow the President to invade a neighboring nation in order to repel invasion was to allow him to make war at pleasure, in contradiction of the constitutional provision giving the power to declare war to Congress. The action also violated the framers' intent that no one man should hold the power to take the country into war.[12] In 1852 Lincoln defended Whig presidential candidate Winfield Scott against Stephen A. Douglas's charge that a proposal by Scott to change the naturalization laws, creating different classes of aliens, showed he had never read the Constitution, which Douglas said required one uniform rule of naturalization. Citing the action of the first Congress, including signers of the Constitution, in passing a naturalization law that created different classes of aliens, Lincoln inquired: "Will Judge Douglas sneeringly ask if the framers of *this law* never read the Constitution?"[13] In 1854 Lincoln caught Douglas on a misquotation of the Constitution. Douglas had said the Constitution required the suppression of the foreign slave trade, but not the prohibition of slavery in the territories. "That is a mistake, in point of fact," Lincoln asserted. "The constitution does NOT require the action of Congress in either case; and it does AUTHORIZE it in both."[14]

Lincoln's critique of the *Dred Scott* decision was based on discrepancy between Chief Justice Taney's construction of the Constitution and the written text. Taney had said the right of property in a slave

---

[11] Ibid., 1:171–72.

[12] Ibid., 1:451.

[13] Ibid., 2:142–43.

[14] Ibid., 3:278–79. Lincoln here referred to the territorial clause of the Constitution (Art. IV, sec. 3). He clarified his position in the First Inaugural by stating that the Constitution did not expressly say whether Congress might prohibit slavery in the territories.

was "distinctly and expressly affirmed in the Constitution." Taking this assertion in connection with the supremacy clause, Lincoln said it meant that the right in question was so firmly fixed in the Constitution that it could not be separated from the instrument without breaking it. This was sound reasoning if the premise were correct, Lincoln averred, but it was preposterous in reality because the Constitution affirmed no such right. "I believe that the Supreme Court and the advocates of that decision may search in vain for the place in the Constitution where the right of property in a slave is distinctly and expressly affirmed," Lincoln declared.[15]

We have noted that Lincoln's argument against secession as a valid exercise of the right of revolution turned on the question of violation of clearly written constitutional rights. So too his interpretation of the Union as perpetual appealed to the written Constitution in two senses: the implied perpetuity found in any national organic law, and adherence to the forms of the American Founding. "It is safe to assert that no government proper," Lincoln observed, "ever had a provision in its organic law for its own termination." Appealing to constitutionalist conviction, Lincoln advised, "Continue to execute all the express provisions of our national Constitution, and the Union will endure forever—it being impossible to destroy it, except by some action not provided for in the instrument itself."[16]

During the Civil War Lincoln repeatedly turned to the text of the Constitution as a guide to statecraft. Of numerous examples a few may be cited to illustrate his belief that running the Constitution meant keeping within "the four corners of the document."[17] Replying to Democratic critics who contended that the government could make no arrests nor suspend the privilege of the writ of habeas corpus " 'outside the lines of necessary military occupation, and the scenes of insurrection,' " Lincoln reasoned: "Inasmuch, however, as the constitution itself makes no such distinction, I am unable to believe that there is any such distinction."[18] On another occasion

---

[15] Ibid., 3:230–31.

[16] Ibid., 4:264–65.

[17] The "four-corners" metaphor is used by contemporary legal theorists to describe constitutional interpretation that is confined to enforcing norms stated or clearly implied in the written Constitution. See John Hart Ely, *Democracy and Distrust: A Theory of Judicial Review* (Cambridge, Mass.: Harvard University Press, 1980), p. 1.

[18] Basler et al., eds., *Collected Works of Lincoln*, 4:265.

critics sought to illustrate the force of civil liberties protections by suggesting that the Constitution be thought of without the habeas corpus clause. "Doubless [sic] if this clause of the constitution . . . were expunged," Lincoln wrote, "the other guaranties would stand; but the question is, not how those guaranties would stand, with that clause *out* of the constitution, but how they stand with that clause remaining in it." He added: "If the liberty could be indulged, of expunging that clause letter & spirit, I really think the constitutional argument would be with you."[19] But of course the liberty could not be indulged.

Lincoln expressed what may be described as a sense of constitutional fundamentalism in responding to criticism of the Conscription Act of 1863 as unconstitutional. "Whether a power can be implied, when it is not expressed, has often been the subject of controversy," he noted, "but this is the first case in which the degree of effrontery has been ventured upon, of denying a power which is plainly and distinctly written down in the constitution."[20] Citing the pertinent constitutional language, he wrote: "The case simply is the constitution provides that congress shall have power to raise and support armies; and, by this act, the congress has exercised the power to raise and support armies. This is the whole of it. It is a law made in litteral [sic] pursuance of this part of the United States Constitution."[21]

II

Throughout his life Lincoln thus showed a strong attachment to the text and forms of the Constitution. Yet the existence of a written constitution was not enough to ensure adherence to constitutional limitations, or, as Lincoln was forced to consider, the necessary exercise of constitutional powers. To give the Constitution effect beyond that of mere "parchment barriers," the framers had created "auxiliary precautions," in the form of checks and balances within the separation of powers, to supplement the primary limitation on government imposed by its dependence on the people.[22] Further to

---

[19] Ibid., 6:302.
[20] Ibid., 6:446.
[21] Ibid.
[22] *The Federalist*, ed. Edward Mead Earle (New York: Modern Library, 1938). pp. 336–38.

ensure observance of the ends and purposes of government, as well as restraints upon it, the framers would inculcate reverence for the Constitution. In a nation of philosophers, explains Publius, the voice of enlightened reason would produce reverence for the laws. In a democratic nation, however, where popular passion must play a role, "the most rational government will not find it a superfluous advantage to have the prejudices of the community on its side."[23] This advantage—what might be called the benefit of constitutionalist conviction—could be secured by teaching adherence to the text of the Constitution and respect for constitutional forms, as well as by reasoned argument applying the language of the document to specific political questions.

Employing the legislative science of *The Federalist*, Lincoln adapted it to the political realities of a democratic age that demanded greater recognition of popular passion and prejudice than did the era of the Founding.[24] It was all the more important therefore to encourage constitutionalist conviction by teaching attachment to the text and forms of the Constitution.[25] In the Springfield Lyceum Address of 1838, in which he discussed the perpetuation of republican political institutions, Lincoln dwelt on this problem.

In the Lyceum speech Lincoln analyzed the democratic distemper of his time: the unlawful actions and the spirit of lawlessness evident in mob outrages occurring from New England to Louisiana. Ultimately to be feared was the undermining of the people's "attachment" to the government, resulting in its destruction at the hands of ambitious men who would seek distinction in tearing down the temple of liberty. To prevent such an outcome Lincoln urged "the support of the Constitution and Laws," citing as an example the way Americans during the Revolution supported the Declaration of Independence. "Let reverence for the laws," he proposed, "be taught in schools, in seminaries, and in colleges. . . . let it be preached from the pulpit, proclaimed in legislative halls, and enforced in courts of justice; and, in short, let it become the *political*

---

[23] Ibid., p. 446.

[24] Thomas S. Engeman, "Utopianism and Preservation: The Rhetorical Dimension of American Statesmanship," in *The American Founding: Politics, Statesmanship, and the Constitution*, ed. Gary L. McDowell and Ralph A. Rossum (Port Washington, N.Y.: Kennikat Press, 1981), pp. 143–56.

[25] On the general subject of constitutionalist conviction, see Robert Eden, "Tocqueville on Political Realignment and Constitutional Forms," *The Review of Politics*, 48 (Summer 1986), 349–73.

religion of the nation." Revolutionary passion had helped found the nation, he pointed out, but in the future it would be a liability. "Reason, cold, calculating, unimpassioned reason, must furnish all the materials for our future support and defence." Lincoln advised: "Let those [materials] be moulded into *general intelligence*, [sound] *morality* and, in particular, *a reverence for the constitution and laws.*"[26]

In recent years the Springfield Lyceum Address has been made to yield psychohistorical meaning expressive of a darker side to the Lincoln story, against the view of Professor Jaffa and others who find in it the essential elements of Lincoln's political philosophy.[27] In the present context we observe that the object of reverence, by which the attachment of the people to the government is to be maintained, is the formal written Constitution of the Founding. Lincoln was saying in effect that to guard against the destructive effects of popular passion and the danger of democratic dictatorship, statesmen must use rational arguments to shape and instill constitutionalist conviction in the public mind, such that in a time of crisis the people will rise to the defense of constitutional forms and institutions.

So important are constitutional forms and symbols that one is inclined to say they are the essence of the political way of life known as constitutionalism. Like the rest of the Constitution with which they are identified, constitutional forms and formalities are ordinarily taken for granted, and considered secondary in importance to supposedly more substantive matters of passion, interest, and ideology. Yet in their configurative effect, resulting from constitutionalist conviction and commitment, constitutional forms shape the course of events.[28] Constitutional forms are impartial means by which political conflict is directed into peaceful, demilitarized modes of civil action.[29] The urge to go beyond forms on the one hand, or the pres-

---

[26] Basler et al., eds., *Collected Works of Lincoln*, 1:109–15.

[27] See, for example, George B. Forgie, *Patricide in the House Divided: A Psychological Interpretation of Lincoln and His Age* (New York: W. W. Norton, 1979), pp. 61–63, passim; Charles B. Strozier, *Lincoln's Quest for Union: Public and Private Meanings* (New York: Basic Books, 1982), pp. 59–61; Harry V. Jaffa, *Crisis of the House Divided: An Interpretation of the Issues in the Lincoln–Douglas Debates* (New York: Doubleday, 1959; repr. Chicago: The University of Chicago Press, 1982), pp. 183–232; Major L. Wilson, "Lincoln and Van Buren in the Steps of the Fathers: Another Look at the Lyceum Address," *Civil War History*, 29 (September 1983), 197–211.

[28] Arthur Bestor, "The American Civil War as a Constitutional Crisis," *American Historical Review*, 69 (January 1964), 327–52.

[29] Eden, "Tocqueville on Political Realignment and Constitutional Forms," 365.

sure for political informality on the other, is a source of tyranny and rebellion, especially in a democratic age.[30]

Consistent with his teaching in the Lyceum speech, Lincoln in later years appealed to the constitutionalist conviction based on the forms and text of the document. In 1848, answering the Democratic view that internal improvement legislation required amendment of the Constitution, Lincoln expressed disapproval of frequent constitutional alteration. As a general rule he thought the Constitution ought to be left alone, in order to reinforce constitutionalist conviction. "No slight occasion should tempt us to touch it," he said. "Better not take the first step, which may lead to a habit of altering it. Better, rather, habituate ourselves to think of it, as unalterable. . . . New Provisions would introduce new difficulties, and thus create, and increase appetite for still further change."[31] In 1852 Lincoln commented on Seward's "higher law" doctrine in relation to the issue of constitutional stability: ". . . in so far as it may attempt to foment a disobedience to the constitution, or to the constitutional laws of the country, it has my unqualified condemnation."[32] In December 1859 Lincoln criticized John Brown's raid on Harper's Ferry, stating: "We have a means provided for the expression of our belief in regard to Slavery—it is through the ballot box—the peaceful method provided by the Constitution."[33]

In dealing with secession Lincoln placed still greater emphasis on adherence to constitutional forms, perhaps believing that constitutionalist conviction would carry the country through the crisis. Noting that "We everywhere express devotion to the Constitution," he said southerners had the same fundamental law they had had for seventy years, and all their constitutional rights as in the past.[34] Acclaimed as he journeyed to Washington in February 1861, Lincoln said the treatment accorded him showed "the devotion of the whole people to the Constitution, the Union, and the perpetuity of the liberties of this country."[35] During the war, in the face of rumors that a Democratic victory in the election of 1864 might provoke him

---

[30] Harvey C. Mansfield, Jr., "The Forms and Formalities of Liberty," *The Public Interest*, No. 70 (Winter 1983), 123.

[31] Basler et al., eds., *Collected Works of Lincoln*, 1:488.

[32] Ibid., 2:156.

[33] Ibid., 3:496.

[34] Ibid., 4:215–16.

[35] Ibid., 4:220.

to ruin the government, or his opponents to seize it straightaway, Lincoln promised to follow the forms of the Constitution. "Whoever shall be constitutionally elected therefore in November," he stated publicly, "shall be duly installed as President on the fourth of March." Lincoln went so far as to say that the people's "will, constitutionally expressed, is the ultimate law for all," and if they should determine to have immediate peace, "even at the loss of their country, and their liberty, I know not the power or the right to resist them."[36]

This assertion is surely testimony to Lincoln's democratic commitment, but is it not tantamount to placing form over substance in the ethic of constitutionalism? Does it signify a purely positivist view of the Constitution as a set of rules and procedures divorced from normative ends? An exclusive concern with constitutional forms might warrant this conclusion. In fact, however, Lincoln regarded constitutionalist trust and conviction, shaped by the forms and formalities of the organic law, as inseparable from the ends and purposes of the Founding. Lincoln expressed this nonpositivistic (though text-based) aspect of constitutionalism in referring to the spirit of the Constitution.[37]

Disputing Douglas's charge that Republicans desired to attack slavery in the South, Lincoln said in July 1858: ". . . we agree that, by the Constitution we assented to, in the States where it exists we have no right to interfere with it because it is in the Constitution and we are by both duty and inclination to stick by that Constitution in all its letter and spirit from beginning to end."[38] In February 1861, en route to Washington and reluctant to comment on the secession trouble, he observed: "And when I do speak, fellow-citizens, I hope to say nothing in opposition to the spirit of the Constitution, contrary to the integrity of the Union, or which will in any way prove inimical to the liberties of the people or to the peace of the whole country."[39] In judging the constitutionality of West Virginia's admission into the Union after its separation from Virginia, Lincoln declared it "absurd" to count loyal and disloyal citizens as equals in

---

[36] Ibid.

[37] For discussion of positivistic and nonpositivistic views of the Constitution, see Gary J. Jacobsohn, *The Supreme Court and the Decline of Constitutional Aspiration* (Totowa, N.J.: Rowman & Littlefield, 1985), pp. 57–73.

[38] Basler et al., eds., *Collected Works of Lincoln*, 2:494.

[39] Ibid., 4:210

assessing the validity of the claim for admission. He wrote: "It is said, the devil takes care of his own. Much more should a good spirit—the spirit of the Constitution and the Union—take care of it's own. I think it can not do less, and live."[40] In discussing the problem of habeas corpus suspension, moreover, as we have seen, Lincoln attended to the "letter & spirit" of the constitutional clause permitting irregular arrests under certain conditions.[41]

While it would be difficult to establish a universally agreed upon meaning for the "spirit of the Constitution" in our constitutional history, Lincoln was probably representative in using the term to refer generally to the purposes and intentions of the framers as expressed in the instrument itself. Of course, reference to specific provisions in the text could make the spirit of the Constitution bewilderingly particularistic. The vitality of the concept derives from the sense it conveys of the central purpose of the Founding Fathers in writing the Constitution, namely, to establish liberty. In a sense, therefore, the spirit of the Constitution could be said to be political liberty. Lincoln at any rate expressed this central idea or spirit of American institutions in referring to the "philosophy of our government" or the "principles of true republicanism." He meant the right of individuals to govern themselves under the Constitution, according to the principle of majority rule.

III

As a candidate for the state legislature in 1832 Lincoln said he was under a duty, in accordance with "the principles of true republicanism," to express his views on local affairs.[42] As a member of Congress in 1848 he said an elected representative was obligated "to carry out the known will [wishes] of his constituents," calling this "the primary, the cardinal, the one great living principle of all Democratic representative government." Lincoln contrasted this principle to the Democratic party practice of adopting a platform and forcing the people to ratify it, "however unpalatable" it might be. He explained that the Whig party, in contrast, distinguished between selection of

---

[40] Ibid., 6:27.
[41] Ibid., 6:302.
[42] Ibid., 1:5.

the President and legislation for the country, "so that the people can elect whom they please, and afterwards, legislate just as they please, without any hindrance, save only so much as may guard against infractions of the constitution, undue haste, and want of consideration."[43] The "true philosophy of our government," he said at the time, was that "in Congress all options and principles should be represented, and that when the wisdom of all had been compared and united, the will of the majority should be carried out."[44]

Lincoln inflexibly defended this philosophy of government in the secession crisis. In words intended for a Kentucky audience though never delivered, he rejected the notion that as incoming President he was somehow under an obligation to say something to "restore peace to the country." Insisting that he "should be inaugurated, solely on the conditions of the constitution, the laws," he declared that if an elected President "can not be installed, till he first appeases his enemies, by breaking his pledges, and . . . betraying his friends, this government, and all popular government, is already at an end." Lincoln believed acquiescence to such demands "would not merely be the ruin of a man, or a party; but as a precedent they would ruin the government itself." His position on this issue was not "a matter of mere personal honor." It was necessary to defend both constitutional form and principle together.[45]

Lincoln at this time extended the republican majority principle beyond policy matters to the determination of constitutional questions. Observing that both North and South professed devotion to the Constitution, he said the sectional dispute centered on the meaning of the organic law in respect of southerners' rights. "To decide that," Lincoln asked, "who shall be the judge? Can you think of any other, than the voice of the people?" If the majority did not control, the minority must, and "Would that be just or generous? Assuredly not!" he asserted. Lincoln conceded that the majority might be wrong, wrong even in electing him as President. "Yet we must adhere to the principle that the majority shall rule," he insisted. "By your Constitution you have another chance in four years."[46] The First Inaugural restated the principle. Describing the nature of the sectional disagreement over the meaning of the Con-

---

[43] Ibid., 1:506–507.
[44] Ibid., 2:2–3.
[45] Ibid., 4:200.
[46] Ibid., 4:207.

stitution, Lincoln noted the argument that constitutional questions should be decided by the Supreme Court. He believed Court decisions were binding on the parties in a case and were entitled to high respect and consideration in all parallel cases by the other departments of government. "At the same time," he said, "the candid citizen must confess that if the policy of the government, upon vital questions, affecting the whole people, is to be irrevocably fixed by decisions of the Supreme Court, the instant they are made, in ordinary litigation between parties, . . . the people will have ceased, to be their own rulers." Pronouncing the idea of secession to be "the essence of anarchy," Lincoln memorably summarized his philosophy of government: "A majority held in restraint by constitutional checks, and limitations, and always changing easily, with deliberate changes of popular opinions and sentiments, is the only true sovereign of a free people."[47]

In the constitutional controversy preceding the Civil War Lincoln underscored the fact that his philosophy of government was based on the ideas of liberty and equality as expressed in the Declaration of Independence. Attacking the Kansas–Nebraska Act in 1854, he asserted: "The theory of our government is Universal Freedom. 'All men are created free and equal,' says the Declaration of Independence."[48] The " 'central idea' in our political public opinion," he said in 1856, was "the equality of all men."[49] Disputing the Democratic reading of the document, Lincoln held that the equality principle in the Declaration meant that all men were equal at least in respect of the rights of life, liberty, and the pursuit of happiness. This principle, he reasoned, was intended as "a standard maxim for a free society, which should be familiar to all, and revered by all; constantly looked to, constantly labored for, and even though never perfectly attained, constantly approximated, and thereby constantly spreading and deepening its influence."[50] When secession became the preeminent political issue facing the nation, Lincoln focused on liberty as the central idea of the Declaration of Independence. "I am exceedingly anxious that this Union, the Constitution, and the liberties

---

[47] Ibid., 4:267–68.
[48] Ibid., 2:245. Lincoln's quotation of the Declaration was inaccurate. The text states that "all men are created equal."
[49] Ibid., 2:385.
[50] Ibid., 2:406.

of the people," he said in February 1861, "shall be perpetuated in accordance with the original idea" for which the Revolution was fought. This was not merely national independence, "but something in that Declaration giving liberty, not alone to the people of this country, but hope to the world for all future time."[51]

The inference can be drawn that Lincoln viewed the Declaration of Independence as the nation's primary constitutive document, and as the source of the substantive principles of the Constitution.[52] The

---

[51] Ibid., 4:240.

[52] This argument has been made most persuasively by Harry V. Jaffa in a number of works. For a concise statement of the thesis, see his essay, "Abraham Lincoln," in *Encyclopedia of the American Constitution*, ed. Leonard W. Levy, Kenneth L. Karst, and Dennis J. Mahoney (New York: Macmillan, 1986), 3:1162–66. Jaffa's analysis of the Declaration of Independence in Lincoln's thought is central to his interpretation of Lincoln's relationship to the Founding Fathers. His general view is that Lincoln preserved the Union and the Constitution of the framers. In *Crisis of the House Divided: An Interpretation of the Issues in the Lincoln–Douglas Debates* (1959), however, Jaffa introduced a specific argument about Lincoln's view of equality that strikes a somewhat different note. He argued that Jefferson, following Locke, regarded equality as the immanent and effective basis of legitimate government and viewed civil society as constituted by a movement away from the state of nature and the condition in which the equality of all men was actual. Lincoln, in contrast, according to Jaffa, treated the equality of all men "as a transcendent goal, and viewed civil society as constituted by the movement toward a condition in which the equality of men is actual. Jaffa said further that in Lincoln's thought the principle of equality "is so lofty a demand that the striving for justice must be an ever present requirement for the human and political condition" (*Crisis of the House Divided* [Chicago: The University of Chicago Press, 1982], p. 321). Lincoln "transforms and transcends the original meaning" of the Declaration, Jaffa wrote, giving it "a new dimension" and effecting a "'reconstruction' of the meaning of the Fathers" (ibid., p. 328.) This argument, which is central to Jaffa's natural-right interpretation of Lincoln, places Lincoln at a greater distance from the Founding than does the present analysis. In subsequent writings, however, Jaffa has not, to the best of my knowledge, elaborated on the "transcendental reconstruction" thesis about Lincoln's conception of equality, but, rather, has underscored the similarity of Lincoln's views to those of the Founding generation. See Jaffa, *How to Think About the American Revolution: A Bicentennial Cerebration* (Durham, N.C.: Carolina Academic Press, 1978), pp. 13–48, wherein he refutes Willmoore Kendall's view of Lincoln as a modern egalitarian. In a recent essay, moreover, Jaffa states that in asserting the principle of equality as "a standard maxim for free society," constantly to be "revered" and "labored for" though never perfectly attained, Lincoln cannot be seen as giving warrant for contemporary judicial activism in pursuit of egalitarian social policies. In asserting the principle of equality as a fundamental goal, Jaffa observes, "Lincoln is speaking of the Declaration of Independence apart from the Constitution and before there was a Constitution." He adds that equality as "a standard maxim of society intended to guide public policy" was understood by Lincoln as shaped and implemented primarily through "legislative prudence"

Declaration created the Union, making liberty, equality, and consent the fundamental principles of republican government. The Constitution in turn was written in order to make a more perfect Union that would preserve those principles. Lincoln expressed this understanding of the seminal importance of the Declaration in the fragment on the Constitution and the Union, dated January 1861. In it he stated that the principle of liberty for all, announced in the Declaration of Independence, was the primary cause of national prosperity. "The assertion of that *principle*, at *that* time, was the word '*fitly spoken*' which has proved an 'apple of gold' to us," he wrote. "The *Union* and the *Constitution*, are the *picture* of *silver*, subsequently framed around it. The picture was made, not to *conceal*, or *destroy* the apple; but to *adorn*, and *preserve* it."[53]

As an expression of the Declaration of Independence and as applied to the slavery question, Lincoln's constitutionalism has been described as a theory of constitutional aspiration.[54] In contemporary legal philosophy this theory holds that within the Constitution it is possible to identify certain higher political values or principles that express the framers' aspirations toward a good and just society. In view of these aspirations, some parts of the Constitution can be considered temporary expedients or compromises, reflecting immediate interests, wants, or fears, which the framers expected to be abrogated at some future time in order to achieve a "truly constitutional" state of affairs. Moreover, as one contemporary theorist has written, "therapeutic constructions" can be given to words and phrases that do not fit the aspirations of the Constitution.[55]

Not without reason, proponents of constitutional aspiration find support for their theory in Lincoln's words and actions. Lincoln undoubtedly regarded the Declaration of Independence as a statement

---

(Jaffa, "What Were the 'Original Intentions' of the Framers of the Constitution of the United States?" *University of Puget Sound Law Review*, 10 [Spring 1987], 370–71). It may be said that Professor Jaffa in his recent writings has not modified his original view of Lincoln and equality, but rather has extended it to apply to different historical conditions and theoretical arguments. Persuasive as he so often is in his analysis of Lincoln, I am inclined on this matter to introduce a distinction that Professor Jaffa himself makes between "the character of Lincoln's thought" and "the articulation of that thought in *Crisis of the House Divided*" (*How to Think About the American Revolution*, p. 21).

[53] Basler et al., eds., *Collected Works of Lincoln*, 4:168.

[54] Jacobsohn, *Supreme Court and the Decline of Constitutional Aspiration*, pp. 95–112.

[55] Sotirios A. Barber, *On What the Constitution Means* (Baltimore: The Johns Hopkins University Press, 1984), pp. 23–37 and passim.

of national purpose and aspiration. From time to time he referred, aspirationally, to "the hopes of our constitution, our Union, and our liberties."[56] And it was of course an article of faith with Lincoln that the Founding Fathers believed slavery would one day disappear or be eliminated. Noting that the Constitution did not contain the word *slavery*, he said the omission was intended deliberately, so that when in the future slavery had passed away "there should be nothing on the face of the great charter of liberty suggesting that such a thing as negro slavery had ever existed among us."[57] Nevertheless, slavery was mentioned in "covert language," in words that Lincoln said were "ambiguous, roundabout, and mystical," and thus was arguably approved in the Constitution.[58] Moreover, although Lincoln did not underscore the fact, he acknowledged that while the equality of all men was the fundamental principle on which free institutions rested, "by our frame of government that principle has not been made one of legal obligation."[59]

The very idea of making a constitution from reflection and choice necessarily implies aspiration and intention to fulfill the ends and purposes of the government to be formed. Beyond this obvious point the theory of constitutional aspiration as expounded in contemporary jurisprudence is intended as an alternative to a strictly positivistic view of the Constitution as text-defined forms and procedures on the one hand, and as a non–text-bound, subjective, unwritten constitution on the other.[60] One may be skeptical, however, of the attempt to present Lincoln as a theorist of constitutional aspiration in a technical jurisprudential sense.[61]

This is not to deny the relevance of the Declaration of Independence for Lincoln's interpretation of the Constitution, especially his

---

[56] Basler et al., eds., *Collected Works of Lincoln*, 2:353.

[57] Ibid., 3:307.

[58] Ibid.; 4:22.

[59] Ibid., 3:327.

[60] Jacobsohn supports the theory of constitutional aspiration for this reason, seeing it as the approach favored by the framers, in contrast to what he calls "judicial aspiration" which he identifies with contemporary theories of judicial activism and judicial supremacy. See *Supreme Court and the Decline of Constitutional Aspiration*, p. 6.

[61] This point applies especially to the theory of constitutional aspiration as developed by Barber, *On What the Constitution Means*. For discussion of the theory of constitutional aspiration, see Gary L. McDowell, *The Constitution and Contemporary Constitutional Theory* (Cumberland, Va.: Center for Judicial Studies, 1985), pp. 34–40.

view of constitutional questions not expressly answered by the document as discussed in the First Inaugural. This is different, however, from saying that the Declaration of Independence was part of the Constitution, a construction entertained in contemporary legal theory that has been attributed to Lincoln.[62] The Declaration was a constitutive document, but it was not the Constitution or a part of it. The Constitution, in Lincoln's view, was the written document of the framers as ratified and amended. Insofar as Lincoln's theory of constitutionalism contained an aspirational element, it was consistent with the philosophy of government that sought the expression of opinions and principles leading to the choice of wise policies, within constitutional checks and limitations.

IV

Relevant to the problem of judicial review if not fully consistent with the theory of constitutional aspiration, Lincoln's constitutional teaching is more obviously pertinent to the problem of presidential government. Lincoln's significance in this respect is the subject of a well-established historical interpretation—the constitutional dictatorship thesis—which holds that as President he exercised absolute power or one-man rule.[63] Acting "on no precedent and under no restraint" Clinton Rossiter wrote in a typical expression of this view, Lincoln at the start of the war, and intermittently throughout it, "was the government of the United States."[64] What writers sympathetic to Lincoln saw as constitutional dictatorship has in recent years been described more harshly as unconstitutional dictatorship in works that view him as destroying the framers' Constitution and founding the nation anew on the basis of supreme executive power.[65] In either old or new version, however, the dictatorship thesis divorces Lincoln from the legislative science of the Founding—that is,

---

[62] Murphy, "Who Shall Interpret? The Quest for the Ultimate Constitutional Interpreter," 290; Harold M. Hyman and William M. Wiecek, *Equal Justice Under Law: Constitutional Development, 1835–1875* (New York: Harper & Row, 1982), p. 278.

[63] See Herman Belz, "Lincoln and the Constitution: The Dictatorship Question Reconsidered," *Seventh Annual R. Gerald McMurty Lecture* (Fort Wayne, Ind.: Louis A. Warren Lincoln Library, 1984), reprinted above as Chapter 2.

[64] Clinton Rossiter, *Constitutional Dictatorship: Crisis Government in the Modern Democracies* (Princeton, N.J.: Princeton University Press, 1948), pp. 212, 224.

[65] See works cited in note 2 above.

limited government based on constitutional text and forms, separation of powers and checks and balances, restricted judicial review,
and policy making by the legislature. It makes him a prototype of
twentieth-century presidential government, ruling through rhetorical leadership of public opinion rather than adherence to the text
and forms of the Constitution.

The basic question in evaluating Lincoln's governance is whether
he violated the Constitution in taking emergency actions at the start
of the war, and in dealing with problems of internal security, emancipation, and reconstruction during the conflict. Lincoln denied that
he violated or acted outside the Constitution. Explaining the administration's policy of irregular arrests in his message to Congress of
July 4, 1861, he asked: ". . . are all the laws, but *one*, to go unexecuted, and the government itself go to pieces, lest that one be violated?" If so, Lincoln reasoned, he would be guilty of violating his
constitutional oath to preserve, protect, and defend the Constitution. Lincoln rejected this construction, however, denying that the
government's policy of irregular arrests violated any law. Citing constitutional text, he declared: "The provision of the Constitution that
'The privilege of the writ of habeas corpus, shall not be suspended
unless when, in cases of rebellion or invasion, the public safety may
require it,' is equivalent to a provision—is a provision—that such
privilege may be suspended when, in cases of rebellion, or invasion,
the public safety *does* require it." Under the Constitution, therefore,
he decided that a case of rebellion existed and that qualified suspension of the habeas corpus privilege was warranted.[66]

Concerning emergency actions increasing the size of the army and
navy and causing public monies to be spent, Lincoln said these measures, whether strictly legal or not, were undertaken on popular demand and public necessity, in the belief that they were within the
authority of and would be ratified by Congress.[67] Without more, this
statement might be regarded as a concession to the argument that
his actions were against the law or lawless. In May 1862, however,
Lincoln commented further on actions taken at the start of the war.

---

[66] Basler et al., eds., *Collected Works of Lincoln*, 4:430. As for whether Congress or
the President might suspend the writ, the Constitution did not say. Consulting
original intention, however, Lincoln said it could not be believed that the framers
of the document intended that in every case nothing should be done until Congress
could be convened (ibid., 4:431).

[67] Ibid., 4:429.

Under the circumstances, he wrote, "It became necessary for me to choose whether, using only the existing means, agencies, and processes which Congress had provided, I should let the government fall at once into ruin, or whether, availing myself of the broader powers conferred by the Constitution in cases of insurrection, I would make an effort to save it with all its blessings for the present age and for posterity." Choosing the latter course, Lincoln said he took measures "some of which were without any authority of law." But "the government was saved from overthrow," in accordance with constitutional design and on the basis of constitutional powers.[68] The action thus was not constitutionally lawless.

Lincoln perceived that the Constitution provides an extremely broad grant of power for dealing with national crisis or emergency. In *Federalist*, No. 23, Publius states that when the public safety is endangered, ". . . in any matter essential to the *formation, direction,* or *support* of the NATIONAL FORCES," there can be "no limitation of that authority which is to provide for the defense and protection of the community."[69] A sound constitution makes necessary power available in time of emergency; if it does not, and the constitution is simply set aside, its legitimacy and effectiveness as a political law for peacetime government will be eroded.[70] It is not unrealistic of course to see extraordinary executive power as a threat to the rule of law. It is worth recalling, however, that emergency prerogative power capable of having such an effect is meaningful only in the context of defined and limited constitutional forms and institutions.[71] The question is: How best can a crisis in public safety be dealt with, and the rule of the Constitution in noncrisis times, both as a limitation on government and a source of power, be maintained and promoted? The fact is there can be no full resolution of the conflict between executive discretion and the rule of law. Moreover, there are times when the rule of law is threatened by further adherence to the rule

---

[68] Ibid., 5:240–43. Lincoln's explanation was made in response to a resolution of the House of Representatives censuring Simon Cameron, secretary of war in April 1861.

[69] *The Federalist*, ed. Earle, p. 143.

[70] Joseph M. Bessette and Jeffrey Tulis, eds., *The Presidency in the Constitutional Order* (Baton Rouge: Louisiana State University Press, 1981), pp. 17–19.

[71] Thomas S. Engeman, "Presidential Statesmanship and the Constitution: The Limits of Presidential Studies," *The Review of Politics*, 44 (April 1982), 272.

of law. In those situations not only is decisive action by a single individual to be risked, it is required.[72]

Consistent with his view of the Constitution as the supreme and binding political law for the nation, and his desire that reverence for it be as a political religion, Lincoln the President adhered to the forms and text of the Constitution. Charged by political opponents with regarding the Constitution as different in time of insurrection from what it was in peacetime, he denied the accusation. His position, he explained in June 1863, was "that the constitution is different, *in its application* in cases of Rebellion or Invasion, involving the public security, from what it is in times of profound peace and public security." He added: ". . . this opinion I adhere to, simply because, by the constitution itself, things may be done in the one case which may not be done in the other."[73] Ultimately actual circumstances, not the extent to which a threat is perceived by the people or the legislature, must determine whether emergency powers in the Constitution can be applied.[74] Lincoln insisted on this point. Replying to Democratic critics who asked whether he could override the guaranteed rights of individuals, Lincoln said the question, "divested of the phraseology calculated to represent me as struggling for an arbitrary personal prerogative, is either simply a question *who* shall decide, or an affirmation that *nobody* shall decide, what the public safety does require, in cases of Rebellion or Invasion." He reasoned: "The constitution contemplates the question as likely to occur for decision, but it does not expressly declare who is to decide it. By necessary implication, when Rebellion or Invasion comes, the decision is to be made, from time to time; and I think the man whom, for the time, the people have, under the constitution, made the commander-in-chief, of their Army and Navy, is the man who holds the power, and bears the responsibility of making it."[75]

Lincoln reiterated his position in the Hodges letter of April 1864. His oath to preserve the Constitution, he observed, "imposed upon

---

[72] Bessette and Tulis. *Presidency in the Constitutional Order*, p. 26; E. A. Goerner, "Letter and Spirit: The Political Ethics of the Rule of Law Versus the Political Ethics of the Rule of the Virtuous," *The Review of Politics*, 45 (October 1983), 553–75.

[73] Basler et al., eds., *Collected Works of Lincoln*, 4:302.

[74] Bessette and Tulis, eds., *Presidency in the Constitutional Order*, p. 24.

[75] Basler et al., eds., *Collected Works of Lincoln*, 6:303.

me the duty of preserving, by every indispensable means, that government—that nation—of which that constitution was the organic law." Accordingly, he "felt that measures, otherwise unconstitutional, might become lawful, by becoming indispensable to the preservation of the constitution, through the preservation of the nation."[76] This statement has been taken to signify Lincoln's view that the nation was more important than the Constitution, and his belief that a narrow constitutionalism must not interfere with "the living processes and necessities of nationalism."[77] In fact it expresses Lincoln's adherence to the constitutionalism of the Founding.

At bottom the issue was one of statesmanship, which, while it cannot be guaranteed by the Constitution, must be given scope for expression in times of crisis if the "parchment provisions" of the document are to remain effective after an emergency has passed.[78] Lincoln was aware of this reality. Explaining why it was necessary for the commander in chief to decide what the public safety required in time of invasion or rebellion, he wrote: "If he uses the power justly, the people will probably justify him; if he abuses it, he is in their hands, to be dealt with by all the modes they have reserved to themselves in the constitution."[79] Lincoln thus understood that the Constitution provides necessary emergency power, and that the statesmanship of Presidents who exercise this power will always be controversial. Moreover, his reference to the people's reserved powers under the Constitution explains why dictatorship is an inapt description of American government in times of crisis. The text and forms of the Constitution—most especially the separation of powers—make it possible and indeed virtually ensure that political criticism will be brought to bear by coordinate institutions as a restraint on the exercise of emergency power. The American Constitution,

---

[76] Ibid., 7:281.

[77] Willard L. King and Allan Nevins, "The Constitution and Declaration of Independence as Issues in the Lincoln–Douglas Debates," *Journal of the Illinois State Historical Society*, 52 (Spring 1959), 17.

[78] *The Federalist*, ed. Earle, p. 158. Observing that "parchment provisions" are unequal to "a struggle with public necessity," Publius comments: "Wise politicians will be cautious about fettering the government with restrictions that cannot be observed, because they know that every breach of the fundamental laws, though dictated by necessity, impairs that sacred reverence which ought to be maintained in the breast of rulers towards a constitution of a country, and forms a precedent for other breaches where the same plea of necessity does not exist at all, or is less urgent and palpable."

[79] Basler et al., eds., *Collected Works of Lincoln*, 6:303.

though making extreme power available when the public safety is threatened, does not provide for the kind of unlimited, absolute power implied in the term *dictatorship*, whether constitutional or otherwise.[80]

V

As defender of the Union in its most profound crisis, Lincoln has been regarded as a precursor of the kind of organic nationalism and constitutionalism, "not bound to the letter of the Constitution nor fettered by state rights," that has characterized American government in the twentieth century.[81] Although Lincoln expressed his love of the nation in prose that perhaps evoked "mystical and emotional forces,"[82] one may question use of the organic metaphor to describe his views on government and the constitutional order. Indeed it is a good question what an organic concept of politics and government means in the American context. Consider, for example, an authentic expression of organic nationalism from a European source: " 'The constitutions of states cannot be invented; the cleverest calculation in this matter is as futile as total ignorance. There is no substitute for the spirit of a people, and the strength and order arising therefrom, and it is not to be found even in the brightest minds or in the greatest geniuses.' "[83] This outlook has no application to political action and constitution making in the United States, where the Union was formed and the Constitution adopted through reflection and rational choice. Nor is the organic view persuasive in relation to Lincoln's political thought, which was grounded in the natural rights philosophy of the eighteenth century, if not that of classical natural right.[84]

---

[80] Bessette and Tulis, eds., *Presidency in the Constitutional Order*, p. 25.

[81] Rawley, "Nationalism of Abraham Lincoln," 283, 292, 298.

[82] Alan P. Grimes, *American Political Thought* (New York: Henry Holt, 1955), p. 281.

[83] Quoted in Karl Mannheim, *Ideology and Utopia* (New York: Harcourt, Brace, 1963), p. 234.

[84] As in the study of Lincoln's life and political career in general, a major issue in the analysis of his political thought has been the relationship of the prewar and wartime periods. Many historians and political scientists identify Lincoln with the natural rights philosophy in discussing the sectional struggle, while identifying him with organic nationalism in discussing his actions during the Civil War. See, for example, Grimes, *American Political Thought*, pp. 236–38, 280–86; Charles E. Merriam, *A History of American Political Theories* (New York: Macmillan, 1903),

If the organic nationalist interpretation of Lincoln is inaccurate, the view which links him to the rights-conscious egalitarianism of contemporary liberalism is no more satisfactory.[85] To be sure, Lincoln referred to Union, Constitution, and liberty as a trinity.[86] To argue, however, that he went beyond the idea of liberty as the pursuit of individual rights and "perceived liberty as equality, as obligations under society actively to support individuals in their efforts to enjoy rights," appears to go beyond the evidence.[87]

It has been argued that in emancipating slaves Lincoln embraced a concept of positive liberty, defined as the exercise of government power in a manner that anticipates welfare-state liberalism of the twentieth century.[88] In fact, the use of government power to emancipate slaves and abolish slavery promoted liberty in its classic nineteenth-century sense, what the twentieth century calls negative liberty. Removing the legal disabilities of slavery, emancipation and abolition was intended to secure liberty defined as a basic right of noninterference. It consisted in specific rights of person and property that created legal and moral space in which individuals were free to exercise their personal capacities and talents in pursuit of their interests.

Lincoln viewed the Declaration of Independence as a constitutional document in the making of the Union, and he understood the Constitution in a political–philosophical sense as an expression of the Declaration's principles.[89] But it seems mistaken to say, as some have claimed, that Lincoln "insisted . . . that the Declaration of Independence was part of the Constitution."[90] The Constitution

---

pp. 221–25, 291. An able presentation of Lincoln as a consistent natural rights thinker is Mark E. Neely, Jr., "Abraham Lincoln's Nationalism Reconsidered," *Lincoln Herald*, 76 (Spring 1974), 12–28. The most thorough and satisfying analyses of Lincoln's political thought view him in the tradition of classical natural right. See Jaffa, *Crisis of the House Divided*, and Glen E. Thurow, *Abraham Lincoln and American Political Religion* (Albany: State University of New York Press, 1976).

[85] This view is propounded by left-wing as well as right-wing writers. For the leftist argument, see Otto H. Olson, "Abraham Lincoln as Revolutionary," *Civil War History*, 24 (September 1978), 213–24. For the rightist analysis, see Kendall and Carey, *Symbols of the American Political Tradition*.

[86] Harold M. Hyman, *A More Perfect Union: The Impact of the Civil War and Reconstruction on the Constitution* (New York: Alfred A. Knopf, 1973), p. 57.

[87] Hyman and Wiecek, *Equal Justice Under Law*, pp. 277–78.

[88] James M. McPherson, *Abraham Lincoln and the Second American Revolution* (New York: Oxford University Press, 1991), pp. 62–63, 137.

[89] Jaffa, "Abraham Lincoln," in *Encyclopedia of the American Constitution*, 3:1162.

[90] Hyman and Wiecek, *Equal Justice Under Law*, p. 278.

was the document drafted and ratified by the Founding generation, containing forms, principles, and procedures for securing republican government. Stated alternatively and negatively: the Constitution was not the nation, or the people, or the government, though it was of course related to all these things as a political and historical reality.

If community, constitution, and government are the component parts of any polity, community and Constitution in the United States are so closely related as to be virtually identical in popular perception, while government is distinctly separate.[91] Lincoln's theory of constitutionalism conforms with this description. Justifying wartime measures in the Hodges letter of April 1864, Lincoln referred to his oath-based constitutional duty to preserve "that government—that nation—of which the constitution was the organic law." "Was it possible to lose the nation, and yet preserve the constitution?" he asked. Lincoln answered this question metaphorically, stating that although "By general law life *and* limb must be protected; yet often a limb must be amputated to save a life; but a life is never wisely given to save a limb." "I felt," he continued, "that measures, otherwise unconstitutional, might become lawful, by becoming indispensable to the preservation of the constitution, through the preservation of the nation." Reasserting this as his ground of action, Lincoln said: "I could not feel that, to the best of my ability, I had even tried to preserve the constitution, if, to save slavery, or any minor matter, I should permit the wreck of government, country, and Constitution all together."[92]

If, in Lincoln's metaphor, the nation is life and the Constitution is the limb that may have to be amputated, he is saying that constitutional forms and rules can be disregarded in an emergency. This is an unnecessarily broad reading, however, which conflicts with Lincoln's view, expressed elsewhere, that the Constitution in express terms provides for a different application in times when the public safety is threatened from what it does in peacetime. Lincoln was not asserting a general justification of constitutional violations in the higher cause of nationalism. Rather, he was expressing his view of

---

[91] Elmer E. Cornwell, Jr., "The American Constitutional Tradition: Its Impact and Development," in *The Constitutional Convention as an Amending Device*, ed. Kermit L. Hall, Harold M. Hyman, and Leon V. Sigal (Washington, D.C.: American Historical Association and American Political Science Association, 1981), p. 1.

[92] Basler et al., eds., *Collected Works of Lincoln*, 7:281.

the virtually inseparable relationship (though not identity) of national community and Constitution in his political philosophy.[93] Lincoln was saying that in order to preserve the Constitution, it was necessary to preserve the nation. His point was that without the nation, for which it was made, to talk about the continued existence of the Constitution was meaningless. Lincoln was also saying that American nationality was defined by the Constitution, just as before the war he identified the nation with the ideas of liberty and equality in the Declaration of Independence. In a sense, therefore, the nation was the Constitution. The Constitution, however, was not the nation, or the "instinctive forces" or "living processes and necessities of nationalism."[94] In other words, the Constitution, in Lin-

---

[93] Lincoln's reference to the possible wrecking of "government, country, and Constitution all together" might suggest that he equated the particular administration of which he was the head with the constitutional regime and the nation. This reading is contradicted, however, by his willingness to accept the possibility of electoral defeat and relinquishment of the machinery of government to his political opponents in 1864.

[94] Merriam, *History of American Political Theories*, p. 296; King and Nevins, "Constitution and Declaration of Independence as Issues in the Lincoln–Douglas Debates," 17. Compare the view of Chief Justice Earl Warren, a twentieth-century liberal constitutionalist who has sometimes been seen as carrying on the tradition of Lincolnian Republicanism. Concerning the conflict between national security and individual rights, Chief Justice Warren wrote: "Lincoln once asked, '[Is] it possible to lose the nation and yet preserve the Constitution?' His rhetorical question called for a negative answer no less than its corollary: 'Is it possible to lose the Constitution and yet preserve the Nation?' Our Constitution and Nation are one. Neither can exist without the other." This thought should be kept in mind, Chief Justice Warren advised, in judging the claims of political officers who assert that national security requires what the Constitution appears to condemn ("The Bill of Rights and the Military," in *The Great Rights*, ed. Edmond Cahn [New York: Macmillan, 1963], p. 109). We observe first that Chief Justice Warren does not carefully consider, or at least does not give evidence of having considered, Lincoln's answer to his own question. He implies that Lincoln answered the question as he, Warren, does and, moreover, that Lincoln asked, or should have asked, the corollary question about the possibility of losing the Constitution. The latter of course is Warren's invention which enables him to assert an equivalence or identity between the Constitution and the nation that was not present in Lincoln's thought. The significance of equating Constitution and nation in modern liberal constitutionalism, or of defining the Constitution in terms of the nation, is that it removes restraints on the judiciary and places the judiciary on a par with the political branches in determining national security and other policy questions. If the Constitution is the nation, as Chief Justice Warren says, and if the Supreme Court is the final authority on the meaning of the Constitution, as the Court often said during Warren's tenure as chief justice, then the standard for judicial determination of the constitutionality of government action would appear to be infinitely variable, limitless, and politically subjective.

coln's view, was not an organic and unwritten thing. It was the document handed down by the Fathers to which, in its forms and substantive principles, popular attachment was to be maintained through constitutionalist conviction.

It is fitting, in conclusion, to recall the analysis of Lincoln and the Constitution offered half a century ago by the constitutional historian Andrew C. McLaughlin. Fusing constitutional theory and historical observation, McLaughlin wrote: "A constitution need not be looked upon as only a piece of parchment stored away in a safe, free from the prying eyes of the multitude, consigned to the clever exposition of politicians and subjected to the astute arguments of jurists." A constitution includes "the actual life and the living philosophy of a nation," McLaughlin suggested, adding that the "real Constitution" of the United States was "the underlying character of America as a political entity." Moreover, "To the extent that a formal written constitutional system or any other kind of constitution is at variance with the character of a people," he said, "it is wanting in substantial reality." Applying these insights historically, McLaughlin wrote that while Lincoln had respect for the formal principles and checks of the Constitution, he looked beyond forms to character, and penetrated to the foundations of a democratic government restrained by law. Lincoln acted on the assumption, McLaughlin concluded, that devotion to procedure should not be regarded as a paramount obligation, if it made dissolution of the Union probable.[95]

McLaughlin's interpretation of Lincoln has recently been described as revealing "a profound debt to the currents of German scholarship, with its emphasis on organismic theories of the state and its hostility to formulated doctrines and written plans of society."[96] The author of this assessment, Dr. Mark E. Neely, Jr., expressing ambivalence about McLaughlin's scholarly objectivity, states that McLaughlin's view of the Constitution "may well be too misty and mystical to offer much in the way of aid to the study of the United States Constitution during the Civil War."[97] In defense of McLaughlin, I should like to suggest on the contrary that his view of constitutionalism is sound, and that use of the organic interpreta-

---

[95] Andrew C. McLaughlin, "Lincoln, the Constitution, and Democracy," *International Journal of Ethics*, 47 (October 1936), 1–24.

[96] Neely, "Andrew C. McLaughlin on Lincoln and the Constitution," *Lincoln Lore*, No. 1761 (November 1984), 2.

[97] Ibid., 3.

tion misunderstands not only McLaughlin's contribution but also, by implication, Lincoln and American constitutionalism.

The Constitution, to be sure, is not simply words inscribed on paper. Moreover, a constitution at variance with the character of a people, as McLaughlin recognized, lacks historical reality. What needs to be pointed out, however, and what McLaughlin never doubted, was that the Constitution can never be something less than the document, something other than the forms, procedures, and principles embodied in the text. McLaughlin is right in reminding us that the choice of a constitution must conform to the general character of a people. The framers' creation of a commercial republic for the people of America in the Constitution of 1787 well illustrates the point. Nevertheless, the theory of constitutionalism requires that the character of the people in their everyday activities, in the sense of popular passions, interests, and public opinion, conform to the principles and forms of the Constitution, rather than that the Constitution conform or constantly be adapted to reflect the quotidian tendencies of public opinion. Looked at in this light, the Constitution is not misty or mystical; nor is it maintained by mysticism or spiritualism. It is created and preserved by persuasive reasoning and moral teaching, producing reverence for the Constitution and the laws that result in constitutionalist conviction. In this way, as Lincoln and, I dare say, McLaughlin understood, "the *attachment* of the People" to the government—"the strongest bulwark of any Government, and particularly of those constituted like ours"—is assured.[98]

Quoting Lincoln's appeal to "the mystic chords of memory, stretching from every battlefield and patriot grave to every living heart and hearthstone," McLaughlin warned that if memories are benumbed and achievements and aspirations forgotten, "the nation loses its character . . . and constitutional forms are likely to give way to tumult or be dissipated by the spirit of distraction and essential uncertainty."[99] Precisely so! The way to prevent such an eventuality, however, is not to invoke an unwritten, organic constitution that ultimately is nothing other than the actions of government officers taken in response to ideology, interest, or popular passion. The proper way, following Lincoln's example, is to insist on fidelity to the text, forms, and principles of the framers' Constitution.

---

[98] Basler et al., eds., *Collected Works of Lincoln*, 1:111.
[99] McLaughlin, "Lincoln, the Constitution, and Democracy," 2.

4

Protection of Personal Liberty in Republican Emancipation Legislation

THE MOTIVATION OF REPUBLICAN EMANCIPATION POLICY in 1862 has been a perennial imponderable of Civil War historiography. In 1948 Richard Hofstadter gave pointed expression to what has come to be known as the revisionist view of the matter in stating that Lincoln adopted emancipation only after all other policies failed, that he resorted to it in an unhappy frame of mind, and that the Emancipation Proclamation "had all the moral grandeur of a bill of lading." "It contained no indictment of slavery," Hofstadter wrote, "but simply based emancipation on 'military necessity.' "[1] In 1963, believing that a good point had been carried too far, Mark M. Krug contended that Lincoln undertook emancipation not just for military reasons but also to right a moral wrong. Krug advanced this conclusion as a reasonable inference based on Lincoln's expressions of hatred for slavery and on the judgment of contemporaries that moral conviction sustained the emancipation edict.[2] Similarly, Harry V. Jaffa, viewing Lincoln's career as a consistent whole, the rationale of which was to remove the curse of slavery from the American republic and from both the black and the white races, concluded in 1965 that Lincoln deserved to be regarded, as he traditionally had been, as the great emancipator.[3]

Something of a fusion of the revisionist and traditionalist interpre-

---

An earlier version of this chapter appeared in *The Journal of Southern History*, 42, No. 3 (August 1976), 385–400.

[1] Richard Hofstadter, *The American Political Tradition and the Men Who Made It* (New York: Vintage, 1954), p. 132.

[2] Mark M. Krug, "The Republican Party and the Emancipation Proclamation," *Journal of Negro History*, 48 (April 1963), 98–114.

[3] Harry V. Jaffa, *Equality and Liberty: Theory and Practice in American Politics* (New York: Oxford University Press, 1965), pp. 140–68.

tations appeared in the work of V. Jacque Voegeli a few years later. Emphasizing the political and military expediency of Lincoln's emancipation policy, Voegeli noted also that in private Lincoln tended to adopt an abolitionist view of the war. In the Emancipation Proclamation itself, Voegeli pointed out, Lincoln called emancipation an act of justice and thus took "a meaningful step toward higher ground."[4] More recently, James A. Rawley has described the Emancipation Proclamation in revisionist terms as a weapon of war and instrument of nationality and not as a torch of freedom or a program of social reform, while Don E. Fehrenbacher in a more traditionalist vein has suggested that confusion in understanding the Emancipation Proclamation arises from taking too seriously Lincoln's verbal concessions to conservatives and the fiction that slave liberation was strictly a military measure.[5]

As this brief review of representative writings suggests, the problem of motivation in Republican emancipation policy has been conceived of almost entirely as a question of Lincoln's motivation in issuing the Emancipation Proclamation. Looked at in this way, however, the problem is unlikely to be resolved, for there is evidence to support both the revisionist and the traditional points of view. Lincoln based emancipation on thoroughly pragmatic grounds of military and political expediency, and he had compelling ideological and humanitarian reasons for adopting a policy of slave emancipation. It may be possible, however, to advance our understanding of wartime emancipation by studying congressional legislation and by asking whether in formulating emancipation measures Republicans evinced an interest in Negro liberty as distinct from a desire to secure military advantage for the Union by depriving the enemy of its labor supply.

Congressional attitudes and actions have generally been regarded as more aggressively antislavery than those of the Lincoln administration. While recognizing that Republican lawmakers desired to make slave liberation a military asset, historians by concentrating on the problem of military expediency *vs.* antislavery moral principle in Lincoln's Emancipation Proclamation have by implication suggested

---

[4] V. Jacque Voegeli, *Free But Not Equal: The Midwest and the Negro During the Civil War* (Chicago: The University of Chicago Press, 1967), pp. 41, 47, 75 (quotation).

[5] James A. Rawley, *The Politics of Union: Northern Politics During the Civil War* (Hinsdale, Ill.: Dryden, 1974), p. 85; Don E. Fehrenbacher, "Only His Stepchildren: Lincoln and the Negro," *Civil War History*, 20 (December 1974), 306.

that Congress, with its contingent of radical Republicans, adopted emancipation quite as much for ideological and humanitarian as for political and military reasons. Congress moved faster and further than Lincoln on emancipation, James A. Rawley writes in a typical expression of this point of view, and took the initiative in promoting civil rights for blacks.[6]

It is of course true that emancipation proposals appeared in Congress far in advance of the Emancipation Proclamation. In examining the motivation of Republican policy, however, the more important question to consider is whether antislavery legislators provided definite emancipation procedures and safeguards that would secure the personal liberty of freed slaves. If they did, a prima facie case might be made that emancipation was undertaken with a view toward promoting the personal liberty and rights of Negro slaves, as well as gaining military advantage for the Union. If, on the other hand, Republicans in Congress ignored the problem of guaranteeing personal liberty, the conclusion would seem to follow that emancipation policy rested exclusively on military expediency.

The question of personal liberty for blacks arose with the first occupation of Confederate territory at the start of the war, when escaped slaves began to enter Union lines. To deal with the problem, federal authorities, following the initiative of General Benjamin Franklin Butler at Fort Monroe in Virginia, adopted the theory that slaves used for insurrectionary purposes were contraband of war, whose services could be appropriated and turned to account for the Union. Although this theory did not recognize the personal liberty and free status of escaped slaves, it contained useful ambiguities. It assumed on the one hand that slaves were property that could be taken and used to defeat the rebellion. Agreeable to conservatives, this notion was criticized by abolitionists who believed that slaves should be recognized as persons under the Constitution with equal rights.[7] On the other hand, although it was not a theory of emancipation, the contraband idea seemed clearly to point in that direction. It seems fair to say, moreover, in view of the prejudice against blacks in the North, the constitutional limitations on federal power over

---

[6] Rawley, *Politics of Union*, p. 88; see also Hans L. Trefousse, *The Radical Republicans: Lincoln's Vanguard for Racial Justice* (New York: Alfred A. Knopf, 1969), pp. 4–5, 203–39; David Donald, *Charles Sumner and the Rights of Man* (New York: Alfred A. Knopf, 1970), pp. 61–63.

[7] *National Anti–Slavery Standard*, January 4, 1862; *Independent*, January 16, 1862.

slavery in the states, and the long-standing disavowal of abolition purposes by Republicans, that the contraband idea made the drift toward emancipation easier and more acceptable than it would have been if justified on the high ground of antislavery moral principle. In November 1861 the abolitionist Edward Lillie Pierce observed that many persons who "would be repelled by formulas of a broader and nobler import" and who were averse to "slaves [being] declared free-men . . . [had] no objection to their being declared contrabands."[8]

The contraband theory provided the general framework both for administration policy toward escaped slaves and congressional eman-cipation legislation in 1861 and 1862. The War Department ap-proved General Butler's application of the theory in May 1861, and several commanders followed this example in using runaway slaves for military labor. Other commanders, however, refused to receive escaped slaves in their lines or otherwise permitted the recapture of fugitives. In this situation Congress, whose antislavery interests naturally drew it to the fugitive question and whose authority to act was clear since it was the Fugitive Slave Act that was involved, intervened by passing an article of war prohibiting military and naval personnel from returning escaped slaves.[9]

In enacting this rule Congress was concerned mainly with depriv-ing the enemy of labor which could then be used for the Union cause. Criticizing the exclusion of fugitives from Federal lines, Sena-tor James Wilson Grimes of Iowa said such a policy denied the Union the benefit of a labor force capable of garrison duty in climates un-congenial to whites as well as information about the enemy that escaped slaves might bring.[10] Although it was a secondary issue, the situation also gave Republicans an opportunity to speak out for Negro freedom by arguing that the purpose of disallowing the return of escaped slaves was to prevent military officers from settling ques-tions of personal liberty outside their jurisdiction. Ironically, this argument placed Republicans in the position of regarding the Fugi-tive Slave law, with which the army was now prohibited from inter-fering, as a chance at least in theory to vindicate the idea that slaves

---

[8] [Edward Lillie Pierce], "The Contrabands at Fortress Monroe," *Atlantic Monthly*, 8 (November 1861), 627.

[9] *Congressional Globe*, 37 Cong., 2 sess., 959, 1143 (February 25, March 10, 1862); Louis S. Gerteis, *From Contraband to Freedman: Federal Policy Toward Southern Blacks, 1861–1865* (Westport, Conn.: Greenwood, 1973), pp. 11–15.

[10] *Cong. Globe*, 37 Cong., 2 sess., 1651–52 (April 14, 1862).

were persons under the Constitution and protected by due process of law.[11]

More directly pertinent to evaluating the motivation behind emancipation policy were bills introduced into the Thirty-Seventh Congress to free the slaves of rebels. Generally consistent with the contraband theory, these measures were concerned with using black manpower for military purposes rather than establishing the free status of former slaves. Nearly all of them, however, failed to provide means of guaranteeing freed blacks' personal liberty.

The First Confiscation Act, for example, passed in August 1861, provided that if slaves were employed in military labor or service in support of the rebellion, persons claiming their services forfeited the claim. But the act did not declare that slaves so employed were free. Nor was the omission inadvertent. A provision stating that slaves used for insurrectionary purposes were discharged from labor was rejected on Republican initiative, lest the inference be drawn that Congress intended to abolish slavery as a municipal institution.[12] The Confiscation Act of 1861 thus deprived the enemy of slave labor but did not in express terms confer liberty on blacks released from service to rebel masters.[13]

When Congress met in December 1861 the continued failure and inactivity of Union arms made Republican lawmakers more willing to undertake an aggressive antislavery policy. Accordingly, numerous emancipation and confiscation bills were introduced which declared unequivocally that slaves of persons aiding the rebellion were free men, state laws to the contrary notwithstanding. These proposals did not, however, supply means of actually securing the right of personal liberty for freed slaves. Only the requirement that persons seeking to enforce claims to slave labor must prove their past loyalty served as possible protection for freed blacks, and this was intended

---

[11] Ibid., 358 (January 16, 1862), remarks of Jacob Collamer; ibid., 956–57 (February 25, 1862), remarks of John A. Bingham; ibid., 1894 (May 1, 1862), remarks of Charles Sumner.

[12] Ibid., 37 Cong., 1 sess., 409–11, 430–31 (August 2, 3, 1861), remarks of Orlando Kellogg and John A. Bingham.

[13] *Statutes at Large of the United States of America, 1789–1873*, 17 vols. (Washington, D.C.: Government Printing Office, 1850–1873), 12:319. The only part of the act that could be construed as a defense of personal liberty was a provision stating that any attempt to claim services of slaves released from labor could be denied on the basis of the insurrectionary employment of the slave. Representative John A. Bingham of Ohio said that under this section blacks might go to court to enforce a claim of personal liberty (*Cong. Globe*, 37 Cong., 1 sess., 410 [August 2, 1861]).

to guard the interests of loyal masters as much as the freedom of emancipated slaves.[14]

Although military expediency remained the controlling consideration in the congressional approach to emancipation, Republican lawmakers in limited ways began to recognize protection of personal liberty as a problem that needed to be dealt with. Ironically, in its first manifestation this broader outlook was joined with a proposal to colonize emancipated slaves on abandoned plantations. Under legislation submitted by Republicans John Addison Gurley of Ohio and Francis Preston Blair, Jr., of Missouri, special federal commissioners would issue certificates of freedom to slaves of persons engaging in rebellion. These certificates would be conclusive of the right of personal liberty against any private individual or state officer seeking to claim the service of a freed slave. Yet, even with their certificates of freedom the blacks would not really be free. Rather, they were to be subject to regulations of the federal commissioners and were to be employed in military labor or indentured as apprentices to loyal plantation proprietors. Only after an apprenticeship of either six years or until reaching the age of twenty-five were freed slaves declared to be "at liberty to make contracts and to buy and sell real and other property . . . in like manner as other free persons. . . ."[15]

As antislavery pressures increased in the first half of 1862 a more straightforward interest in securing the freed slaves' personal liberty appeared. Thus, bills were introduced to enable slaves freed under the First Confiscation Act to establish their right to freedom through certificates acquired from United States courts, special commissioners, or military officers, and to prohibit kidnapping and enslavement of free persons.[16] While these measures were not inconsistent with

---

[14] 37 Cong., H.R. 106, December 2, 1861; H.R. 107, December 3, 1861; H.R. 126, December 9, 1861; H.R. 199, January 8, 1862; H.R. 421, April 24, 1862; H.R 440, April 30, 1862; H.R. 456, May 5, 1862, Bills and Resolutions, 1789–1962, Records of the House of Representatives, Record Group 233 (National Archives, Washington, D.C.; cited hereinafter as HBR, RG 233); S. 331, May 26, 1832, Bills and Resolutions, 1789–1968, Records of the United States Senate, Record Group 46 (National Archives; cited hereinafter as SBR, RG 46).

[15] 37 Cong., H.R. 121, December 9, 1861, introduced by Gurley; H.R. 214, January 15, 1862, introduced by Blair, HBR, RG 233. The quoted material is from a provision that was the same in each bill. Gurley's bill proposed colonization in Florida; Blair's, in a foreign country.

[16] 37 Cong., S. 335, May 31, 1862, SBR, RG 46, introduced by Henry Wilson; H.R. 493 June 2, 1862, HBR, RG 233, introduced by James Falconer Wilson.

the purpose of denying slave manpower to the Confederacy, coming as they did from radical Republicans it seems fair to regard them in some degree as reflections also of a humanitarian-ideological concern for liberty.

As the number of freed slaves increased, a further consideration behind the interest in securing personal liberty was the pragmatic judgment that reenslavement was a practical impossibility because emancipated blacks would not allow it to happen. They would fight against it and make their own guarantee of liberty. In July 1862 Lincoln acknowledged this factor in expressing his belief that it would be impossible to return freed blacks to slavery. "I believe there would be physical resistance to it, which could neither be turned aside by argument, nor driven away by force," he stated to Congress in approving the Second Confiscation Act.[17] The enlistment of Negro soldiers in the Union army in 1863 strengthened the perception that blacks would not simply be acted upon or disposed of passively in the aftermath of emancipation. This prudential concern in conjunction with ideological tendencies of antislavery reformers informed the Republicans' limited attempt in 1862 to deal with the problem of the freed slaves' personal liberty.

The first measure in which Congress actually made provision for freed slaves' personal liberty was the District of Columbia abolition act of April 1862. As originally reported, the bill specified no emancipation procedure but simply released slaves from service. After lengthy discussion of compensation for slaveowners, however, conservative Republican senator Jacob Collamer of Vermont called attention to the opposite side of the question—the emancipated slaves' personal liberty. If freed blacks went into neighboring Maryland, Collamer pointed out, they would be presumed to be slaves and would need evidence of their freedom to prevent being captured. Persuaded by this advice, the Senate amended the district abolition bill by adding a definite procedure for carrying out emancipation and securing personal liberty.

The procedure required slaveowners, in order to qualify for compensation, to pay a fee of fifty cents and place on record in federal court a description of their slaves. Emancipated slaves in turn were authorized—upon payment of a twenty-five-cent fee—to receive

---

[17] Roy P. Basler et al., eds., *The Collected Works of Abraham Lincoln*, 9 vols. (New Brunswick, N.J.: Rutgers University Press, 1953–1955), 5:329.

certificates of freedom from the same federal court. In addition, the act prohibited the kidnapping or transporting of freed persons out of the district with the intent of reenslaving them. In July Congress passed a supplementary act permitting slaves not yet freed because the absence of their owners had prevented the emancipation process from being initiated to petition the federal court for a certificate of personal freedom. For this the slave must pay a fifty-cent fee.[18] Here indeed was emancipation "with all the moral grandeur of a bill of lading" and with actual bureaucratic details to boot.

The concern for an emancipation procedure in the District of Columbia notwithstanding, in their principal antislavery undertaking of 1862—the formulation of a confiscation policy that would emancipate the slaves of rebels—Republicans were interested mainly in military and political considerations. Confiscation of property and slave emancipation were intended to weaken the enemy, raise money for the Union, and lay the foundation for postwar reform of southern society.[19] In a political and strategic sense, therefore, and in accordance with the contraband theory, slaves were considered along with property as a military and economic asset in war planning.

Yet an interest in personal liberty, though it was not in the end embodied in congressional policy, also figured in the deliberations on the Confiscation Act. To begin with, in the actual formal terms of their legislation Republicans departed from the implications of the contraband theory and regarded slaves as persons rather than property. Although both issues were ordinarily dealt with in the same measure, emancipation was provided for separately from confiscation of property. This distinction was more apparent in the House of Representatives, where separate bills were introduced for slave emancipation and property confiscation. In the emancipation bill, moreover, which the House passed in June 1862, Republicans went so far as to articulate a definite emancipation procedure and provide a guarantee of the freed slaves' personal liberty, even though the overall purpose of the measure was to deprive the enemy of labor and end the war without abolishing slavery as a municipal institution.

---

[18] *Cong. Globe*, 37 Cong, 2 sess., 1479 (April 1, 1862), remarks of Collamer; ibid, 1522, 3136, 3138 (April 3, July 7, 1862); *U.S. Statutes at Large*, 12:376–78, 538–39.

[19] John Syrett, "The Confiscation Acts: Efforts at Reconstruction During the Civil War," Ph.D. diss., University of Wisconsin, 1971, points out the postwar orientation of Republican thought on the confiscation question.

As originally reported by radical Thomas Dawes Eliot from the Select Committee on Confiscation and Emancipation, the emancipation bill contained no means of actually securing slave liberation. It merely provided that all persons willfully engaging in rebellion forfeited all claims to the labor of slaves. The sole protection for persons released from labor was the provision that if a master sought to enforce a claim to service the slave was authorized to plead the claimant's participation in rebellion as a defense or the claimant must establish his loyalty.[20] The broad sweep of the bill affecting all who voluntarily supported the rebellion gave it a radical character and led sixteen Republicans to join with the Democratic opposition in defeating it 74 to 78. Subsequently, however, in a compromise move supported by radical Republicans, the House agreed to consider a substitute bill that was less extensive in its emancipation scope but more thorough in its provisions for slave liberty.[21]

Drafted by conservative Republican Albert Gallatin Porter of Indiana, who had opposed Eliot's measure, the new emancipation bill proposed to liberate only the slaves of Confederate and state military and civil officers rather than those of all willful participants in the rebellion.[22] As though to compensate for this more limited scope, however, the bill contained an emancipation procedure and safeguards. It directed that special commissioners be appointed by the President in each slave state to compile and publish lists of slaves belonging to persons in the designated classes and required the latter to appear in federal court and prove their loyalty if they wished to avoid forfeiture of the services of their slaves. Upon failure of the rebel owner to appear or on proof of his participation in rebellion if he should appear, the court was to declare his slaves free and give them certificates of freedom guaranteeing personal liberty in all state and federal courts. Further to protect personal liberty, Porter's bill took the seemingly obvious and elementary step, yet one that had not previously been contemplated, of authorizing the federal courts to issue writs of habeas corpus to secure the release of any

---

[20] *Cong. Globe*, 37 Cong., 2 sess., 2233 (May 20, 1862).

[21] Leonard P. Curry, *Blueprint for Modern America: Nonmilitary Legislation of the First Civil War Congress* (Nashville, Tenn.: Vanderbilt University Press, 1968), pp. 68–69.

[22] The categories were Confederate and state military and civil officers, former U.S. officers who became Confederate officers, and all persons who willfully participated in rebellion and, after sixty days' warning by presidential proclamation, refused to return to allegiance to the United States (*Cong. Globe*, 37 Cong., 2 sess., Appendix, 295 [June 4, 1862], remarks of Albert G. Porter).

freed slaves or their descendants who should subsequently be held by any person. Persons illegally detaining freedmen were in turn to be tried for kidnapping. Finally, slaves not included in the published lists drawn up by the commissioners to initiate emancipation could apply directly to a federal court and receive the benefits of the act.[23]

Porter defended this emancipation plan on pragmatic and conservative grounds. In the first place, he said, it would affect the leaders of the rebellion without interfering with the rights of loyal persons in the South. Liberating an estimated one million slaves, it would assist the Union and undermine slavery "as a mere political and governing power," without, however, destroying slavery as a domestic institution. Indeed, Porter said, the slavery interest would best be served by withdrawing the institution from political strife in the manner thus proposed. Nor, he added, would emancipation conducted in this way, which would operate more as a postwar than a wartime undertaking, produce social upheaval.[24] Pointing to the existence of the considerable free black populations in the border states, Porter argued that large numbers of slaves could be freed without disrupting southern society or causing alarm among Unionist planters in the South. Plainly, he envisioned a peace settlement facilitated and made possible perhaps by emancipation but based nonetheless on the continued coexistence of slavery and freedom.[25]

At the same time, however, Porter emphasized the superiority of his bill to the original emancipation plan as far as Negro freedom was concerned. Eliot's bill in particular he regarded as defective because it took into account only the possibility that a slaveowner would go into court to claim the service of a freed slave. It provided

---

[23] Ibid.; U. S. House of Representatives, *Journal*, 37 Cong., 2 sess., 887–89 (June 18, 1862).

[24] *Cong. Globe*, 37 Cong., 2 sess., Appendix, 295 (June 4, 1862). The estimate of one million emancipated slaves is found in the minority report of the Select Committee on Confiscation and Emancipation, written by John William Noell of Missouri (*House Reports*, 37 Cong., 2 sess., No. 120: *Emancipation of Slaves of Rebels* [Serial 1145, Washington, 1862], p. 2). Like most of the confiscation bills of 1862, Porter's emancipation plan was to be executed in the federal district court for the district in which the slaves affected by the act resided. As no federal courts existed in the South at this time, it was apparent that the legal process on which confiscation and emancipation depended would not become available until the restoration of civil order. This Reconstruction aspect of confiscation appealed more to moderate and conservative Republicans than to radicals, who criticized it because it would not contribute directly to the war effort.

[25] *Cong. Globe*, 37 Cong., 2 sess., 2393 (May 27, 1862); ibid., Appendix, 294–96 (June 4, 1862).

no safeguard against seizure of emancipated slaves, which Porter thought more likely, or against the prejudice that blacks would encounter in state courts if these were to be the only forums available for defending the freedmen's liberty. For this reason Porter said it was essential, in order to make emancipation secure, to give freed slaves the privilege of the writ of habeas corpus in federal courts. Observing that under existing law federal habeas corpus jurisdiction extended only to cases of detention by United States officers, Porter illustrated the centralizing or nationalizing logic of emancipation.[26] His was the first proposal to recognize the necessity, which wartime emancipation under federal authority created, permanently to alter the federal-state balance by giving the national government, in this instance the judiciary, power to protect the right of personal liberty against interference from any state officer or private person.[27]

Porter's conservative argument for emancipation did not satisfy the Democratic opposition. From the Select Committee on Confiscation and Emancipation John William Noell of Missouri objected that the bill treated slaves as persons and purported to alter their status in disregard of local law. Congress might legislate the seizure of slaves as property as a war measure, Noell contended, but it had no power even in time of war to change the relations between persons or the status of individuals under state law.[28] Republicans, however, especially those who found Eliot's emancipation bill too radical, approved Porter's substitute measure 82 to 54.[29] Thus the House, which had already passed a property-confiscation bill, enacted and sent to the Senate a companion emancipation plan.

The interest in freedmen's guarantees evinced in the House was not shared by the Senate, which was more exclusively concerned

---

[26] Ibid., 297 (June 4, 1862). Federal habeas corpus jurisdiction was actually slightly broader, applying to the state officers in cases where they might detain federal revenue collectors acting under the authority of a foreign nation. These exceptions were made after the tariff and nullification crisis of 1832 and the Caroline affair of 1837. See William M. Wiecek, "The Great Writ and Reconstruction: The Habeas Corpus Act of 1867," *The Journal of Southern History*, 36 (November 1970), 534–35.

[27] *Cong. Globe*, 37 Cong., 2 sess., Appendix, 297 (June 4, 1862). Substitute emancipation bills introduced by Eliakim Persons Walton of Vermont, Justin Smith Morrill of Maine, and Samuel Lewis Casey of Kentucky also contained the habeas corpus provision (ibid., 37 Cong., 2 sess., 2362 [May 26, 1862], remarks of Walton and Morrill; 37 Cong., H.R. 472, HBR, RG 233, substitute amendment, June 11, 1862).

[28] *House Reports*, 37 Cong., 2 sess., No. 120: *Emancipation of Slaves of Rebels*, p. 1.

[29] *Cong. Globe*, 37 Cong., 2 sess., 2793 (June 18, 1862).

with legitimizing or confirming the *de facto* emancipation that resulted as Federal armies moved South and with turning to account for the Union the black manpower thus made available. This became clear when Republican Lyman Trumbull of Illinois in June 1862 urged passage of the House emancipation bill as a substitute for the confiscation bill containing emancipation features then being considered by the Senate.

The Senate confiscation bill declared the slaves of rebels free but offered no sanctions or any safeguards for personal liberty. Arguing the importance of such guarantees, Trumbull pointed out that the House emancipation bill gave freed slaves the right of personal liberty and the ability to vindicate this right through the writ of habeas corpus. In Trumbull's view the House measure answered what he perceived as a growing popular demand that something practical be accomplished toward promoting actual slave liberation. Other Republicans, however, preferring to leave the status of freed slaves indefinite, objected. Trumbull then withdrew his motion to adopt the House bill, and the Senate went on to approve its own confiscation bill, which included an emancipation section, instead of the separate House confiscation and emancipation measures. When the House in turn rejected the Senate bill a committee of conference on confiscation was formed.[30]

The conference report compromised the differences between the House and the Senate as far as the manner of property confiscation was concerned[31] but followed the Senate bill with respect to emanci-

---

[30] Ibid., 2998–3006 (June 28, 1862), remarks of Lyman Trumbull, John Sherman, and James Rood Doolittle; ibid., 3107 (July 3, 1862), House rejection.

[31] The main disagreement over the method of confiscation was that the House wished to use *in rem* proceedings to seize property while the Senate preferred trial and conviction for treason or rebellion. *In rem* proceedings were directed against property where the owner could not be reached, as in revenue cases or where the violators were not citizens or were beyond the jurisdiction of the government. As adapted by the Union government the idea behind the use of *in rem* proceedings was that property used to destroy the government was guilty and could be attacked directly without jury trial of the owner to the property. This approach was more expeditious and hence more radical than the alternative of trial and conviction of the owner. In the latter method, which was more conservative, the punishment for treason was death or, at a minimum, five years' imprisonment and $10,000 fine, while for rebellion it was a maximum of ten years' imprisonment or $10,000 fine and liberation of slaves or both. The bill contained both methods (Syrett, "The Confiscation Acts," p. 74; James G. Randall, *Constitutional Problems Under Lincoln*, rev. ed. [Urbana: University of Illinois Press, 1951], pp. 80, 278–79; Curry, *Blueprint for Modern America*, p. 94).

pation. It did not, in other words, contain an emancipation procedure and a guarantee of personal liberty. On its face the antislavery scope of the conference plan was broader than either the House or the Senate proposals. Instead of basing emancipation only on judicial process either in the form of conviction for treason or rebellion or by *in rem* proceedings leading to forfeiture of slaves' services, the bill declared that slaves of rebels who escaped to Union lines, were captured from or abandoned by rebels, or were found in places occupied by Union arms were "captives of war" and forever free. This meant a policy of complete emancipation if Federal armies were victorious and no compromise peace settlement took place.[32] The bill also prohibited the return of fugitive slaves by the army.

Nevertheless, the conference report contained no means of implementing the broad emancipation decree or any guarantee of the freed slaves' personal liberty. Rather, in a clear demonstration of pragmatic military purpose, it authorized the President to employ, organize, and use persons of African descent "in such manner as he may judge best for the public welfare." The bill also authorized the President to initiate voluntary colonization of slaves freed by the act. Its earlier interest in emancipation safeguards notwithstanding, the House joined the Senate in approving the Confiscation Act in July 1862.[33]

Many years ago James G. Randall observed that the antislavery sections of the Second Confiscation Act raised puzzling questions of enforcement and implementation. In such an unfamiliar undertaking as slave emancipation, Randall wrote, a definite procedure was to be expected, yet none was provided.[34] Logical as this observation appears in retrospect, it is really somewhat unhistorical and beside the point, for Republicans in Congress did not in the final analysis conceive emancipation to be a matter of securing personal liberty and civil rights. Rather, emancipation was intended to deprive the Confederacy of slave labor and to range black manpower on the side of the Union. John Sherman of Ohio, for example, objecting to Trumbull's assertions regarding the House emancipation bill with its guarantee of personal liberty, explained that he opposed general emancipation of slaves until there existed "some provision for their

---

[32] Syrett, "Confiscation Acts," p. 84.

[33] *Cong. Globe*, 37 Cong., 2 sess., 3267, 3275 (July 11, 1862); *U.S. Statutes at Large*, 12:589–92 (quotation on p. 592).

[34] Randall, *Constitutional Problems*, pp. 359–60.

government, for their education, for their protection, and for their colonization." But as the government could seize and use the property of rebels, so Sherman believed the labor of escaped and freed blacks should be used in ending the rebellion.[35] Furthermore, although Sherman looked forward to a more articulated freedmen's policy, most Republicans evidently thought the Confiscation Act, with its provision for employment of blacks as the President saw fit, adequately supplied the post-emancipation needs of the freed people, for the time being at least.[36]

Although freedmen's personal liberty and military expediency were not incompatible considerations, few Union men were convinced of the wisdom or necessity of pursuing both ends. Yet some did, indicating the growth of an interest in the civil rights side of emancipation. A perceptive critic of congressional policy was Henry Winter Davis of Maryland, who at the time Eliot's emancipation bill was being considered in the House advised Republican members that it was defective because it guaranteed no legal protection to freed slaves. It did not give the blacks it declared free the right to bring suit to vindicate personal liberty or to enjoy the privilege of the writ of habeas corpus, Davis pointed out, and hence offered no real freedom.[37] Similarly, the radical *Independent* stated that although the army could enforce emancipation in time of war, after the return of peace there would be need of civil-law guarantees to enable slaves entitled to freedom but ignorant of their rights or still in the control of their masters to gain personal liberty. The personal rights conferred by emancipation, the *Independent* reasoned, would need to be made explicit and protected by specific remedies at law.[38]

Many abolitionists criticized the Confiscation Act for being insufficiently radical. Moncure Daniel Conway believed southern whites would circumvent it with impunity by getting loyal border-state men to buy slaves and then send them south when the rebellion was over.[39] For the most part, however, abolitionists seemed to object to the restricted scope of the act rather than to the lack of procedural

---

[35] *Cong. Globe*, 37 Cong., 2 sess., 2999 (June 28, 1862).

[36] Ibid., 3000 (June 28, 1862), remarks of James R. Doolittle.

[37] Henry Winter Davis, *Speeches and Addresses Delivered in the Congress of the United States* . . . (New York: Harper & Brothers, 1867), pp. 298, 301.

[38] *Independent*, January 30, 1862.

[39] Monecure Daniel Conway, *The Golden Hour* (Boston: Ticknor & Fields, 1862), p. 150.

safeguards of personal liberty. In a typical expression Maria Weston Chapman called it "an Emancipation bill with clogs on."[40]

Henry Winter Davis offered the most pointed objections to the Confiscation Act from the standpoint of Negro liberty. Like Porter in the House, Davis desired to use emancipation as an instrument of war, without, however, abolishing slavery as a municipal institution. Eager to wage aggressive war, he criticized the Confiscation Act for freeing only the slaves of persons convicted of treason or rebellion or slaves of rebels who escaped into Union lines. But Davis also attacked the failure to make legal provision for securing the freed slaves' personal liberty. ". . . I suppose no body thought of any *legal* process," he wrote; "*all* was concentrated in the authority to the President to *use* all the negro population at his pleasure against the rebels!" Yet Davis's concern for legal process took into account more than the condition of freed blacks. Calling the Confiscation Act a measure of "revolutionary suppression," he complained that in view of the power given the President to use blacks for military purposes, "he will be a *smart* man who can hold a slave in any State!" Praising Porter's House emancipation bill because it freed slaves "absolutely," Davis was chiefly concerned with making emancipation effective for the sake of the Union. Nevertheless, his critique of the Confiscation Act, like Porter's emancipation bill, identified important issues for the protection of freedmen's liberty.[41]

A radical correspondent evaluating the Confiscation Act confirmed Davis's interpretation of congressional motives as concerned solely with military expediency. "We have a good Confiscation bill from the hands of a Conference Committee," wrote D. W. Bartlett in the *Independent*. "A section authorizes the President to make any use he pleases of black men, bond or free, in this struggle. . . . Congress has solemnly asked the President . . . *to use the black man in this war!* This is something."[42]

The disposition of freed slaves after their use by the government loomed as a great unresolved issue in 1862. In the limited discussion

[40] James M. McPherson, *The Struggle for Equality: Abolitionists and the Negro in the Civil War and Reconstruction* (Princeton, N.J.: Princeton University Press, 1964), p. 112.

[41] Davis to Mrs. S. F. DuPont, July [?], 1862, Papers of Samuel Francis DuPont and His Wife, Sophie Madeleine DuPont, Eleutherian Mills Historical Library, Greenville, Delaware.

[42] *Independent*, July 17, 1862.

that had developed by this time the principal question concerned *where* freed slaves would reside, not what status or rights they would enjoy. Some Republicans believed they would remain on southern soil as a free labor force and that free blacks from the North would join them in reconstructing free states in the South.[43] The only suggestion that emancipated slaves should go north to be distributed in the free states according to population came from conservatives trying to provoke and embarrass Republican emancipationists.[44] The readiest answer to the question of the future disposition of freed slaves was colonization.

On several occasions in 1862, including the passage of the Second Confiscation Act, Congress endorsed the voluntary removal of freed Negroes in a way that cast ironic light on the emancipation policy of the Republican party and the problem of the freedmen's liberty. Colonization was of course an old idea that had never worked and that must have seemed, even in the altered circumstances of 1862, somewhat chimerical. The best explanation of its revival is that it was politically useful as a corollary of emancipation, for it would allay apprehensions about large-scale migration of blacks into the North.[45] What was notable about colonization as it appeared in the Second Confiscation Act was the attempt to connect it with the idea of the freed slaves' rights. Thus, the act stated that Negro emigrants, assuming the President chose to initiate colonization, would be settled in a tropical country "with all the rights and privileges of freemen."[46] The fact that this provision was found in none of the earlier colonization measures of 1862 suggests that it was intended to express the interest in the emancipated slaves' personal liberty which was beginning to appear at this time.[47] Pessimistic about the possibility of securing civil equality for blacks in race-conscious America, several Republicans said that real freedom for emancipated slaves would come only through colonization with equal rights abroad.[48]

---

[43] Robert Dale Owen, *Letter to S. P. Chase: The Cost of Peace, November 10, 1862* (N.p, n.d.), p. 5; *National Anti–slavery Standard*, July 13, 1861; *Cong. Globe*, 37 Cong., 2 sess., 2243 (May 20, 1862), remarks of Albert G. Riddle.

[44] *Cong. Globe*, 37 Cong., 2 sess., 1356 (March 25, 1862), remarks of Anthony Kennedy and Willard Saulsbury.

[45] Voegeli, *Free But Not Equal*, pp. 22–24 and passim.

[46] *U.S. Statutes at Large*, 12:592.

[47] Ibid., 12:278, 425, 582, 592.

[48] *Cong. Globe*, 27 Cong., 2 sess., 1492 (April 2, 1862), remarks of John Sherman; ibid., 1520 (April 3, 1862), remarks of Orville H. Browning; ibid., 1604 (April 10,

Designed to confirm the *de facto* emancipation that was taking place with the advance of Union armies, the Confiscation Act of 1862 aimed principally at placing black manpower at the service of the Union. Though it declared slaves of rebels free upon entering Federal lines, it neglected to guarantee the right of personal liberty. Perhaps most significant, in authorizing colonization, albeit voluntary, it failed by implication to secure the right of remaining within the American republic. Republicans, sensitive to the demands of politics and the strength of race prejudice, were willing to make a promise of equal rights for emancipated slaves only in a foreign country.

A critic of colonization pointed out the obvious inadequacy of this position. "However it may have failed to be his country," Union publicist William Aikman wrote in 1862 concerning the black man in the United States, "this is his home. . . . after, by a great act of justice, you have raised him from chattelhood into citizenship, and have given him a country, by what rule of right do you propose . . . to banish him from it?"[49]

Congressional Republicans, then, no less than the Lincoln administration, failed to deal with the problem of the freed slaves' personal liberty. Some of them, it is true, were beginning to see that the issue needed attention, even if like Porter of Indiana and Henry Winter Davis they were not prepared to demand the abolition of slavery. Although it is not at all certain that the guarantee of personal liberty was a decisive consideration, the House in approving Porter's emancipation bill showed to some extent at least an awareness that emancipation to be effective required something more than well-intentioned political rhetoric, even if the rhetoric was incorporated in statutory provisions. Yet, more compelling was the desire to sustain the war effort politically by declaring for slave emancipation and militarily—so it was hoped—by depriving the enemy of slave labor. The authorization in the Confiscation Act for the President to use

---

1862), remarks of Lyman Trumbull; ibid., Appendix, 83 (March 19, 1862), remarks of James R. Doolittle.

[49] William Aikman, *The Future of the Colored Race in America* (New York: A. D. F. Randolph, 1862), p. 13. This criticism did not necessarily signify, however, a more sympathetic view toward blacks than was held by colonizationists. Aikman went on to argue that Negroes were an inferior race, that blacks and whites could not live together in North America, and that blacks would eventually go to Africa on their own initiative after they had improved themselves and became more capable and self-reliant (ibid., pp. 17–18, 26–27, 33.

Negroes as he saw fit, and in the militia act which Congress passed at the same time providing for enlistment of blacks into the army, clearly revealed the Republicans' expedient purpose. Motivated by pragmatic considerations rather than by concern for slaves' personal liberty, they were content to declare the slaves of rebels free and to leave to future developments the determination of their status and rights in the civil order.

5

Race, Law, and Politics in the Struggle for Equal Pay During the Civil War

THE ENROLLMENT OF EMANCIPATED SLAVES and free blacks in the Union army signified a major advance toward citizenship and equality before the law for American Negroes. Despite its long-range egalitarian tendency, however, at its inception, the policy was beset with internal contradiction in the form of lower pay and allowances for black soldiers in comparison with whites. After vigorous protest against this discrimination, which saw at least one black soldier court-martialed and sentenced to death for mutiny, Congress in June 1864 legislated equal pay for Negro troops. In the accomplishment of this goal, however, law, politics, and race—the essential elements in Union policy toward emancipated slaves during the Civil War—interacted in an unusual way. A decisive stand on behalf of equal pay for blacks was taken by conservative legalist Attorney General Edward Bates, who on this issue adopted an uncharacteristically radical political approach, while Secretary of War Edwin M. Stanton, who usually took the radical side of issues concerning slavery and emancipation, adopted a conservative legalist position. He did so moreover in accordance with the advice of the Solicitor of the War Department, William Whiting, who was also radical in outlook. What follows is an analysis of the issues that led to this reversal of radical and conservative roles within the Lincoln administration, and the manner in which they were resolved in the equal pay act of 1864.

Employment of black manpower in the Union cause was the principal corollary of the policy of military emancipation toward which President Lincoln and Congress moved in 1862. In different ways the Confiscation and Militia Acts of July 17, 1862, were directed to

An earlier version of this essay appeared in *Civil War History*, 22, No. 3 (September 1976), 197–213.

this end. The former measure, after declaring that slaves of rebels who entered Union lines were free, authorized the President to organize and use as many persons of African descent as he thought best for the public welfare. The Militia Act, in a specific and pointed way, authorized the President to receive Negroes into the service of the United States for the purpose of constructing trenches, laboring in camps, and performing any other military or naval service for which they might be found competent. Furthermore, unlike the Confiscation Act, the militia law directed that blacks employed in military labor or service be paid a definite wage, $10 per month, of which $3 could be in clothing.[1]

Lincoln did not hesitate to use the Confiscation Act to organize blacks for military labor. On July 22, 1862, he instructed Secretary of War Stanton to prepare an executive order authorizing the seizure of rebel property and the employment as laborers of as many colored persons as could be used for military or naval purposes.[2] Stanton's ensuing order required military commanders to employ Negroes as laborers, pay them reasonable wages, and keep accounts of their property and labor in order that fair settlement might subsequently be made.[3] At the same time Lincoln publicly stated that he was not prepared to use the contrabands as soldiers.[4] This policy soon changed, however, for, at the end of August, Stanton, presumably with the President's approval, directed General Rufus Saxton in South Carolina to raise five thousand colored volunteers and authorized them to receive the same pay and rations allowed by law to volunteers in the service.[5]

The Emancipation Proclamation, in which Lincoln announced that freed slaves would be received into the armed service for garrison duty, reflected growing pressure to use Negroes in the army and augured more widespread recruitment of both contrabands and free

---

[1] *Statutes at Large of the United States of America, 1789–1873*, 17 vols. (Washington, D.C.: Government Printing Office, 1850–1873), 12:592, 599.

[2] Roy P. Basler et al., eds., *The Collected Works of Abraham Lincoln*, 9 vols. (New Brunswick: N.J.: Rutgers University Press, 1953–1955), 5:337.

[3] William Whiting, *War Powers Under the Constitution of the United States*, 43rd ed. (Boston: Lee & Shepard, 1871), pp. 487–88.

[4] Basler et al., eds., *Collected Works of Lincoln*, 4:356–57.

[5] Benjamin P. Thomas and Harold M. Hyman, *Stanton: The Life and Times of Lincoln's Secretary of War* (New York: Alfred A. Knopf, 1962), p. 241; Dudley T. Cornish, *The Sable Arm: Negro Troops in the Union Army, 1861–65* (New York: W. W. Norton, 1956), p. 184.

blacks. In January 1863, under War Department authorization, Governor John A. Andrew of Massachusetts raised the first colored regiment from a northern state, and by April eight black regiments had been approved and six were in existence. In May the War Department created the Bureau for Colored Troops and put into operation the enlistment effort that by the end of the war brought 186,000 blacks into the national service.[6]

Although Stanton had authorized Saxton to pay Negroes equally with whites, this action did not establish a settled, uniform policy. Many colored troops in fact served months without receiving any pay at all.[7] In creating the Bureau for Colored Troops and launching a serious recruiting campaign, therefore, it was necessary for the War Department to consider the legal question of the pay that Negro soldiers were entitled to receive under the legislation of Congress. The result of this consideration was an official opinion of the Solicitor of the War Department, William Whiting, on the pay of colored troops.

Beginning with the proposition that before July 1862 blacks were legally excluded from the militia, the regular army, and the volunteers, Whiting's opinion reviewed the provisions of the Confiscation Act and the Militia Act under which Negroes might be enrolled in the service. One or the other of these statutes must provide the basis for a uniform pay policy. The Confiscation Act, Whiting pointed out, authorized the organization and use of Negroes as laborers, but made no reference to pay. The Militia Act, in contrast, provided that blacks employed in military labor or service were to be paid $10 per month, of which $3 might be in clothing, and one ration per day. Whiting argued further that Congress had confirmed this policy in March 1863 by passing an act authorizing the enlistment of Negro cooks at the same $10-per-month pay. Under congressional statutes, he concluded, Negro soldiers were entitled to the pay and allowances specified in the Militia Act. Stanton accepted Whiting's opinion, and on June 4, 1863, it became official War Department policy in the form of a general order to all commanders.[8]

Criticism of the War Department decision began immediately, led by Colonel Thomas Wentworth Higginson, commander of the First

---

[6] Cornish, *Sable Arm*, p. 99.
[7] Ibid., p. 183.
[8] *OR*, Ser. III, Vol. V, 632–33.

South Carolina Colored Volunteers, and Governor John A. Andrew of Massachusetts. Higginson's unit had been receiving the standard army pay of $13 per month; now, however, under Whiting's ruling it would be paid $10, less $3 in clothing. In protest most of the South Carolina troops refused any pay at all, on the advice, one may suppose, of their commanding officer.[9] Governor Andrew, for his part, sought equality for his state's black regiments through the political process. Visiting Washington in September 1863, Andrew suggested to Lincoln that the Attorney General might issue an opinion interpreting existing laws as requiring equal pay for Negro soldiers, while Congress could be asked to enact legislation clarifying and approving an equal pay policy. Though his main interest was to secure equal rights for Massachusetts's colored troops, Andrew was willing to subordinate this purpose to the broader objective of equal pay for all black soldiers.[10]

At first Andrew was encouraged by the reception accorded his views.[11] By the winter of 1863–64, however, neither Lincoln nor Stanton had shown any inclination to reverse the pay policy adopted on the basis of Whiting's opinion. In Congress, moreover, proposals to place black and white soldiers on the same footing with respect to pay and emoluments produced controversy within the Republican party which delayed legislative action. At length, in June 1864, Congress passed a military appropriations bill with a section equalizing the pay of colored soldiers.

Senator Henry Wilson of Massachusetts began proceedings in February 1864 with a joint resolution that would give colored persons mustered into military service the same pay, clothing, equipment, rations, medical attendance, and emoluments other than bounty as other soldiers received. In this initial proposal, moreover, equalization of pay was to be retrospective as well as prospective, applying to the whole time blacks had been and would be in the

---

[9] Senator James Grimes of Iowa claimed that the officers of the 1st South Carolina Volunteers persuaded the black soldiers to accept no pay. *Congressional Globe*, 38 Cong., 1 sess., p. 636 (February 13, 1864).

[10] Thomas Wentworth Higginson, *Army Life in a Black Regiment* (East Lansing: Michigan State University Press, 1960), p. 218; Tilden G. Edelstein, *Strange Enthusiasm: A Life of Thomas Wentworth Higginson* (New Haven, Conn.: Yale University Press, 1968), p. 293; Henry Greenleaf Pearson, *The Life of John A. Andrew, Governor of Massachusetts, 1861–65*, 2 vols. (Boston and New York: Houghton Mifflin, 1904), 2:99–100.

[11] Ibid., 2:100.

service. Only with respect to bounty payment were black troops denied formal equality, the resolution providing that they should receive such bounty as the President should order but in no case exceeding $100.[12]

For a variety of reasons, chief of which was alleged to be the straitened condition of the Treasury, objection arose to Wilson's comprehensive, retroactive equalization formula. The Massachusetts senator then offered a bill giving all black troops equal pay as of January 1, 1884, but restricting back pay to those colored units which had been enlisted on a promise of equal pay. This was designed to reach the few regiments of South Carolina and Massachusetts black troops who had been the initial object of concern in the protests of Governor Andrew and Colonel Higginson.[13]

The Senate passed this modified equalization bill in March 1864, but it was allowed to die in the House Committee on Military Affairs. Wilson succeeded in reviving it, however, in the form of an amendment to a military appropriations bill which the House had already passed.[14] Intraparty disagreement on the Negro pay issue, which was indicated in the treatment accorded Wilson's bill in the military affairs committee, became manifest when the House ways and means committee in turn rejected the Senate amendment to the appropriations bill. Instead of singling out a few black regiments for back pay as the Senate preferred to do, the ways and means committee, led by Thaddeus Stevens, proposed to give back pay to all black troops who were free as of April 19, 1861, the date on which the war had been determined legally to have begun.[15]

To resolve disagreement between the two houses a committee of conference was appointed which reported a bill basically like that of the Senate. It gave back pay to colored soldiers who had received a promise of equal pay upon enlistment. Blacks who had not been promised equal pay were also taken into account, but only in a tentative and uncertain way. The conference committee report stated that they could be given back pay to the time of enlistment if in the judgment of the proper authorities they were determined to be

---

[12] 38 Cong., Joint Res. S. No. 23, February. 3, 1864. In January 1863 the House had passed a bill for recruiting Negro regiments which equalized pay, but not retroactively. The Senate took no action on this measure.

[13] *Cong. Globe*, 38 Cong., 1 sess., p. 990 (March 8, 1864).

[14] Ibid., 1030 (March 10, 1864), p. 1805 (April 22, 1864), p. 2056 (May 3, 1864).

[15] Ibid., pp. 2470, 2473 (May 25, 1864), remarks of Robert C. Schenck.

entitled to it. This section was apparently written at least in part with an eye to the opinion on Negro pay issued in April 1864 by Attorney General Edward Bates, which declared that a colored chaplain was legally entitled to the same pay as a white chaplain. Nevertheless, the committee report did not specify the Attorney General as the proper authority for deciding questions about the pay of Negro troops, which meant that the Solicitor of the War Department, William Whiting, might also be regarded as the official most appropriately concerned.[16]

Standing by its opposition to retrospective pay for the few colored units that had been promised equal pay, the House rejected the conference report. A second committee of conference was then formed which took a position closer to the House view.[17] Its report declared black soldiers who were free at the start of the war entitled to the pay and emoluments allowed them by law retroactive to the time of enlistment. Knowing that the meaning of the law was a matter of dispute, and obviously with Bates's opinion in the Negro chaplain's case in mind, the committee then expressly authorized the Attorney General to determine all questions of law concerning the pay of colored troops. Finally, the committee directed the War Department to alter its pay policy in accordance with the legal determinations of the Attorney General.[18] In mid-June both houses agreed to this proposal, which ironically denied back pay to the colored troops of South Carolina on whose behalf the campaign for equal pay had in part originally been undertaken.[19]

In analyzing the issues raised in the equal pay controversy it is important to note that congressional opinion divided not on whether blacks should receive the same pay as whites in the future—all but a few extreme conservatives agreed they should—but on whether black soldiers should be given equal pay retroactively. Warning against the expense it would involve and recalling both the experimental nature of Negro enlistment in 1862 and the express terms of the Militia Act, a few Republicans held that prospective equal pay satisfied the requirements of the principle of equality. The real

---

[16] Ibid., p. 2471 (May 25, 1864).

[17] Ibid., p. 2475 (May 25, 1864). The second conference committee consisted of Stevens, Thomas T. Davis, a Unionist, and George Pendleton, a Democrat, from the House, and Timothy Howe and Lot M. Morrill, Republicans, and Charles Buckalew, Democrat, from the Senate.

[18] Ibid., p. 2851 (June 10, 1864).

[19] Ibid., Appendix, p. 178.

question, said Senator James Grimes of Iowa, was not what the country or Congress thought of colored troops at any time in the past, but what Congress thought of them now. Grimes believed the widespread sentiment in favor of equal pay for blacks was a sign of great progress which ought to satisfy the demands of antislavery reformers and abolitionists.[20] Most Republicans, however, were of opinion that equal treatment of Negro soldiers required some degree of compensatory back pay.

Although a consensus existed on this general point, the reasons offered in support of retroactive equalization revealed important differences in attitude toward blacks. The principal contention, for example, behind both Governor Andrew's efforts and the bill introduced by Henry Wilson in February 1864 was that the government was honor-bound to keep the promise of equal pay that it had given to colored soldiers from South Carolina and Massachusetts. More than a pledge, the government had in effect made a contractual obligation with these soldiers which must be upheld, declared Representative John F. Farnsworth of Illinois.[21] This approach, which characterized the outlook of the Senate, implied, however, that blacks should receive back pay not because they were equal to or worth as much as white soldiers, but because the government had incurred a contractual commitment to them. In contrast, the preference of the House for broader retroactive application of the equalization principle came closer to expressing the idea that black soldiers were equal in value to whites.[22]

The interest of the Senate in basing back pay on the idea of a contractual obligation made for a distinction among colored troops which further revealed differences in attitude toward blacks. Although Wilson's original joint resolution covered all Negro troops, the measure that he steered through the Senate and that formed the basis for the first conference report extended retroactive equalization only to the few colored regiments from South Carolina and

---

[20] Ibid., p. 636 (February 13, 1864).

[21] Ibid., p. 2472 (May 25, 1864), remarks of John W. Farnsworth. See also ibid., pp. 480–81 (February 4, 1864), remarks of Henry Wilson; pp. 481–82 (February 4, 1864), remarks of John Ten Eyck; pp. 484 (Feb. 4, 1864), remarks of Charles Sumner, p. 2472 (May 25, 1864), remarks of James A. Garfield.

[22] Ibid., p. 2851 (June 10, 1864), remarks of Timothy Howe. That the House proposed to give back pay to free blacks did not mean that freed slave soldiers were not valued as highly, for in this view the latter were compensated in part by the freedom they had received.

Massachusetts. The principal reason for rejecting this plan in the House was that it created a distinction among blacks that seemed unwise and unfair.

According to Republican Senator John B. Henderson of Missouri, House members wanted free Negroes from New York, Pennsylvania, and other free states to receive equalization benefits, as well as those from Massachusetts.[23] Republican Theodore Thayer of Pennsylvania said that while it was arguable whether black and white soldiers should receive equal pay, no valid reason existed for discriminating among Negro troops.[24] Border-state conservatives joined in pointing up the inconsistency and unfairness in the Senate approach. Reverdy Johnson of Maryland asked why Massachusetts colored men should receive more than those of Maryland, while Representative William H. Wadsworth of Kentucky held that if Congress should go beyond the provisions of the Militia Act, it must treat all colored soldiers the same.[25]

Objecting to the discriminatory nature of the Senate bill, House Republicans themselves in turn proposed to create a distinction among blacks by awarding back pay to all who had been free on April 19, 1861. Several Republicans and War Democrats critically observed that this discriminated against colored soldiers who had been slaves at the start of the war.[26] At the very least, said Samuel C. Pomeroy of Kansas, if former slave status were to be considered relevant, the burden should lie upon the government to prove that certain blacks had been slaves.[27] Senators Morton Wilkinson of Minnesota and Jacob Howard of Michigan attacked the distinction among colored troops on broader grounds, arguing that slaves were persons under the Constitution who owed allegiance to the government. Subject like all other persons within the jurisdiction of the Union to military service, slaves who enlisted in the army should receive the same benefits as other soldiers and should suffer no discrimination because of color or previous status. The power to call upon "the people of the United States," in whose number slaves were included, said

---

[23] Ibid., p. 2854 (June 10, 1864).

[24] Ibid., p. 2473 (May 25, 1864).

[25] Ibid., p. 635 (February 13, 1864), remarks of Reverdy Johnson; p. 2475 (May 25, 1864), remarks of William H. Wadsworth.

[26] Ibid., p. 2472 (May 25, 1864), remarks of Thaddeus Stevens and Rufus P. Spalding; p. 2851 (June 10, 1864), remarks of John Conness.

[27] Ibid., p. 2851 (June 10, 1864).

Howard, "must regard all alike free and equal."[28] Henry Wilson disapprovingly pointed out that the result of distinguishing among blacks on the basis of prewar status was to discriminate against the very troops, recruited from among South Carolina's contraband population, whose rights it was the original purpose to uphold.[29]

Retroactive equalization raised questions not only about differences among blacks, but also about distinctions between blacks and whites that some Republicans viewed as discriminatory against the latter. Noting that white troops had been treated differently with respect to bounties, Senator William Pitt Fessenden of Maine said that if the demand for justice to the Negro should prevail, "let us have the same kind of justice for the white man, and go back and equalize everybody from the beginning."[30] James Doolittle of Wisconsin and James A. Garfield of Ohio agreed that blacks should not be given special treatment that was denied to whites. As white soldiers had often been recruited with promises for which no legal authorization existed and had gotten relief only through prospective equalization, said Garfield, so blacks should be paid as provided in the Militia Act of 1862 until Congress legislated otherwise. Declaring his support for prospective equal pay, Garfield criticized those who would make political capital "by showing an excessive zeal for the black man."[31]

It is difficult in retrospect to understand how the solution to the equal pay problem arrived at in June 1864 could fairly be seen as inimical to the interests or the equal status of white soldiers. Nevertheless, some Republicans not only viewed back pay in that light, but also believed that lower pay for blacks was not really discriminatory because of the different circumstances in which black soldiers were placed. Doolittle of Wisconsin, for example, proposed an amendment to Wilson's equal pay bill that would have set aside $3

---

[28] Ibid., pp. 821–24 (February 25, 1864). Wilkinson and Howard were here opposing an amendment by Wilson to the equal pay bill that would have made only free Negroes eligible for retroactive payment of the bounty given to volunteers enlisted under the call of October 17, 1863. Negro troops received no bounty until passage of the Military Appropriations Act in June 1864.

[29] Ibid., p. 2853 (June 10, 1864).

[30] Ibid., p. 870 (February 29, 1864).

[31] Ibid., p. 483 (February 4, 1864), remarks of James Doolittle; p. 2472 (May 25, 1864), remarks of James A. Garfield. Garfield desired legislation giving back pay to Negro units which had been promised equal pay, while Fessenden favored a private bill to accomplish this purpose.

per month from the pay of black troops to provide care for families of Negro soldiers who were being supported by the army out of the Union Treasury. Since white soldiers had legal obligations to their families which former slave soldiers did not, Doolittle reasoned, the $3 deduction would put the races on a basis of equality.[32]

Doolittle's proposal was rejected, as was a House amendment to the final equal pay bill that would have marked one-third of the pay of colored troops for the relief of Negro families in the South.[33] The argument that such an arrangement really equalized the situation of colored and white soldiers simply could not be sustained, especially in view of the fact that several northern states and local communities provided support for the families of white soldiers beyond their regular pay and allowances.[34] Nevertheless, the idea that different circumstances justified different yet equitable treatment of blacks found partial expression in the provision for lower bounties for Negro recruits that was contained in the equal pay act of 1864. Even Henry Wilson, the chief sponsor of the bill, gave limited endorsement to this point of view. Conceding that free Negroes enlisting in northern states should receive the same bounty as whites, Wilson nevertheless observed, first, that white troops did not all receive the same bounty, and, second, that in the occupied South where the government supported the families of contraband soldiers it was not unfair that the latter should be given a smaller bounty than whites.[35]

Notwithstanding the desire to give "perfect equality," Republican lawmakers were forced to recognize what they regarded as practical realities—the state of the Treasury, for example—in formulating an equal pay policy.[36] The distinction drawn in the equalization act of 1864 between free black and former-slave soldiers may similarly be seen as an accommodation to reality that, while not according with strict, formal equality, was nonetheless thought of as equitable.

---

[32] Ibid., p. 566 (February 10, 1864), pp. 638–41 (February. 13, 1884), remarks of James Doolittle. See also remarks of John Sherman, ibid.

[33] Ibid., p. 2000 (April 30, 1864), remarks of Robert C. Schenck.

[34] Fred A. Shannon, *The Organization and Administration of the Union Army, 1861–1865*, 2 vols. (Cleveland: A. H. Clark, 1928) 2:50–52; Higginson, *Army Life in a Black Regiment*, p. 222. James Doolittle claimed that Wisconsin deducted from the pay of white troops to provide family support, but Shannon, the authoritative source, contains no evidence of this alleged practice.

[35] *Cong. Globe*, 38 Cong., 1 sess., p. 769 (February 23, 1864).

[36] Ibid.

The reality here, at least from the Republican point of view, was that black soldiers who had been slaves at the start of the war received a substantial bounty in the form of personal liberty. Explaining why the second conference committee recommended a distinction among black troops, Timothy Howe of Wisconsin reported the view of several members that slaves freed during the war received thereby a very large compensation for their services as soldiers.[37] This argument did not persuade radicals, who thought the distinction between free black and former-slave soldiers merely reflected a petty desire to save a few dollars by denying equality to those whom the war had made free.[38] Yet Republicans who supported the distinction among blacks did so because they regarded the freedom that contraband soldiers received as, in Thaddeus Stevens's words, "a sufficient equivalent" for a money payment.[39] Henry Wilson also, although at first wishing to give back pay to all Negro troops, agreed to the distinction on the ground that freed slaves were compensated by the guarantee of freedom.[40] In similar fashion the Militia Act of 1862 provided compensation for service in the form both of $10 per month and of a guarantee of freedom. Colored persons enrolled in the army and their families if owned by loyal masters were entitled to freedom.[41] Henry Wilson and Thaddeus Stevens both agreed, considering that the act was intended to enlist former slaves, that the compensation it offered was fair and gave no ground for complaint.[42]

The basic practical question in the equal pay controversy, as already noted, was whether all or only some black soldiers should receive back pay. Two further considerations lay behind this issue:

---

[37] Ibid., p. 2851 (June 10, 1864).

[38] Higginson, *Army Life in a Black Regiment*, p. 225.

[39] *Cong. Globe*, 38 Cong., 1 sess., p. 1996 (April 30, 1864).

[40] Ibid., p. 820 (February 25, 1864). The specific issue was whether the equal pay bill should give all blacks, or only free blacks enrolled under the call of October 1, 1863, the same bounty as whites received. Wilson argued that former slaves should not receive the bounty because they were already provided for by the Enrollment Act of February 1864. This act, the main purpose of which was to declare all blacks part of the national forces and eligible for military service, gave to loyal masters of slaves who were drafted into the army a bounty of $100 (and $300 bounty if the slave volunteered), while to the slave soldier it gave a guarantee of freedom. *U.S. Statutes at Large*, 12:11.

[41] Ibid., 12:599; Whiting, *War Powers*, p. 486.

[42] *Cong. Globe*, 38 Cong., 1 sess., p. 873 (February 29, 1864), remarks of Henry Wilson; p. 1996 (Apr. 30, 1864), remarks of Thaddeus Stevens.

first, whether Negro troops possessed the same value as whites, and, second, what the law provided concerning the pay of colored troops.

Senator Timothy Howe of Wisconsin, a member of the second conference committee, said the majority of the committee believed Negroes were not worth as much as white soldiers. Hence, they rejected the more comprehensive back pay plan favored by the House. Nor did they think, however, that a contract to give equal pay, as the Senate proposed, should determine policy if it meant paying soldiers more than they were worth. On the other hand, there was the question of the pay that the law authorized Negro troops to receive. This proved to be the key to the situation, for despite their negative attitude toward colored soldiers, a majority of the committee believed that existing law made no distinction in the pay of black and white troops.[43]

Those, evidently a majority, who regarded blacks as inferior soldiers, Howe explained, had little good reason to oppose giving them what the law provided.[44] Yet, because of the political liability involved in declaring, in effect, that Negroes were worth as much as whites, the committee did not wish Congress to make this determination. The way out of the difficulty was to declare black soldiers who were free before the war entitled to the pay and emoluments allowed them by law at the time of enlistment; then to charge the Attorney General with deciding any legal question arising under this provision or, in other words, what the law allowed. By this time of course Attorney General Edward Bates had published his opinion stating that a colored chaplain was entitled to the same pay as a white chaplain, and the logic of this pointed to equal back pay for all colored troops. Without itself making a formal determination, therefore, Congress could resolve the practical political issue at the heart of the controversy—namely, the valuation of black soldiers in comparison with whites—by turning it into a legal question for the Attorney General to settle.

The irony in all of this is that Edward Bates, who was usually a conservative legalist, dealt with the Negro pay question in what appears to have been a thoroughly political manner. Bates's involvement in the dispute began when Lincoln requested an opinion from him on whether Samuel Harrison, a Negro chaplain in the 54th Mas-

---

[43] Ibid., p. 2851 (June 10, 1864), remarks of Timothy Howe.
[44] Ibid.

sachusetts, was entitled to the $100 per month pay that white chaplains received or the $10 per month that black soldiers received under the Militia Act and the War Department policy of 1863. Lincoln, for his part, had taken this action at the instance of Governor Andrew of Massachusetts, who on seeing the equal pay bill stalled in Congress determined to seek justice for his state's colored regiments through executive action.[45] Harrison's was to be a test case designed to force abandonment of the government's discriminatory pay policy.

Bates's opinion, which was issued on April 23, 1864, held in essence that although Negroes were barred from the militia by act of Congress in 1792, nothing in the laws of the United States excluded them from the regular army or the volunteer service. If there was any doubt about this, which of course there was, it was removed, Bates said, by the Confiscation Act of 1862, which authorized the President to organize and use blacks in any way he saw fit. This, rather than the Militia Act, was the specific peg on which Bates hung his opinion. Chaplain Harrison, he reasoned, manifestly did not belong to the class of military laborers or garrison troops which the Militia Act, with its $10 pay provision, had contemplated. Harrison must therefore have been enrolled under the Confiscation Act, and specifically in accordance with the terms of the volunteer service act of July 1861 by which Lincoln chose to be guided in the actual organization of Negro troops.[46]

Although Bates's opinion was entirely satisfactory, Governor Andrew was disappointed when Lincoln refused to use it as the basis for equalizing the pay of all Negro soldiers. When Andrew inquired further into the matter, Lincoln replied that while he supported equal pay, it was not within his constitutional power to bring it about.[47] Meanwhile, however, as we have seen, Congress in its own way took the initiative and charged the Attorney General with deciding whether free colored troops should receive back pay. Bates at first demurred, on the ground that as Attorney General his duty was not to decide legal questions but simply to advise about them. Only when Lincoln requested an opinion on the pay of colored troops designated in the military appropriations act did Bates respond in the manner intended by Congress.[48]

---

[45] Pearson, *Life of John A. Andrew*, 2:105–106.

[46] OR, Ser. 3, Vol. IV, pp. 271-73.

[47] Pearson, *Life of John A. Andrew*, 2:111.

[48] Lincoln to Bates, June 24, 1864, in Basler et al., eds., *Collected Works of Lincoln*, 7:404–405.

Bates's second opinion on Negro pay, which was published on July 14, 1864, followed the logic of his earlier one. Now, however, he flatly asserted—rather astonishingly it must be admitted—that the Militia Act of 1862 gave no authority to enlist colored soldiers, that its purpose was simply to bring black labor into the service. Authority to enroll Negroes as soldiers, Bates contended, was provided instead in the Confiscation Act of 1862. Accordingly, not having been enlisted under the Militia Act, black troops were not subject to the $10 limitation in pay provided therein. Enrolled under the authority of the Confiscation Act, which contained no pay provision, and in specific accordance with the terms of the act of July 1861 for raising volunteers, which contained no racial exclusion, the black troops referred to in the equal pay act were entitled to receive the same pay as other volunteers. Bates thus concluded that existing law guaranteed equal pay to Negro soldiers.[49] In accordance with the act of Congress, the War Department implemented the Attorney General's opinion on August 1, 1864, by ordering back pay to be given to colored troops who were free as of April 19, 1861.[50]

According to his biographer, Bates's opinion in the Negro chaplain's case did not express his true feelings, but rather was influenced by the fact that blacks were fighting for the Union. Bates reached the only conclusion he could under the circumstances.[51] Justice—and one may think politics, meaning by that appreciation of what most Republicans considered necessary, wise, or expedient—demanded equal pay for Negro soldiers. Yet Bates, evidently enjoying the uncharacteristic role of friend of the freedmen that was now thrust upon him, went along with the view that it was simply the law, properly understood, which was responsible for the change in policy. Meeting Charles Sumner at the White House and learning from him that he, Bates, was much in favor in abolition circles for his opinion on Negro soldiers' pay, Bates related what a friend had told him: that the radicals "would never forgive me for proving that negroes had some rights by law, whereas they insist that all the rights of negroes are derived from their bounty!"[52]

[49] OR, Ser. 3, Vol. IV, 490–93.

[50] Ibid., 565.

[51] Marvin R. Cain, *Lincoln's Attorney General: Edward Bates of Missouri* (Columbia: University of Missouri Press, 1965), p. 234.

[52] Howard K. Beale, ed., *The Diary of Edward Bates, 1859–1866*, (Washington, D.C. Government Printing Office, 1933), p. 371.

Bates's official opinion notwithstanding, the evidence suggests that blacks were in fact excluded by law from the regular army before 1862, that the Militia Act was designed to place them under arms as soldiers, and that William Whiting's opinion on the pay of Negro troops, on which the War Department policy until 1864 rested, was legally sound. It will be recalled that much depended in Whiting's view on the contention that blacks were legally ineligible for recruitment into the regular army and volunteers, as well as from the militia, before July 1862. This seems to be correct. It was true that Negroes had fought in the Revolution and in the War of 1812. They were excluded from the militia by the act of 1792, however, and although legislation barring them from the army and navy was never enacted by Congress, the War Department after 1816 excluded Negroes by administrative order. At the start of the Civil War, therefore, army regulations, which were recognized as having legal effect, restricted the regular army and volunteers to white men only.[53]

Theoretically, perhaps, the United States as a sovereign government had the power to enlist all persons under its jurisdiction in military service.[54] Yet if this power existed, it had not been used by the President, and in the political circumstances of 1862 was not likely to be. Politically as well as legally, legislation was needed to make blacks available for armed service in defense of the Union. This, it seems clear, was the purpose of the Militia Act, which authorized the President to receive colored persons into the national forces for the purpose of constructing trenches or performing any military or naval service. The act also stated that Negroes enlisted in the army should receive $10 per month plus a guarantee of freedom. The Confiscation Act, in contrast, looked simply to the organization of Negroes as laborers. Containing no references to qualifications needed for military service, pay, or period of service, it was not intended to make soldiers out of emancipated slaves. With these facts in view, it is difficult to accept Attorney General Bates's

---

[53] OR, Ser. 3, Vol. V, 654; Whiting, *War Powers*, pp. 479–80; Cornish, *Sable Arm*, p. ix; Russell F. Weigley, *History of the United States Army* (New York: Macmillan, 1967), p. 212; Frank A. Flower, *Edwin McMasters Stanton: The Autocrat of Rebellion, Emancipation, and Reconstruction* (New York: W. W. Wilson, 1905), p 186.

[54] Conservative Unionists held that the laws did not bar blacks from the regular army and that the President had the power to enroll them. They adopted this view in opposing the Militia Act. *Cong. Globe*, 37 Cong., 2 sess., p. 3253 (July 11, 1862), remarks of Edgar Cowan. On the question of theoretical power see also Whiting, *War Powers*, p. 479.

conclusion that blacks were intended to be and were enlisted as soldiers under the Confiscation Act. In fact, as War Department records showed, Negroes were mustered in under the Militia Act.[55]

Congressional deliberation on the Militia Act in 1862 shows beyond doubt that the act was intended to place blacks in the army, primarily as laborers but also as fighting men. This was most clearly indicated in the rejection of an amendment to strike from the bill language authorizing Negroes to perform "any military and naval service." Conservative Republicans who wished to restrict blacks to camp labor supported the amendment, but a majority of Republicans, agreeing with Senator Preston King of New York that Negroes should be used as armed soldiers and not just as menial laborers, defeated it.[56] Further evidence that Republicans envisioned Negroes serving as combat troops emerged in discussions of the provision in the Militia Act guaranteeing liberty to slaves who enlisted. "You arm these slaves, and fight them in the Army of the United States," declared James H. Lane of Kansas, "and when that is done, I say it is out of the power of the . . . Congress of the United States, or the General Government to return them to the loyal master in a state of slavery. . . ."[57]

The Militia Act was intended to reach southern freedmen, not free blacks in northern states. In formal terms, however, the act made no distinction between these two classes but comprehended all "persons of African descent." In 1863 this provision made for difficulty when recruiting of free Negroes at the North began and the question arose concerning the pay they were entitled to receive. What seemed fair compensation—freedom plus $10 per month—for contraband soldiers and laborers whose employment was considered experimental was not necessarily appropriate for free blacks.[58] Nevertheless, as we have seen, the War Department, guided by William Whiting's opinion, treated all blacks the same with respect to pay and allowances.

Whiting's opinion and the policy based upon it were criticized as

---

[55] Whiting, *War Powers*, pp. 482, 489.

[56] *Cong. Globe*, 37 Cong., 2 sess., p. 3231 (July 10, 1862), p. 3252 (July 11, 1862), remarks of Preston King, p. 3239 (July 10, 1864), remarks of James Doolittle.

[57] Ibid., pp. 3338, 3339 (July 15, 1862), remarks of James H. Lane, James Harrison, Jacob Howard; p. 3251 (July 11, 1862), remarks of Preston King.

[58] Ibid., 38 Cong., 1 sess., p. 873 (Feb. 29, 1864), remarks of Henry Wilson, p. 1996 (Apr. 30, 1864), remarks of Thaddeus Stevens.

racist. Arguing that no change in the law was needed in order to equalize pay, the Chicago *Tribune* declared that "the chief disability of the black race, lies in prejudice and not in law." The War Department, suggested the *Tribune*, could just as well have concluded in 1863 that no bar existed to giving all soldiers equal pay irrespective of color.[59] Yet while such a view was plausible, and was maintained by Governor Andrew and Charles Sumner among others, it lacked historical soundness and legal cogency. The fact was that Negroes were legally excluded from the army until the Militia Act of 1862 authorized their enrollment. If the law were to control, as Whiting supposed it should, the War Department had little choice but to treat all black troops the same, regardless of whether they were contrabands from the South or northern free Negroes.

This is not to say that the War Department policy was entirely free of any political content or motivation. No decision in a matter of this sort could be completely nonpolitical. The motive that led Stanton to accept Whiting's opinion in disregard of Governor Andrew's urging for equal pay is somewhat obscure, however. One theory might be that while the use of Negro troops was politically expedient, any recognition of their equality with whites was not because of the prejudice against blacks at the North. Andrew's biographer many years ago argued that Stanton as a Democrat shared the hostility of his party against the friends of the Negro, and for that reason rejected Andrew's appeal for equal pay.[60] More recently Harold M. Hyman and Benjamin P. Thomas have suggested that Stanton acted as he did because Andrew had disregarded a ruling by the Secretary of War that Massachusetts could not recruit free Negroes from other northern states.[61]

For his own part, Whiting's opinion seems to have gone counter to his political and social views, which were radical and in this instance supported equal pay for blacks.[62] In a letter to a meeting of colored

---

[59] Chicago *Tribune*, Jan. 28, 1864, quoted in Cornish, *Sable Arm*, p. 191.

[60] Pearson, *Life of John A. Andrew*, 2:97–98.

[61] Thomas and Hyman, *Stanton*, p. 264.

[62] Whiting, a patent lawyer brought to Washington in December 1862 as Solicitor of the War Department, was well known for a treatise he wrote in 1862 arguing for sweeping war powers of President and Congress. The Democratic leader S. S. Cox called him the "fertile brain" and "reservoir of all the Republican heresy and legislation proposed in the House" (*Cong. Globe*, 38 Cong., 1 sess., p. 709). Charles Sumner, in a letter introducing Whiting to John Bright in England, referred to him as being "in the full confidence of the President, and my personal friend, agreeing

citizens in Poughkeepsie, New York, Whiting observed that the Militia Act and its $10 pay provision were framed with reference to southern freedmen, not northern free blacks. Trying to suggest some remedy for the latter, he said that under the recently passed Conscription Act, which made no distinction of color, black volunteers who were citizens of states might be enlisted on an equal footing with whites.[63] A few years later Whiting wrote that the injustice of his opinion on Negro pay was a source of great regret. Yet when he issued it, he explained, blacks had in fact been enrolled under the Militia Act, correctly as it seemed to him, and he felt that the law required payment of $10 per month to all Negro troops.[64] In general, it seems fair to characterize Whiting's position as conservative and legalistic.

Bates's opinion, in contrast, which by a kind of ironic legislative fiction was to be brought forward as an impartial statement of the law, was more political in nature than legalistic. Bates interpreted the Confiscation and Militia Acts in precisely the opposite manner intended by Congress, in order to avoid the $10 pay limitation imposed by the latter. In contradiction of the facts he held that Negroes had been enlisted under the Confiscation Act. Political expediency rather than the plain meaning of the law seemed to guide the usually legalistic Attorney General.

The Military Appropriations Act of June 1864 did not entirely resolve the equal pay problem, for it denied back pay to colored troops who were slaves at the start of the war. Accordingly antislavery radicals kept up their criticism, denouncing what they termed "the miserable delusion of the 19th of April provision." Rejecting the logic which regarded freedom as partial compensation for contraband soldiers, they insisted that all regiments formed from emancipated slaves in the southern and border states should receive back pay to the time of enlistment.[65] Congress responded in the Enroll-

---

with me positively in policy and object" (Edward L. Pierce, *Memoir and Letters of Charles Sumner*, 4 vols. [Boston: Roberts, 1877–1894], 4:143).

[63] *Liberator*, July 31, 1863, letter of William Whiting on Colored Troops, July 10, 1863. The defect in this suggestion was that not all Negroes were citizens in the states in which they resided. Whiting was not proposing that they be regarded as citizens of the United States, it being his view that the *Dred Scott* decision denying national citizenship to blacks was still valid constitutional law at this time. Apparently nothing came of Whiting's suggestion concerning the Conscription Act.

[64] Whiting, *War Powers*, pp. 486–87.

[65] Boston *Commonwealth*, January 7, 1865.

ment Act of March 3, 1865, by giving back pay to the Negro troops who were enlisted by Generals Hunter and Saxton in South Carolina, under the War Department order of August 25, 1862, with a promise of equal pay. As for other contraband troops, back pay would be given them retroactively where the Secretary of War was satisfied that they had been mustered in on an assurance of equal pay.[66]

Important as this measure was in rectifying what had come to be regarded as a most egregious injustice, it did not grant back pay categorically to all freed slaves who had been enlisted as soldiers. The principle on which it rested was not that black troops of this class were inherently equal to and worth as much as white troops, but rather that where the government had promised equal pay it must uphold its contractual obligation. With respect to Negro soldiers who had received no such promise, and it is not known how many there were, freedom remained the compensation for military service, along with $10 per month, from the time of enlistment until the equalization required by the act of June 1864.

In a general sense one may conclude that the difficulty experienced in equalizing the pay of colored troops was related to and reflected the belief in Negro inferiority that prevailed among white Americans in the Civil War era. Many years ago Fred A. Shannon in effect reached this conclusion when he wrote that "the federal administration during the Civil War had but very rudimentary notions concerning the rights which were proper to be offered to negro soldiers."[67] Without disputing the accuracy of this view, one can perhaps place it in clearer historical perspective by calling attention, as this essay has tried to do, to the additional exigencies of law, politics, and wartime circumstances in general, which caused Republican lawmakers in resolving issues growing out of emancipation to be as much concerned with achieving equitableness as strict, formal equality, if not more so.

---

[66] *U.S. Statutes at Large*, 13:488.

[67] Shannon, *Organization and Administration of the Union Army*, 2:168.

6

The Freedmen's Bureau Act of 1865 and the Principle of No Discrimination According to Color

FROM THE TIME Benjamin F. Butler issued his famous contraband order of May 1861, that escaped slaves would be employed as military laborers, the Union government was engaged in attempts to deal with the results of emancipation. The culmination of these wartime efforts was the Freedmen's Bureau Act of March 3, 1865. Historically, this measure has been best remembered for its provision assigning forty acres of land to every male freedman. Yet at the time of its passage it contained a civil rights dimension that was as important as, if not more important than, its economic content. The result of two years of legislative deliberation on freedmen's affairs, it was intended to recognize the former slaves as free men with ordinary civil rights.

The principle of no discrimination according to color played a conspicuous part in the formation of the Freedmen's Bureau. Ironically, however, in the shaping of the 1865 act it was not Radicals with a reputation for being the special friends of the freedmen who insisted on this principle, but rather Republicans who sought to uphold the interest of loyal white refugees in the South. These same spokesmen for southern refugees were advocates, moreover, of laissez-faire legal equality as a basic approach to the freedmen's question. Regarding the proposal for a permanent department of freedmen's affairs, advocated by Radicals, as an unwholesome and unsound form of guardianship, they believed that emancipated blacks should be recognized as free men or citizens and, as the phrase had it, left severely alone

---

An earlier version of this essay appeared in *Civil War History*, 21, No. 3 (September 1975), 197–217.

to make their own labor arrangements and provide for themselves. How the famous civil rights principle of no distinction according to color was joined with laissez-faire legal equality in creating the only federal agency that represented an institutional commitment to blacks in the Reconstruction era forms the subject of this essay.

Freedmen's Bureau legislation took shape in the context of the government's wartime policy toward emancipated slaves. Though varying in detail according to military command, as antislavery pressures and actual liberation increased in 1862 and 1863, this policy came to comprise three possible courses of action for the former slaves. They might choose voluntary colonization, seek employment as military laborers or agricultural workers on plantations leased under government authority, or enlist as soldiers of the United States. The chief concerns of this policy were military and political: emancipated slaves coming within Union lines were to be kept from placing an excessive burden upon the army, were indeed now expected to contribute to the war effort. Through employment on the soil or in the ranks the freedmen would furthermore be kept from going north, where public opinion was uniformly fearful of large-scale Negro immigration. Though not insubstantial, benefits for the freed blacks were a secondary consideration in this general approach to dealing with the results of emancipation.[1]

Although Congress helped to determine this policy, in 1863 many Republican lawmakers took a more critical view of it and began to seek alternatives that would promote more directly the interests of the freed people. In particular, the idea of creating a federal agency exclusively for the purpose of assisting blacks in the transition from slavery to freedom gained in favor and was expressed in legislative proposals. The accomplishment of this end, however, involved two distinct considerations which in the opinion of many Republicans might be contradictory. On the one hand, it seemed necessary to provide temporary support for the freed slaves and protect them against injury and hostile treatment, especially in the form of apprenticeship arrangements that might be merely *de facto* serfdom. On the other hand, almost all Republicans desired to recognize the emancipated people as free men with the same rights, responsibilities, and personal freedom as ordinary citizens, understanding, of

---

[1] V. Jacque Voegeli, *Free But Not Equal: The Midwest and the Negro During the Civil War* (Chicago: The University of Chicago Press, 1967), pp. 34–38, passim.

course, that this did not entail political or social equality. While many Republicans had no difficulty in finding both these purposes satisfactorily and compatibly expressed in the Freedmen's Bureau proposals that were introduced, others saw a contradiction between what they regarded as paternalistic supervision or guardianship and genuine civil liberty.

In 1864 the Senate and the House of Representatives passed separate Freedmen's Bureau bills which, though placing the proposed agency in the Treasury and War Departments respectively, adopted essentially the same outlook toward the immediate post-emancipation situation. The outstanding feature of each measure was the organization of freedmen's labor on a voluntary contractual basis, on abandoned plantations that were either operated directly by the government or leased to private businessmen and planters. Intended to provide relief and support for the displaced and often destitute blacks, the two proposals also tried to resolve uncertainty about the future status of the freedmen by guaranteeing basic rights. Thus the Senate bill declared that ". . . every such freedman shall be treated in every respect as a freeman, with all proper remedies in courts of justice; and no power or control shall be exercised with regard to him except in conformity with law."[2]

While supporters of the Senate bill thought this provision a sufficient guarantee, other Congressmen, including a substantial number of Republicans, regarded it as an inadequate recognition and safeguard of the free status and rights of the former slaves. It established in their view an undesirable system of guardianship. Democrats trying to embarrass the opposition and prevent any freedmen's bill from passing were one source of criticism from the laissez-faire point of view. The leading laissez-faire critics, however, were antislavery Republicans from the Middle West. "Are they free men or are they not?" asked Senator James Grimes of Iowa.[3] Questions such as this reflected political rivalry between western and eastern Republicans,

---

[2] 38 Congress, H.R. No. 51, Senate amendment, June 27, 1864, sec. 4; *Congressional Globe*, 38 Congress, 1 sess., 3299 (June 27, 1864). The House bill contained a briefer and more general reference to protecting the rights of freedmen which its supporters interpreted as a guarantee of civil rights. 38 Cong., H.R. No. 51, sec. 4, Dec. 7, 1863; *Cong. Globe*, 38 Cong., 1 sess., 572–73 (February 10, 1864), remarks of Thomas D. Eliot.

[3] Ibid., 2972 (June 15, 1864).

as well as hostility toward Negroes.[4] But Grimes's question, and the opposition to the Freedmen's Bureau bills of 1864, also reflected attachment to the principle of laissez-faire legal equality.

Having passed separate measures, Republicans left the differences between the two bills to be composed at the second session of the Thirty-Eighth Congress in December 1864. Two main features marked the legislative situation at this time with respect to freedmen's affairs. The first was continued conflict between the War and Treasury Departments for control of post-emancipation policy. Evident in the disagreement between the House and the Senate, this rivalry during the legislative proceedings that ensued took the form of a debate over civilian-*vs.*-military regulation of the freedmen and reflected the tension existing between the apparent need to supervise the transition from slavery to freedom and the simultaneous recognition of southern blacks' new status as free men.[5] The second circumstance affecting the legislative situation was a recently inaugurated movement to aid loyal white refugees in the South. This undertaking was to have an important influence on the evolution of the Freedmen's Bureau bill and so requires a brief accounting.

Assisted early in the war by the Sanitary Commission, southern refugees by 1864 were attracting more widespread attention.[6] The

---

[4] Midwestern Republicans who in June 1864 led the opposition to the Freedmen's Bureau bill in the Senate, where Charles Sumner was its chief advocate and manager, were in part reacting against efforts by Sumner and Henry Wilson of Massachusetts to secure a bill allowing the states to fill their draft quotas by recruiting southern freedmen. The westerners charged that such an arrangement would place their states, less wealthy than Massachusetts, at a disadvantage. Ibid., 3334 (June 28, 1864); Richard H. Abbott, "Massachusetts and the Recruitment of Southern Negroes, 1863–65," *Civil War History*, 14 (September 1968), 202–203.

[5] Since 1862 both military officers and treasury agents had undertaken to supervise freedmen's affairs in the occupied South. Army involvement came as escaped slaves entered the lines of advancing Union forces, while Treasury supervision of freedmen developed as an aspect of congressionally authorized management of abandoned and confiscated lands, the idea being that the former slaves should remain on the plantations as a free labor force. Although by December 1864 the army had gained a larger share of control, treasury agents still sought to extend their influence over freedmen's policy. The most comprehensive account of freedmen's police in occupied areas is Louis S. Gerteis, *From Contraband to Freedman: Federal Policy Toward Southern Blacks, 1861–1865* (Westport, Conn.: Greenwood, 1973).

[6] Boston *Commonwealth*, April 8, 1864; John Eaton, *Grant, Lincoln, and the Freedmen: Reminiscences of the Civil* War (New York: Longmans, Green, 1907), pp. 37–38; Paul S. Pierce, *The Freedmen's Bureau: A Chapter in the History of Reconstruction* (Iowa City: State University of Iowa Press, 1904), p. 31.

American Freedmen's Inquiry Commission, for example, appointed in 1863 by the War Department to report on the condition of emancipated slaves, stated that the aid required by blacks was no different from that which southern whites fleeing from the Confederacy would need. Similarly, the protection given the families of Negro soldiers was compared to that required by the families of white men under the same conditions.[7] Assessing the outlook for southern reconstruction, the Boston businessman and reformer Edward Atkinson suggested that the Freedmen's Bureau might be needed to organize and civilize poor whites more than emancipated blacks.[8] The white refugee problem also contained obvious political significance, for southerners choosing not to remain within the contracting Confederacy formed a potential constituency for the Republican party.[9]

The American Union Commission, some of whose officers played a conspicuous part in shaping the final Freedmen's Bureau bill, was the principal organization for aiding loyal white refugees. Founded in 1864 by moderate antislavery reformers, the A.U.C. from its inception aimed at rebuilding southern society along northern lines.[10] Not only were refugees to be given emergency relief, but their civil and social condition was to be restored "upon the basis of industry, education, freedom and Christian morality."[11] To promote this end the A.U.C. helped southern whites obtain seed and equipment for farming, transported refugees to their homes or relocated them in new ones, operated schools and industrial training homes, advocated temporary occupation of abandoned lands for immediate sustenance and recommended changes in land tenure, and urged emigration,

---

[7] 38 Cong., 1st sess., Senate Executive Documents, No. 53, "Final Report of the American Freedmen's Inquiry, Commission to the Secretary of War," May 15, 1864, p. 109.

[8] [Edward Atkinson], "The Future Supply of Cotton," *North American Review*, 98 (April 1864), 497.

[9] Eaton, *Grant, Lincoln, and the Freedman*, p. 38.

[10] [Lyman Abbott], *The American Union Commission: Its Origin, Operations, and Purposes* (New York: Sanford Harroun, 1865), pp. 1–2; Lyman Abbott, "Southern Evangelization," *New Englander*, 23 (October 1864), 699–708; Pennsylvania Relief Association for East Tennessee, *Report to the Contributors to the Pennsylvania Relief Association for East Tennessee* (Philadelphia: Pennsylvania Relief Association, 1864), pp. 26–27.

[11] Circular of the American Union Commission, National Archives, Record Group 105, M–752, roll 13.

new industry, and a free press in the South.[12] Adopting an argument usually applied only to blacks, the A.U.C. furthermore tried to keep poor whites in the South on the theory that they were unsuited to the climate, business, and customs of the North.[13]

The special significance of the American Union Commission for the evolution of the Freedmen's Bureau bill lies in its assertion of the principle of no discrimination according to color as the basis for extending aid to southern white refugees. According to Lyman Abbott, an officer of the organization, A.U.C. representatives were often asked in 1864–65 whether care of the freedmen was part of its purpose and operations. The answer to this, Abbott explained, was emphatically to affirm that "The American Union Commission recognizes no distinction of caste or color. It is organized to aid the people of the South—not the black men because they are black, nor the white men because they are white, but all men because they are *men*, upon the ground of a common humanity alone." Nevertheless, Abbott went on to say, the association was careful to avoid duplication of charities and conflict of organizations by maintaining cordial understanding and cooperation with freedmen's aid societies.[14] In other words, the A.U.C. acted as a white refugee organization, but it did so under the idea—usually associated with the protection of Negro civil rights—that distinctions should not be made according to race. As in its argument against poor-white immigration into the North, the A.U.C. exhibited an unconventional and ironic attitude of racial impartiality. Partly owing to the efforts of the Commission's leaders, this same attitude was to find expression in the drafting of the Freedmen's Bureau bill.

Alongside the work of the A.U.C. in assisting white refugees, freedmen's aid societies continued their endeavors and pressed their views on Congress with the hope of securing a federal agency to supervise freedmen's affairs.[15] At length, in February 1865, a com-

---

[12] Ibid.; *The American Union Commission Speeches of Hon. W. Dennison, J. P. Thompson, N. C. Taylor, J. R. Doolittle, J. A. Garfield . . . Washington, February 12, 1865* (New York: Sanford Harroun, 1865), pp. 19–22.

[13] Petition of the Refugee Relief Commission of Ohio, National Archives, RG 233, 38A–B1.

[14] [Abbott], *American Union Commission*, pp. 3–4, 23.

[15] George R. Bentley, *A History of the Freedmen's Bureau* (Philadelphia: University of Pennsylvania Press, 1955), pp. 46–48; Josephine S. Griffing to Lyman Trumbull, Aug. 10, 1864, Trumbull Papers, Library of Congress.

mittee of conference formulated a measure to resolve the differences between the House and the Senate freedmen's bills of 1864.[16] As a solution to the problem of choosing between the War and Treasury Departments as a home for the bureau, the committee proposed to create a new department of freedmen's affairs. Furthermore, showing concern for the laissez-faire criticism of the 1864 bills, it sought more clearly to recognize the freed slaves' new status of civil liberty without, however, altering the basic structure of supervision provided by the earlier measures.

The conference committee bill, which was chiefly the work of Radicals Thomas D. Eliot and Charles Sumner, committed to the new department the "general superintendence of all freedmen" in the rebel states and charged the commissioner, or head, with establishing regulations protecting former slaves in the enjoyment of their rights, promoting their welfare, and securing to them and their posterity the blessings of liberty.[17] Agents of the department, described as "advisory guardians," were instructed to aid freedmen in adjusting their wages, protect them against failure of contract, arbitrate their disputes, and ensure fair trial for them if involved in litigation.[18] A provision in the Senate bill of 1864 authorizing the bureau head to find homes and employment for freedmen whom he was unable to employ was retained in modified form in a section which allowed the commissioner, in such a situation, "to make provision" for former slaves with humane and suitable persons at a just compensation for their services.[19] The conference report also stipulated that department agents should be deemed in the military and liable to trial by military commission for, among other crimes, willful oppression of any freedman.[20]

---

[16] The committee consisted of Republicans Thomas D. Eliot and William D. Kelley and Democrat Warren P. Noble from the House, and Republicans Charles Sumner and Jacob Howard and Democrat Charles Buckalew from the Senate.

[17] 38 Cong., H.R. No. 51, sec. 4, Report of the Conference Committee, *Cong. Globe*, 38 Cong., 2 sess., 563 (February 2, 1865).

[18] H.R. No. 51, sec. 6.

[19] Ibid., sec. 9. The provision in the Senate bill was itself a watered-down version of a proposal, introduced by Waitman T. Willey of West Virginia, which authorized the bureau head to initiate correspondence with state and municipal officials for the purpose of relocating freedmen in the North. Willey's proposition occasioned a sharp struggle between western Republicans allied with border state conservatives and Democrats, and eastern Republicans. *Cong. Globe*, 1 sess., 3329–30, 3334–35, 3337 (June 28, 1864).

[20] H.R. No. 51, sec. 12. This feature was found in the Senate bill also.

The conference committee made certain minor changes in the 1864 legislation apparently for the purpose of allaying apprehension about excessive controls' being placed on the freedmen. Department agents were no longer instructed to see that freedmen upheld their part of labor contracts into which they entered, or to "organize" their labor. As though to assure laissez-faire critics that power would not he abused, the bill stated that the object of the department was "the good of the freedmen."[21] And the bill retained the declaration of the Senate measure that every freedman "shall be treated in all respects as a freeman, with all proper remedies in courts of justice, and no power or control shall be exercised with regard to him except in conformity with law."[22]

Land-occupation arrangements in freedmen's bills provided an opportunity to recognize the civil liberty of emancipated Negroes. In this respect the conference committee measure differed appreciably though not fundamentally from the 1864 legislation. The latter, in both Senate and House versions, primarily envisioned a system of plantation leases under which freed slaves would be employed as contract laborers. Only subordinately did it hold out the possibility of independent tenure. The conference bill reversed this order of priority by stating that abandoned lands should be rented or leased to freedmen, or permitted to be cultivated, used, or occupied by them for a one-year period, on terms to be agreed upon by the department and the former slaves.[23] Lands not required for freedmen could be leased to others, in which case former slaves could be employed under voluntary contracts approved by the department.[24] Described by Thomas D. Eliot as a "material modification" of the 1864 legislation, this provision, though not offering a clear expectation of permanent land ownership because of the one-year limitation on freedmen's leases or occupation, in theory pointed more directly to independent landholding than either of the previous bills.[25]

While the conference report tried to obviate the conflict between civilian and military authority evident in the passage of the 1864

---

[21] Ibid., sec. 1.

[22] Ibid., sec. 4.

[23] Ibid., sec. 5.

[24] Ibid.

[25] *Cong. Globe*, 38 Cong., 2nd sess., 564 (February 2, 1865): LaWanda Cox, "The Promise of Land for the Freedmen," *Mississippi Valley Historical Review*, 45 (December 1958), 417.

bills, it failed to do so because the proposed new department, a civilian agency, was in a practical sense the equivalent of the Treasury. At one level, therefore, the issue remained the same as in 1864. But this formal jurisdictional dispute was now bound up with the controversy over how best to recognize freedmen's liberty and rights.

Discussion of these issues outside Congress throws light on the legislative debate of February 1865 that produced the final Freedmen's Bureau bill. As in 1864, the argument for civilian control was in part based on the contention that the free-labor policy of the military regime of General Banks in Louisiana imposed virtual and effective serfdom on emancipated blacks.[26] Proponents of a civilian agency also charged that army officers regarded the freed people as inferior and were indifferent to their interests and advancement.[27] Still another view was that the conference bill should be supported as an experimental measure, on the theory that any freedmen's measure was better than none at all.[28] Supporters of the conference bill believed, too, that it substantially recognized the rights of the freedmen. "Details are of less moment than principles," declared the radical *Independent*. "The point to be gained is that the rights of the freedmen and the obligations of the Government to them should be recognized and authoritatively affirmed. . . . The present bill seems to do that."[29]

Opponents of a civilian agency, who included army freedmen's officials actively lobbying against the conference bill, warned that without military protection the civil liberty of freed blacks was threatened by commercial and speculative interests seeking to control post-emancipation affairs.[30] Placing the freed people under the same authority as abandoned plantations, one critic argued, gave "an unpleasant twinge, as if, after all, we still clung to the idea of slavery."[31] Not only had the Treasury leasing system seemed to fail, but experience showed that blacks did better when they rented or

---

[26] New Orleans *Tribune*, December 10, 1864; Worcester *Daily Spy*, February 6, 24, 27, 1865; *Independent*, March 2, 1865.

[27] Boston *Journal*, February 1, 1865, Washington correspondence; Washington *Chronicle*, February 9, 1865, letter on freedmen's affairs.

[28] Ibid., editorial on freedmen; *Independent*, February 9, 1865, editorial.

[29] Ibid.

[30] Eaton, *Grant, Lincoln, and the Freedmen*, p. 224.

[31] Washington *Chronicle*, February 8, 1865, letter on freedmen's affairs in Congress.

occupied lands assigned them than when they entered labor contracts.[32] Many Negroes themselves emphatically declared that working for a share of the crop and the profit was preferable to working for mere wages.[33] Yet the conference bill, critics pointed out, proposed a scheme of controlled labor as though the former slaves were incapable of supporting themselves.[34]

Political and bureaucratic rivalries formed a large part of the conflict between civilian and military control.[35] Yet ideas about freedmen's rights were also involved. Opponents of a civilian agency believed that military regulation was more consistent with a laissez-faire, equal rights approach to post-emancipation policy. Only the army, they reasoned, had the power to uproot the prejudicial codes and customs of slavery and protect freedmen's rights in the aftermath of abolition.[36] Once the war power had established freedmen's liberty on an equal rights basis, blacks should be left alone under the peacetime powers of the states.[37] A corollary of this laissez-faire outlook was an insistence on treating the races equally. "We do not want a civil control of the black man, while there is no civil control of the white man," an opponent of the conference bill wrote.[38] The military power which protected and aided whites should do the same for blacks.[39] Thus, although many antislavery men and women supported the conference bill, others saw the War Department as the

---

[32] Ibid.; Gerteis, *From Contraband to Freedman*, pp. 169–71.

[33] New Orleans *Tribune*, September 10, 24, 1864, January 28, 1865; New York *Evening Post*, January 26, 1865, report of the National Freedmen's Relief Association meeting.

[34] Washington *Chronicle*, February 13, 1865, letter on freedmen's affairs; *Independent*, January 26, 1865, letter on the Freedmen's Bureau.

[35] Gerteis, *From Contraband to Freedman*, pp. 147–49. Gerteis holds that the conflict was a mere struggle for power which involved no essential difference in proposals for freedmen's supervision. Both the Treasury and the War Department plans were in this view paternalistic, resting on the assumption that the former slaves ought to remain on the plantations as wage laborers (ibid., pp. 150, 153).

[36] John Eaton, public letter of February 6, 1864, enclosed in Thomas D. Eliot to Charles Sumner, March 7, 1864, Sumner Papers, Harvard University Library; Eaton, *Grant, Lincoln, and the Freedmen*, p. 226; *The New York Times*, February 9, 1865, editorial; *Independent*, January 26, 1865, letter on the Freedmen's Bureau by F.A.S.

[37] Washington *Chronicle*, February 13, 1865, letter on freedmen's affairs.

[38] *Independent*, January 26, 1865, letter on the Freedmen's Bureau by F.A.S.

[39] Washington *Chronicle*, February 8, 1865, letter on freedmen's affairs in Congress; Eaton letter of February 6, 1864, in Eliot to Sumner, March 7, 1864, Sumner Papers, Harvard University Library.

proper place for the Freedmen's Bureau in part because they wanted to avoid the danger of overlegislating for the former slaves.[40]

In the context of this public discussion, congressional debate on the conference bill reflected concern with the status of the freedmen and the degree of government regulation to which they should be subjected in contrast to other persons. The basic argument for the proposal, as in 1864, was that temporary care of the former slaves was a necessary corollary of the government's emancipation policy.[41] The freed people were "unused to self-reliance and dependent for a season somewhat upon our sympathy and aid," declared Thomas D. Eliot, manager of the conference report in the House.[42] Reasoning that if the measure failed, blacks would remain under a policy that made them "the mere accident of the Treasury," Charles Sumner said the new department was needed to recognize and protect the freedmen's basic rights.[43]

Elaborating on this theme, Lot M. Morrill argued that because blacks possessed no security of personal right amid the disorder existing in the South, the government must mediate between them and their former masters by providing employment, support, and protection. William D. Kelley of Pennsylvania reasoned that the former slaves had no relationship to the country and its institutions other than life and nativity. In the rebel states, he pointed out, they could not be witnesses or bring suit in court to protect themselves. Implying that the bill would rectify this situation, Kelley asserted: "We are to guide them, as the guardian guides his ward, for a brief period, until they can acquire habits and become confident and capable of self-control." In short, the government must organize the emancipated people into society. More sanguine than most others, Eliot and Sumner, the principal framers of the conference bill, confidently announced that it gave the freedmen every legal and civil right.[44]

As in the Senate debate of 1864, the leading critics of the bill

---

[40] *Liberator*, December 9, 1864, letter of "M. DuPays"; Josephine S. Griffing to Charles Sumner [November 1864], Sumner Papers, Harvard University Library; Springfield *Weekly Republican*, February 11, 1865, editorial.

[41] *Cong. Globe*, 38 Cong., 2 sess., 768 (February 13, 1865), remarks of Charles Sumner; 988 (February 22, 1865), remarks of Lot M. Morrill.

[42] Ibid., 564 (February 9, 1865).

[43] Ibid., 768 (February 13, 1865).

[44] Ibid., 988 (February 22, 1865); 689, 693 (February 9, 1865); 961 (February 22, 1865).

were Republicans who attacked it from a laissez-faire point of view. The power of general superintendence which the bill extended over the freed people, together with the authority given the new department to "make provision" for them when unable to find employment, seemed in particular to subject blacks to undue restriction. Arguing that the fewer restraints imposed by government "the sooner we shall make men of them," Representative James Wilson of Iowa urged letting the freedmen have entire responsibility for disposing of their own labor. In the Senate fellow-Iowan James Grimes objected that the proposal for Negro migration which he had supported in attenuated form in 1864 had been transformed in the present measure into a potential means of hiring out blacks for indefinite periods without their consent.[45]

Several Republicans protested that the bill rested on the assumption that the Negro race needed guardianship. According to John P. Hale of New Hampshire, it gave the lie to twenty years of abolitionist teaching that freed slaves could take care of themselves. Supporters of the bill had insisted that the regulations of the new department would affect the freed people only with their voluntary consent rather than coercively. Why then, asked John B. Henderson of Missouri, should government agents make bargains and contracts for them? Contending that the bill would destroy blacks in the same manner as government policies had destroyed Indians, William Sprague of Rhode Island recommended giving the freedmen the power to protect themselves through the suffrage. Then no special government agency would be needed.[46]

Similar criticism outside Congress suggests that to a greater extent than in 1864 these objections reflected more than mere intra-party political tensions. One Washington correspondent of antislavery outlook wrote sharply that the conference bill "contemplated a sort of serfdom as a substitute for slavery." "A majority of the antislavery men of the North," he added, "believe that if the negro must have a master, as the friends of Sumner's bill admitted by supporting it, it makes very little difference whether that master comes from South Carolina or from Massachusetts."[47]

While criticism of this sort coming from whites might be taken at

---

[45] Ibid., 689 (February 9, 1865), 959 (February 21, 1865). See note 19 above.

[46] Ibid., 985 (February 22, 1865); 960, 963 (February 21, 1865).

[47] *Cincinnati Daily Commercial*, February 28, 1865, Washington letter from "Mack."

a certain discount according to whether its motivation was political, racial, or ideological-humanitarian, the laissez-faire point of view expressed by blacks possessed an undoubted cogency. The New Orleans *Tribune*, representing the substantial free black community in Louisiana, approached the freedmen's question from this perspective. Condemning the Treasury labor plan of 1864 as "mitigated bondage," the *Tribune* rejected the notion that blacks needed superintendence. "Give the men of color an equal chance," advised the black journal, "and this is all they ask. Give them up at once to all the dangers of the horrid competitive system of modern commerce and civilization; and . . . they will, more quickly than their fellow white man, find a happy issue out of all their sufferings." Opposing "protection and tutorship," the *Tribune* recommended the creation of a board of elected freedmen to represent the emancipated population. But what blacks were given instead, complained the *Tribune*, was the conference committee Freedmen's Bureau bill: "the eternal question of tutorage, presented in its most complete and comprehensive form." Urging suffrage as self-protection, the black newspaper thus assailed "this final effort to domination."[48]

The most prominent black advocate of a laissez-faire post-emancipation policy was Frederick Douglass. In January 1862, when reformers and political men first began to ask what should be done with the freed slaves, Douglass professed the view that he maintained throughout the war: ". . . do nothing with them," he wrote. "Your *doing* with them is their greatest misfortune." Three years later, adverting to the evident sympathy for Negroes among antislavery people, he offered the same advice. "I look over this country at the present time," he told the Massachusetts Anti-Slavery Society, "and I see Educational Societies, Sanitary Commissions, Freedmen's Associations, and the like,—all very good: but . . . there is always more that is benevolent, I perceive, than just, manifested toward us." Attempts to "prop up the Negro" or prepare him for freedom were misconceived. The freedmen, Douglass concluded, should be given equal civil and political rights and left to stand alone, and if they could not, then they must fall. Although he offered no specific comment on the Freedmen's Bureau bill, Douglass's laissez-faire arguments were implicitly critical of the articulated supervisory scheme of the conference committee.[49]

---

[48] New Orleans *Tribune*, February 7, 1865, September 10, 24, 1864, January 8, March 12, 1865, editorials.

[49] Philip S. Foner, ed., *The Life and Writings of Frederick Douglass* 5 vols. (New York: International, 1950), 3:188–89, 4:164.

If congressional Republicans' laissez-faire critique reflected concern for the rights of blacks, their second major argument against the conference bill focused on the needs of white refugees in the South. Invoking the principle of no discrimination according to race, Republican critics insisted on equal rights for white southern war victims and attacked the conference report for its exclusive attention to blacks. In part this line of attack originated in the fear, conditioned generally by northern anti-Negro prejudice, that the freedmen might receive privileges and benefits not available to whites. The argument also reflected, however, commitment to the idea that race was not a reasonable basis on which to classify or distinguish among people.

As on the guardianship issue, representatives from the racially sensitive midwestern states led the way in demanding aid for loyal white refugees. Republican Henry S. Lane of Indiana, noting the absence of any provision for white refugees in the conference report, commented sarcastically: ". . . I have an old-fashioned way of thinking which induces me to believe that a white man is as good as a negro if he behaves himself." Pointing to the land provisions of the conference measure, Henderson of Missouri asked why a distinction was made in favor of blacks over white men. James Grimes asserted that destitute Unionist whites deserved the same advantages as emancipated slaves, while John P. Hale objected to giving all the abandoned lands to the freedmen and declared: ". . . in cases of this kind, I let the white and the black stand together." With evident pleasure the Washington correspondent of the conservative New York *Herald* reported that Republicans—to the consternation and despair of Charles Sumner—were coming to the conclusion "that the poor white refugees of the South had some rights as well us the negroes."[50]

Although intraparty criticism was more pronounced than in the previous session, the conference report passed the House on February 9, 1865, with only four Republican votes cast in opposition.[51] One of these votes—that of Robert C. Schenck of Ohio—was particularly significant, however, for it appeared alongside an attempt already begun by Schenck to formulate an alternative freedmen's bill that would satisfy both the laissez-faire critics and those who desired to assist loyal white refugees.

---

[50] *Cong. Globe*, 38 Cong., 2 sess., 985 (February 22, 1865), 962, 959 (February 21, 1865), 984; New York *Herald*, February 23, 1865, Washington correspondence.

[51] *Cong. Globe*, 38 Cong., 2 sess., 694 (February 9, 1865). The vote was 64 to 62.

Indicative of the considerable bipartisan support it would receive, Schenck's alternative plan originated in a Democratic resolution of January 1865 urging legislation to aid loyal southern refugees.[52] As chairman of the Committee on Military Affairs to which the resolution was referred, Schenck on January 24 introduced a bill combining this purpose with aid to the freedmen. On February 9 he reported this freedmen and refugees bill back from committee with amendments.

Schenck's plan was to create in the War Department a bureau of refugees and freedmen, to continue during the rebellion and to have effect in rebel states and in loyal districts within the operation of the army. Notably brief in comparison to previous freedmen's proposals, the bill contained only two substantive provisions. The first gave the bureau authority to supervise, manage, and control all subjects relating to refugees and freedmen, while the second authorized the President to provide relief assistance to freedmen and refugees and assign to the bureau for their benefit the temporary use of abandoned lands.[53]

On the same day as the House voted on the conference report, Schenck, who was regarded as an influential Radical, presented his freedmen and refugees bill as a laissez-faire, equal rights alternative.[54] Assuming that a military framework was necessary for any freedmen's legislation, Schenck in presenting his plan stressed the temporary nature of the problem facing Congress. The condition of the freedmen was merely an incident of the war, he reasoned, and would end about the time the war concluded. Accordingly, he believed there was no need to create a permanent department of government to deal with post-emancipation affairs.[55]

Schenck's most telling argument, however, invoked the principle

---

[52] Resolution introduced by John Law of Indiana, January 5, 1865, National Archives, RG 233, 38A–B1.

[53] 38th Congress, H.R. No. 698, sec. 1–2, MS, National Archives, RG 233, 38A–BI *Cong. Globe,* 38 Cong., 2 sess., 691 (February 9, 1865).

[54] Schenck was a former Whig who served as brigadier general of volunteers in 1861–62. Injured at the second battle of Bull Run, he left the army and, partly at the request of Lincoln and Secretary of War Stanton, ran against Democrat Clement L. Vallandigham for a seat in the Thirty-Eighth Congress. The correspondent of the Cincinnati *Gazette* characterized Schenck as "particularly hated of all Democrats, who make it a point sometimes not to listen to him, but after Thad Stevens and Winter Davis no Unionist is surer of attention to what he has to say" (Kenneth W. Wheeler, ed., *For the Union: Ohio Leaders in the Civil War* [Columbus: Ohio State University Press, 1968], pp. 24–25; Cincinnati *Gazette,* January 24, 1865, Washington correspondence).

[55] *Cong. Globe,* 38 Cong., 2 sess., 691 (February 9, 1865).

of no distinction according to color within the framework of laissez-faire legal equality. In contrast to the bill of the conference committee, he pointed out, the proposal of the military affairs committee "makes no discrimination on account of color. . . ." This was, he said, a "peculiarity" of the plan. Faithful to the laissez-faire point of view, Schenck added that the principal danger for both freedmen and white refugees was that too much government assistance would encourage them to remain paupers. Thus, the purpose of the bill was to put the former slaves and white refugees "in a condition to shift for themselves and become independent of this help from the authorities of the country at the earliest time. . . ."[56]

Schenck's attempt to formulate and win support for an alternative Freedman's Bureau bill was abetted by the American Union Commission, the white refugee relief organization. In early January, upon learning of the lost resolution directing an inquiry into the condition of loyal refugees, the president of the A.U.C., Joseph P. Thompson, wrote to Schenck describing the work of his organization and requesting a conference.[57] Representatives of the A.U.C. then went to Washington and circulated among members of Congress a memorial outlining the white refugee problem and recommending a course of action.[58] At the invitation of a bipartisan group which included a few members of Congress, the A.U.C. on February 12, 1865, held a public meeting at the capitol to publicize the loyal white refugee issue and win backing for Schenck's bill. Among several speakers in the hall of the House of Representatives, Joseph P. Thompson and the black abolitionist Henry Highland Garnet underscored the laissez-faire theme in rejecting the idea of class legislation and cautioning against a long state of dependence for both black and white.[59] Army freedmen's officials John Eaton and Asa Fiske were meanwhile in Washington trying to influence opinion against the bill of the conference committee.[60]

---

[56] Ibid.

[57] Joseph P. Thompson to Robert C. Schenck, January 9, 1865, National Archives, RG 233, 38A–B1.

[58] Joseph P. Thompson to O. O. Howard, May 20, 1865, Howard Papers, Bowdoin College Library.

[59] *American Union Commission Speeches . . . February 12, 1805*, pp. 6, 19; Henry Highland Garnet, *A Memorial Discourse . . . February 12, 1865* (Philadelphia: J. M. Wilson, 1865), pp. 85–86; Washington *Chronicle*, February 13, 1885; Boston *Journal*, February 13, 1865, Washington correspondence. Garnet spoke earlier in the day, Sunday, February 12, independently of the American Union Commission meeting which was held in the evening.

[60] John Eaton to Alice Eaton, February 3, 1865. Eaton Papers, University of Tennessee Library; Eaton, *Grant, Lincoln, and the Freedmen*, p. 224.

On February 18 Schenck brought the freedmen and refugees bill to the floor of the House. Although the conference bill had already been approved and was awaiting action in the Senate, the chances of passing the new measure appeared good. On its introduction both Republicans and Democrats had expressed support. Democrat John Chanler of New York called it a "pertinent, wise and proper" means of caring for the emancipated blacks. Indicative of moderate Republican opinion, *The New York Times* praised Schenck's bill as much more satisfactory than the "cumbersome, . . . impracticable, and ineffective" bill of the conference committee. Given this favorable response and the subsequent A.U.C. lobbying effort, a solid base of support quickly emerged which enabled the measure to pass without debate. Schenck reminded members as he brought the bill to a vote that it was "broad and general in character and makes no distinction on account of color." By voice vote that was almost unanimous, the House agreed to follow Schenck's recommendation of approving the freedmen and refugees plan and letting the Senate choose between it and the conference bill.[61]

In the upper chamber, meanwhile, Charles Sumner on February 13 had brought forward the conference committee bill, arguing that the choice was between this measure and none at all.[62] Other issues took precedence, however, and by the time Sumner got the matter to the floor again, on February 21, the Schenck bill stood as an alternative. Significantly, it received immediate and bipartisan backing.

As they attacked the conference report for its paternalistic restrictions on blacks and neglect of white refugees, laissez-faire critics referred approvingly to the new House bill. James Grimes stated that it accomplished all that was necessary, in language that had a definite and well-understood meaning in contrast to the merely rhetorical guarantees of liberty contained in the conference proposal. Democrat Reverdy Johnson of Maryland believed the House bill met the needs of both former slaves and loyal white refugees. After two days of debate the Senate rejected the conference report, 14 to 24, with twelve Republicans joining Democrats and border-state conser-

---

[61] *Cong. Globe*, 38 Cong., 2 sess., 693 (February 9, 1865), 908 (February 18, 1865), 989 (February 22, 1865), remarks of Reverdy Johnson; *The New York Times*, February 9, 1865, editorial. During the Senate debate on the conference bill Johnson stated that the vote in the House on Schenck's bill was almost unanimous.

[62] *Cong. Globe*, 38 Cong., 2 sess., 768 (February 13, 1865).

vatives in opposition. A second committee of conference was then requested.[63]

The second conference committee, consisting entirely of members who had sat on neither the House nor the Senate emancipation or freedmen's committees, reported a measure substantially in accord with the Schenck bill.[64] It proposed to establish a bureau of refugees, freedmen, and abandoned lands within the War Department, to continue during the rebellion and for one year thereafter. Within rebel states and in districts embraced by the operations of the army, the bureau was to exercise supervision and management of abandoned lands, and to control all subjects relating to refugees and freedmen. As in Schenck's bill, provision was made for immediate relief of destitute refugees and freedmen. The section of the bill dealing with land, however, was more elaborate and extensive than the corresponding section in the Schenck measure. The commissioner of the bureau was authorized to set aside abandoned or confiscated lands, and assign forty acres to each male citizen, whether freedman or refugee. After three years' use of the land at rent equal to six per cent of its value, the freedman and refugee occupants could purchase it and receive "such title as the United States can convey. . . ."[65]

The most significant feature of this bill was its abandonment of the idea that the freedmen should be contract laborers under the indefinite supervisory power of a new government department. The first conference report, it is true, theoretically gave first call on the land to the freed blacks, with secondary provision for leases to other persons. Nevertheless, defenders of the bill seemed to envision the former slaves continuing as plantation laborers under a contract labor system essentially the same as existing Treasury Department arrangements.[66] The second conference bill, in contrast, envisioned the freedmen as independent farmers, perhaps even as property owners, under their own supervision. Absent were provisions in-

---

[63] Ibid., 959 (February 21, 1865); 989–90 (February 22, 1865). Voting against the conference report were Cowan, Dixon, Doolittle, Grimes, Hale, Harlan, Harris, Henderson, Howe, Lane of Indiana, Ten Eyck, and Trumbull.

[64] The conference committee was composed of Republicans Schenck, Boutwell, and Democrat Rollins from the House, and Republicans Wilson, Harlan and border-state Unionist Willey from the Senate.

[65] H.R. No. 51, sec. 1, 3–4, *Cong. Globe*, 38 Cong., 2 sess., 1182 (February 28, 1865).

[66] Ibid., 689 (February 9, 1865), remarks of Thomas D. Eliot; 988 (February 22, 1865) remarks of Lot M. Morrill.

structing bureau agents to help freed slaves adjust or apply their labor, as well as the stipulation authorizing the commissioner to "make provision" for them. Similarly omitted were all references to bureau agents acting as advisory guardians, arbitrators, or next friends of the freedmen in court proceedings.

To be sure, a degree of federal intervention was necessary, as laissez-faire critics conceded. Placing the bureau in the War Department, however, limiting its existence to a definite period, and charging it with emergency aid and support were ways of minimizing the government's role. The conference committee headed by Schenck further expressed its antipaternalistic attitude in giving the bureau control over "subjects relating to freedmen and refugees," rather than giving the commissioner explicit general power to superintend and regulate the freedmen themselves as in earlier bills. While in practice this emendation would not amount to a significant difference, it reflected the intention of the bill's framers to express more clearly the idea that emancipated slaves were free men with ordinary civil rights.

Although laissez-faire, civil equality purposes characterized the second conference bill, the forty-acre provision has usually seemed the most important feature of the legislation. In particular it has been taken as evidence of a more radical commitment to give land to the freedmen.[67] The intention of Congress in the second conference plan, however, was to allow temporary use of rebel estates, with the rather remote possibility of subsequent ownership, rather than to extend a firm promise of a title in fee simple.

The closest Congress came to promising land to the freedmen was the approval by the House in 1864 of a southern homestead bill which proposed to give outright forty or eighty acres of public land to Union soldiers and army laborers irrespective of color. Only in a very limited and indirect sense, however, can this be viewed as a freedmen's bill.[68] The Freedmen's Bureau legislation of 1864 contained no promise of land to former slaves, and though the first con-

---

[67] Cox, "Promise of Land for the Freedmen"; William S. McFeely, *Yankee Stepfather: General O. O. Howard and the Freedmen* (New York: W. W. Norton, 1968), pp. 104–105; Michael Les Benedict, *The Impeachment and Trial of Andrew Johnson* (New York: W. W. Norton, 1973), p. 38.

[68] 38 Cong., H.R. No. 276, February 29, 1864, introduced by George W. Julian; *Cong. Globe*, 38 Cong., 1st sess., 1187–88 (March 18, 1865), remarks of George W. Julian.

ference report theoretically proposed to place them on the soil, this arrangement was to be only temporary. "The time has come," said Charles Sumner in February 1865, "when they should enjoy the results of their labor at least for a few months."[69]

While friends of the freedmen urged temporary use of rebel estates, proponents of aid to white refugees broached the same idea. Joseph P. Thompson of the A.U.C. thus recommended that white southern refugees be permitted to occupy abandoned lands in order temporarily to support themselves, and Schenck's original bill expressly proposed "the temporary use of abandoned lands and tenements" for the benefit of freedmen and refugees.[70] The second conference bill called for specific assignment of forty-acre plots and omitted the word "temporary," but since Schenck was a member of the committee that drafted this proposal it seems reasonable to suppose that it comported with his original purpose. Whether the conference committee intended anything more depended on the title that Congress could convey after three years, and this was a big question mark.[71]

---

[69] Ibid., 38 Cong., 2 sess. 961 (February 21, 1865).

[70] *American Union Commission Speeches . . . February 12, 1865,* p. 20; H.R. No. 698, sec. 2, February 9, 1865.

[71] The grounds for concluding that Congress intended a policy of permanent confiscation and land redistribution as a corollary of the Freedmen's Bureau bill are slight. Abandoned lands were held under the Captured and Abandoned Property Act of 1863, which aimed neither at permanent confiscation nor at the disturbing of titles to deserted lands. Rather, abandoned lands were to be held under temporary Union control and returned to loyal owners after the war. Rebel lands might also be held under the Confiscation Act of 1862, but this contained a restriction against permanent divestiture of property. The repeal of this restriction in 1864 by separate House and Senate actions is sometimes seen as an indication of a more radical confiscation purpose. (See, for example, James M. McPherson, *The Struggle for Equality: Abolitionists and the Negro in the Civil War and Reconstruction* [Princeton, N.J.: Princeton University Press, 1964], pp. 255–59.) The Senate action, however, was prompted by a desire to prevent lands temporarily occupied by freedmen from reverting to the family of a rebel owner should the owner be killed in battle. The purpose in other words was to protect freed slaves in temporary use of the land. Finally, the Direct Tax Act of 1862 provided a third means of acquiring southern lands. This statute offered the most expeditious method of transferring titles in fee simple, but where it had been applied, in the Sea Islands of South Carolina, whites had been the principal purchasers of the land. Thus there was little basis for concluding that the government would be able to convey title in fee simple after three years' occupation by freedmen or refugees. Temporary occupation seems to have been the main intention and realistic expectation (James G. Randall, *Constitutional Problems Under Lincoln,* rev. ed. [Urbana: University of Illinois Press, 1951], pp. 317–28; *Cong. Globe,* 38 Cong., 1 sess., 3306–3307 [June 27, 1864]; Willie Lee

It is nevertheless true that Congress proposed to assist the freed-men in ways that conceivably could lead to land redistribution. Yet equally important if not more important than this potential economic support was the recognition of the status and rights of free-manship that land occupation, in contrast to contract labor arrangements, implied. The significance of this civil recognition can be seen in the position taken by the black New Orleans *Tribune* on the question of land and the freedmen.

Condemning the Treasury Department plantation leasing and contract labor policy, the *Tribune* in early 1865 proposed that black laborers join black and white managers in a system of associated farming. This would allow emancipated slaves to feed and clothe themselves, go where they pleased, and become self-reliant, the *Tribune* explained. Receiving a low basic wage to cover necessities, freed slaves would most importantly acquire a share of the crop and become partners in the enterprise.[72] A sharecropping arrangement such as this would not only offer an economic incentive, but recognize more clearly than a contract labor system the former slaves' status as free men.[73] A recent study of southern freedmen confirms this finding by pointing out that blacks were more concerned with the form of their labor—that it be consistent and reflect their status as free men—than with the actual level of wages.[74] Thus, by providing for independent land occupation, albeit temporary, Schenck's bill and the second conference committee proposal contained a lais-sez-faire, civil rights dimension not present in earlier Freedmen's Bureau plans.

On March 3, 1865, the final day of the session, Congress enacted the second conference bill by voice vote. Senate approval came after very brief debate, while the House, having already agreed to substantially the same measure in the form of Schenck's bill, concurred with

---

Rose, *Rehearsal for Reconstruction: The Port Royal Experiment* [Indianapolis: Bobbs-Merrill, 1934], pp. 214–15, 287–88).

[72] New Orleans *Tribune*, January 28, 29, February 2, 1865. The only difficulty the *Tribune* anticipated was getting the land, for owners might refuse to lease to associations. The *Tribune* argued, however, that precedents were available for working the land on the plea of public necessity, and cited the example of the Prussian government threatening to take over the operation of factories in 1849 if the owners did not resume production. The *Tribune* did not propose federal confiscation.

[73] August Meier, "Negroes in the First and Second Reconstruction," *Civil War History*, 13 (June 1967), 122, argues that sharecropping began as a compromise between blacks' desire to own or rent land and plantation owners' desire to have the freedmen work for wages under contract.

[74] Gerteis, *From Contraband to Freedman*, p. 167.

no discussion at all.[75] Two years after the first proposal had been introduced, Republican lawmakers had finally created a Freedmen's Bureau.

In analyzing congressional action it appears that clearer recognition of the status of the former slaves as free men was an important difference between the final bill and earlier versions. Yet on this issue disagreement persisted, as a few members on both sides of the aisle objected to what they still regarded as undue coercion of the freedmen.[76] There can be no doubt, however, that the inclusion of white refugees in the bill was a decisive consideration in its enactment. This had not been present in any form in earlier freedmen's legislation, and its rapid acceptance in Schenck's bill after the House had already approved the first conference committee report suggests that in creating the bureau it was as important as, if not more important than, the abandonment of the guardianship idea.

Although they were not disinterested observers, there seems to be no reason to doubt the testimony of American Union Commission representatives that the inclusion of white refugees was decisive. Writing to the commissioner of the Freedmen's Bureau, General O. O. Howard, a few months later, Joseph P. Thompson stated that the principal objections to the first conference bill of Eliot and Sumner were fear of bureaucratic abuse in the creation of a new department and the bill's exclusive concern for blacks. However, the alternative proposal of Robert C. Schenck and the second conference bill based upon it, Thompson explained, attracted much wider support, including that of many Democrats, because it was not exclusive. "This accounts for the naming of the Refugees first; and but for this combination," Thompson averred, "no bill for Freedmen could have passed the last Congress."[77] Lyman Abbott, also an officer of the A.U.C., similarly wrote that prejudice against Negroes threatened to prevent any Freedmen's Bureau bill from passing until a broader approach that included white refugees was undertaken.[78]

---

[75] *Cong. Globe*, 38 Cong., 2 sess., 1307–1308 (March 2, 1865), 1348, 1402 (March 3, 1865).

[76] Conservative Lazarus Powell of Kentucky said the bill placed "overseers and negro–drivers" over the freedmen, while Republican Jacob Howard of Michigan criticized it for imposing a military government on the former slaves. Ibid., 1307–1308 (March 2, 1865).

[77] Joseph P. Thompson to O. O. Howard, May 20, 1865, Howard Papers, Bowdoin College Library.

[78] [Lyman Abbott], *The Results of Emancipation in the United States of America* (New York: American Freedman's Union Commission, 1867), p. 18.

The idea that government should make no distinction among people on the basis of color had been in the past and in the future was to become even more closely associated with the attempt by blacks to secure political and civil equality. It was highly ironic therefore that under this principle southern white refugees were brought under the protection of the freedmen's bureau. The American Union Commission, which helped shape this outcome, was involved a year later in a similar situation concerning the nondiscrimination idea which throws light on its use in the formation of the bureau.

Early in 1866 the American Union Commission and several freedmen's aid societies, run mainly by abolitionists, agreed to merge their organizations. They were unable to decide on a name, however, for agreement had not been reached on the purpose of the merged association. According to Lyman Abbott, the freedmen's groups were reluctant to give up the advantage which their exclusive and limited purpose of assisting blacks, signified in the names of their organizations, gave them in the eyes of a large segment of the northern public. The A.U.C. on the other hand, in order to allay sectional hostility and promote reunification, believed that whites should be aided and that race should not be a consideration in the operations of the new organization. The name of the body, A.U.C. representatives held, should reflect this outlook by containing no reference whatever to race or to the freedmen.[79] The outcome of the negotiations was a compromise in which, though the name "freedmen" was retained, whites were to be included and distinctions of race and color were to be disregarded.[80] Abbott considered the result a vindication of his position. He later wrote: ". . . the radical abolitionists, who had insisted on no distinction because of race or color when that principle was of benefit to the negro, could not deny it because it was of benefit to the white man."[81]

Just this seems to have been what happened in Congress in February 1865. Robert C. Schenck said as much when he pointedly observed that the "peculiarity" of his refugees and Freedmen's Bureau

---

[79] Lyman Abbott, *Reminiscences* (Boston: Houghton Mifflin, 1915), pp. 251, 260–61.

[80] *The American Freedman*, 1 (May 1866), 18, Constitution of the American Freedmen's Union Commission.

[81] Abbott, *Reminiscences*, p. 261.

bill was that it made "no discrimination on account of color—a favorite phrase, as is well understood, in these days among us all."[82]

A further irony in the use of the nondiscrimination principle in the formation of the Freedmen's Bureau lies in the fact that it reflected at once resentment against blacks and commitment to the ideal of racially impartial legal equality. That antislavery Republican as well as Democratic lawmakers could be apprehensive lest blacks receive preferential treatment says much in retrospect about the inability of Americans in the 1860s to comprehend the dimensions and depth of the race question and the circumstances in which emancipation left the freed people. Even before the abolition of slavery had been fully accomplished political representatives were sensitive to what has been described in more recent times as reverse discrimination. At the same time, however, the use of the nondiscrimination principle in conjunction with the doctrine of laissez-faire legal equality represented a concession to racial egalitarianism. Republicans applied the egalitarian idea in opposing the Eliot-Sumner conference bill as a coercive and paternalistic system of guardianship which denied blacks' status as free men, and then in insisting that loyal white refugees had an equal right to any assistance which the federal government might extend to relieve dislocation and suffering caused by the war.

Given the dominance of the idea of equality before the law in mid nineteenth-century America, the logic of the situation made the application and acceptance of the principle of no discrimination according to color irresistible. Yet if it was true that including white refugees was the only way to secure the passage of Freedmen's Bureau legislation, as Thomas D. Eliot later conceded,[83] and if the bureau protected the rights and well-being of the emancipated slaves, as most historical accounts agree it did, then ironic as the use of the nondiscrimination principle was in 1865, in a larger sense it was consistent with the historic purpose of the idea as an instrument for achieving black equality before the law.

---

[82] *Cong. Globe*, 38 Cong., 2 sess., 691 (February 9, 1865). Thomas D. Eliot denied that the first conference bill discriminated in favor of blacks. It merely recognized, Eliot said, that the time had come to pass legislation on their behalf (ibid., 693 [February 9, 1865]).

[83] Eliot said in 1868 that it would have taken another year to create the Freedmen's Bureau had it not been for Schenck's suggestion that white refugees also be brought under the provisions of the bill. (ibid., 40 Cong., 2 sess., 1815 [March 11, 1868]).

7

The New Orthodoxy in Reconstruction Historiography

In the 1960s a survey of Reconstruction historiography concluded that while the interpretation of the Dunning school had been pretty well refuted, no new synthesis had emerged to take its place.* Clearly, this is no longer the case. In recent years studies have begun to appear which signify the crystallization of a view of Reconstruction that will probably remain standard for some time to come. Three new books by Thomas H. O'Connor, Robert Cruden, and Allen W. Trelease give evidence of this synthesis.[1] Directed toward the student and general reader, they confirm that the battle in which the revisionists engaged so long is over. They also suggest, however, that a new orthodoxy is forming which itself is open to question. This new orthodoxy does not go so far as to say, as a new Civil War revisionism would have it, that the new birth of freedom of which Lincoln spoke never occurred, that the Civil War dead died in vain. No one who studies Reconstruction can quite come to that conclusion. Nevertheless, there is a tendency in recent revisionism to conclude not only that Reconstruction failed, but that it was fatally flawed from the very outset because it did not revolutionize landholding in the South. As the conservative southern view no longer finds serious expression, a new line of conflict appears to be emerging between a liberal political interpretation which argues that substantial though short-lived gains were made by blacks during Reconstruction, and a more radical economic interpretation which holds that very little of significance was accomplished, or at least very little relative to what was possible.

---

*An earlier version of this essay appeared in *Reviews in American History* (March 1973), 106–13.

[1] Thomas H. O'Connor, *The Disunited States: The Era of the Civil War and Reconstruction* (New York: Dodd, Mead, 1972); Robert Cruden, *The Negro in Reconstruction* (Englewood Cliffs, N.J.: Prentice-Hall, 1969); Allen W. Trelease, *Reconstruction: The Great Experiment* (New York: Harper & Row, 1971).

Revisionist conclusions arrived at over the past thirty years provide the underpinning and interpretive framework of the three books under consideration. Howard K. Beale established the fundamental theme of revisionist inquiry in 1940 when he asked whether it was not time to study the period without assuming that carpetbaggers and southern white Republicans were wicked, that Negroes were incompetent, and that white southerners owed a debt of gratitude to the restorers of white supremacy. Beale also urged an analysis of the motivating forces in Reconstruction. To the early revisionists, concerned with the Radical governments, issues of economic and political power stood out. As attention turned to understanding how Radical policies came to be adopted anyway, it began to appear that democratic idealism was involved as well. Racism, a force that was candidly acknowledged if differently described in the conservative interpretation, has also figured in recent studies. However they are related, these are seen as the dynamic forces in Reconstruction.

Cruden, O'Connor, and Trelease all assign major responsibility for bringing on Radical Reconstruction to Andrew Johnson, who by refusing to compromise forced moderate Republicans to join with Radicals in adopting the Reconstruction Act of 1867. Only slightly less responsibility belongs to southerners themselves for rejecting the Fourteenth Amendment and adopting the foolish tactic of "masterly inactivity." This is to say that the Republican party at the very least found it expedient—there is disagreement as to whether anything more was involved—to take an increasingly hard line in an attempt to protect southern freedmen and Unionists. Within the Republican party moreover, moderates rather than Radicals occupied the most influential positions, though the latter pointed the way. Accordingly, the congressional policy was harsher than it need have been. But when all is said and done, these books argue, it was not by any objective standard a harsh policy. Military rule did not fall hardly on the South, and in establishing new governments only a small proportion of adult white males was disfranchised. Cruden, O'Connor, and Trelease also show that blacks were a majority in only one legislative body, and in no state did they hold office in approximate proportion in their numbers. Radical Reconstruction was not Black Reconstruction. Nor was it alien rule which depended mainly on outsiders. Trelease makes the simple but sensible point that what was at stake was not home rule, but who should rule at home. Without being doctrinaire, the three authors interpret the policies of the Radical governments as an enlightened response to problems that the planter–professional–business class had ignored before the war. A lot of money was spent and taxes went sky high, but it was to good purpose. Pointing to the establishment of a public school system, the extension of social services, and the passage of legislation protecting poor people, Cruden, O'Connor, and Trelease conclude that democracy made notable advances during Reconstruction.

While these works ably summarize the revisionist outlook, they also contain distinctive points of interpretation. The motivation of congressional Reconstruction is one of them. Cruden holds that economic and political interests determined Republican policy toward the South. He does not deny that the Black Codes made Republicans apprehensive about the safety and well-being of the freedmen, and he notes that business interests in the Republican party did not agree on all aspects of national economic policy. He contends, however, that because each interest had something to lose from a restoration of southern power, northern capitalists were willing to go along with the Radical plan of Negro suffrage. But it was not just a matter of going along. Cruden states that business interests made an offer of collaboration, on terms ensuring the protection of private property, which the Radicals could not afford to turn down (p. 25). Cruden seems to have got this idea from Du Bois, and it does not seem any less schematic, any better documented, than it did in 1935. Although Cruden adds that the purely political logic of staying in power also led to the policy of 1867, the structure of the argument compels the inference that the purpose of keeping power was to promote economic interests. Trelease and O'Connor, in contrast, contend that ideals of liberty and equality motivated Republicans. "Most Republicans," Trelease asserts, "were sincerely interested in the welfare of the Negro" and recognized that emancipation alone was not enough. At the least blacks were entitled to civil and legal equality. While acknowledging the motive of party rule, Trelease identifies this with genuine commitment to "the heart and soul of the entire Union war effort, . . . the successful crusade against slavery and disunion" (pp. 47, 49).

Although none of these books argues the containment thesis— that the purpose of giving blacks equal rights in the South was to keep them from coming North—they devote much attention to racism. Cruden's fairness in handling southern white supremacy is noteworthy. He explains it as a psychological necessity following the destruction of an independent southern yeomanry and as a response to the trauma of defeat and the emergence of blacks as free men (pp. 42, 91). Trelease, in contrast, simply describes southerners' belief that Negroes were less than human and ought to be treated kindly, like dumb animals (pp. 21–22). All three authors see racism, northern as well as southern, as the basis of the restoration of conservative control. Yet because racial prejudice was pretty much a constant, though assuming different forms, it does not by itself explain the failure of Reconstruction.

Blacks became free, but not equal: that is the major and irrefutable fact which informs these works as it has most recent considerations of Reconstruction. Still, these books add, not all was for naught. For all the adversities they suffered, blacks did not lose citizenship; nor was public education denied them. The Fourteenth and Fifteenth Amendments were not upheld, but neither were they repudiated; together with parts of civil rights laws they provided a basis for the Second Reconstruction a century later. Expediency forced the assertion of principle, Cruden observes, but "the principle enunciated was equality" (p. 160). Cruden argues further, however, that Reconstruction provided blacks with meaningful freedom at the time and must be counted "a qualified success" (p. 111). For black power was a reality during Reconstruction. Blacks were not mere pawns in a struggle between whites. The right to vote gave them bargaining power which they used to win gains in education, civil rights, and social reform. The dependence of white politicians on black votes was further evidence of black power. Defending the tactics of maneuver rather than confrontation that black leaders employed, Cruden describes a system of interest group liberalism that enabled blacks to feel that their problems were being dealt with.

Yet as an attempt to integrate blacks into American society on an equal basis, Reconstruction failed. And the reason it did, Cruden and Trelease suggest in company with a number of other historians in recent years, is that it did not give land to the freedmen. Cruden states that congressional policy was "radically defective" because it paid little attention to the economic adjustments needed to make blacks truly free. "If freedom were to be meaningful and equality assured," he writes, "then the federal government must assume physical protection of the black man, promote his welfare, and underwrite his independence by distribution" (p. 161). Trelease is equally certain that what blacks needed most to achieve real free-dom, self-respect, and equality was land. Accordingly, the greatest failure of Reconstruction was its failure to give the freedmen land of their own. This weakened the policy from the outset and contrib-uted to its later overthrow (pp. 24, 27, 75, 138; cf. O'Connor, p. 204).

Behind this argument is the assumption that political equality by itself is largely meaningless, that without economic power we are left with mere bourgeois liberty. That is surely a debatable proposi-tion, yet it serves as the premise of a great deal of recent writing in American history generally and the Civil War era in particular. Events are explained by reference to what might have been, with attention to what ought to have been, until we are led to understand how Reconstruction really could have succeeded. Whatever the value of the idea of property redistribution, it is unhistorical to make it the key to understanding Reconstruction history.

Historians have rediscovered Thaddeus Stevens's proposal to con-fiscate southern property and give forty acres to every freedman. The number of Republicans who supported this is acknowledged to be small, but their existence is taken as proof that an alternative existed, that there was a decisive moment out of which an entirely different and more satisfactory solution to the problem of Recon-struction could have come. Thus historians refer to fateful decisions in which Congress voted down Stevens's confiscation scheme (see O'Connor, p. 207). Yet Stevens's bill never came close to a vote. Freedmen's Bureau legislation of course did, and it contained land allotment features which been interpreted as a golden opportunity if not an outright mandate to give blacks economic security. William McFeely, for example, holds that General O. O. Howard had it in his power to define the nation's commitment to the ex-slaves, but that the "Yankee stepfather" failed to meet his responsibility and let Andrew Johnson give southerners back their land. There is not the slightest attempt in this and other works which lament the lack of economic revolution to examine the legal aspects of confiscation, the definition of abandoned property, the congressional intention with respect to the title to abandoned property, the effect upon it of executive pardon. All this—which is to say the way contemporaries viewed the matter—is ignored. It has seemed necessary only to point out that confiscation threatened private property and was re-jected, as though it were a real issue that hung in the balance.

In contrast to the certainty of historians whose invoking of the land reform thesis assumes the proportions of a new orthodoxy is the uncertainty of people at the time as to the best course to follow. Still, those who cared most about making black freedom meaningful invariably argued for the right to vote. Can we really dismiss this evidence by saying, as Kenneth Stampp does in *The Era of Reconstruction*, that people then did not understand "the sociology of freedom"? Frederick Douglass is often cited for his judgment of 1880 that Reconstruction failed because it did not give land to the freedmen. But in an 1866 analysis of Reconstruction the only reference Douglass made to land was to say that universal suffrage ought to be the law of the land. This was the way to protect black liberty.[2] And in the crisis of 1866–67, when a real turning point seemed to be reached concerning the liberty and rights of Negroes, Stevens did not ask for confiscation. He asked for military protection and Negro suffrage.[3] Like other Republicans he believed in putting first things first.

But suppose land had been given to the freedmen. If historians are going to speculate about land reform they ought to probe further than they have. Charles and Mary Beard held that it was an almost insuperable task to give civil rights to persons who lacked economic power. Yet they saw little reason to believe that if the freedmen had been given land they would have had the capital or the proprietary skill or knowledge to hold it against speculators and sharpers in general. Howard K. Beale asked what would have happened had the planters' estates been divided among the former slaves. The question was perhaps more rhetorical than historical, but sympathetic though he was to the idea, Beale too seemed to see difficulties. Did a description of the freedmen as illiterate, with no conception of the meaning of terms such as government, suffrage, and free labor mean acceptance of the traditional conservative view of the Negro, Beale asked? Nevertheless that description seemed to him accurate. Since Beale's day we have been disabused of racial attitudes that perhaps affected his view of the matter, but what does the evidence suggest? Historians have not generally held that the Homestead Act of 1862 turned the condition of poor white farmers around, and the meliora-

---

[2] Frederick Douglass, "Reconstruction," *Atlantic Monthly* (December 1866), 761–65.

[3] *Congressional Globe*, 39 Cong., 1 sess. (July 28, 1866), pp. 4303–4304.

tive measures of Progressivism and the New Deal often have been judged inadequate if not failures. Why would land reform in Reconstruction have worked any better?

It is easy to criticize Republican policy for not giving land to the freedmen; after all, even in Russia, it is said, the emancipated serfs were given land. Aside from the fact that Russian serfs did not hold the land as private property but rather communally, so that they remained unfree in significant ways, one might ask whether some economic gains were not made by blacks during Reconstruction. In *Black Reconstruction in America*, Du Bois described "exceptional and lucky" Negroes who got land "on a considerable scale." "The land holdings of Negroes increased all over the South," he wrote. Cruden too states that while the number of freedmen who bought land was small, it was significant for it showed that blacks could survive in a competitive society (p. 45). The revisionist scholar Francis B. Simkins believed Reconstruction was not truly radical because it did not give Negroes land, their only effective weapon in battling for economic competence and social equality. Yet Simkins also held that freedmen bargained themselves into an agricultural situation unlike slavery and from their point of view advantageous. "The abandonment of the communal character of the Southern plantation," he wrote, "bestowed upon the Negroes the American farmer's ideal of independent existence."[4] This conclusion seems startling, for while the difference between slavery and sharecropping may be acknowledged, the latter obviously did not give blacks the secure status that Simkins's statement implies. Yet was the establishment of the principle of independent landholding, as in the Southern Homestead Act of 1866, not important? It depends on one's point of view. If historians who emphasize reform endorse this principle, as they seem to, then the change described by Simkin assumes greater significance.

Not all recent students of the period accept what I have called new orthodoxy. John and LaWanda Cox, W. R. Brock, Harold M. Hyman, and Rembert W. Patrick, among others, hold that civil rights was the main issue and that Reconstruction failed because the guarantees of the Fourteenth and Fifteenth Amendments, the Civil Rights and Enforcement Acts, were but fitfully and irresolutely

---

[4] Francis B. Simkins, "New Viewpoints of Southern Reconstruction," *The Journal of Southern History* (February 1939), 52.

maintained. Finally, they were all but abandoned. And why was that? Because liberal theories of government and prevailing constitutional ideas restricted what even the most ardent Radicals thought should be done, and because the drive for political and civil equality was in part a response to a crisis, and the crisis had passed. When this happened it became clear—and the trouble was—not that the grant of political liberty to the freedmen lacked an economic basis, but that it did not rest on a firm emotional and ideological commitment. Underneath it all racial prejudice remained, leading southerners to aggress against blacks and northerners to acquiesce in the aggression. But it is well to recall the Beards' observation on emancipation: "Nothing like this had ever happened in history, at least on such a scale."[5] Instead of saying that Reconstruction failed, it might be more accurate to say that it was, alas, only partially successful. In any event, the crux of it was civil rights and political freedom. These were the essential elements of the republicanism for which the war was fought, and to extend which was the purpose of Reconstruction. Integrating the freedmen into the polity was a principal focus of this undertaking, and it intensified and hastened the process by which it was accomplished. But as the coming of the war involved not only the dehumanizing effect of slavery upon blacks, but also and perhaps more importantly its debilitating and corrupting effect on republicanism, so Reconstruction involved more than adjustment to Negro emancipation. In the largest sense it aimed at improving the system of republican liberty that had flourished in one section of the federal republic, and must now prevail in all of it.

---

[5] Charles A. Beard and Mary R. Beard, *The Rise of American Civilization* II (New York: Macmillan, 1930), p. 116.

8

Equality and the Fourteenth Amendment: The Original Understanding

IN THE WORDS OF Lincoln's Gettysburg Address, the United States "was conceived in liberty and dedicated to the proposition that all men are created equal." It could be expected, therefore, that the meaning of equality should become a central issue in American politics when the liberty of the Founding was augmented by the emancipation of four million Negro slaves during the Civil War. The Thirteenth Amendment, a wartime measure intended to complete the process of emancipation, laid the foundation for a national civil rights policy. When subsequent political events more clearly revealed the nature of post-emancipation race relations, the Thirty-Ninth Congress proposed the Fourteenth Amendment as a plan of reconstruction establishing basic principles for the protection of civil rights. Declaring that all persons born or naturalized in the United States were citizens of the nation and of the state in which they resided, the amendment prohibited the states from abridging the privileges and immunities of U.S. citizens, depriving any person of life, liberty, or property without due process of law, or denying to any person "the equal protection of the laws."

As the meaning of liberty under the due process clause was a major constitutional issue from the end of Reconstruction to the 1930s, so the meaning of equality in the equal protection clause of the Fourteenth Amendment has been a critical issue in the civil rights era that began after World War II. As formulated in judicial and scholarly analysis in the 1980s, the problem of equality poses this question: Was equality in the Fourteenth Amendment a new constitutional principle, concerned primarily if not exclusively with the status and rights of black Americans and intended continually to be redefined

An earlier version of this essay appeared in *Benchmark*, 4 No. 4 (1990), 329–46.

by the national government in accordance with changing public opinion? Or was the equal protection clause intended to confirm and extend to all the states a principle that was part of the existing constitutional order, but imperfectly realized and only partially recognized because of the existence of slavery? More than a century after the events that created the problem of race relations in its modern form, these interpretive choices define the continuing quest for the original understanding of equality in the Fourteenth Amendment as the foundation of national civil rights policy.

Although understood as the embodiment of fundamental political principles, the American Constitution from the outset was construed in the manner of legal documents in the Anglo-American common law tradition. The authors of the Constitution were presumed to have said what they meant to say in the document itself. At times, however, the correct interpretation of the document may depend on the use of sources external to it. With the Constitution, therefore, as with other legal documents, the search for the meaning of the text can become a search for the author's intentions or the intent of the framers.[1] In recent years of course original intent in constitutional interpretation has become a deeply contested issue. Although some theorists deny the intellectual validity of the concept of statutory or constitutional intent, historians confirm the continued reliance on history in constitutional decision-making.[2] Indeed, legal historian William M. Wiecek suggests that history might be considered intrinsic to constitutional adjudication, rather than an extrinsic aid to interpretation as it has usually been regarded.[3]

The search for original intent has been of special importance in the field of civil rights law and policy. In a political and legal sense the problem has been how to rationalize and justify changes in race relations, as well as changes in the constitutional system that they have required or caused. This problem first appeared during the Civil War in arguments over the Constitution, slavery, and emancipation. If the Constitution was a proslavery document, then emancipation worked a profound change in the fundamental law and could be

---

[1] Charles Miller, *The Supreme Court and the Uses of History* (Cambridge, Mass.: The Belknap Press of Harvard University Press, 1969), p. 153.

[2] William N. Eskridge and Philip Frickey, "Statutory Interpretation as Practical Reasoning," *Stanford Law Review*, 42 (1990), 328–37.

[3] William M. Wiecek, "Clio as Hostage: The United States Supreme Court and the Uses of History," *California Western Law Review*, 24 (1987–1988), 227–68.

seen as introducing new principles of liberty and equality. If the Constitution did not sanction slavery, however, but simply recognized it as an existing local institution, if moreover the Constitution contained the principles of equality and consent that condemned slavery to ultimate extinction, then slave emancipation was in a deep sense consistent with the intent of the Founders.

I

Far from conceiving of the Reconstruction amendments as a new constitution to replace the defective organic law of the Founding, the framers in the Thirty–Eighth and Thirty–Ninth Congresses viewed the Thirteenth and Fourteenth Amendments as an extension of existing constitutional principles or as a completion of the Constitution. To begin with, Republicans interpreted the Constitution in light of the Declaration of Independence. They accepted the principle that all men are created equal, and believed that slave and free blacks were men endowed by their creator with certain inalienable rights, including life, liberty, and the pursuit of happiness. Republicans acknowledged that the Constitution recognized the existence of slavery. Where blacks were concerned, therefore, the Constitution did not effectuate the principles of equality and consent, identified in the Declaration, that were otherwise implemented in the constitutional order. The Constitution, however, was not a proslavery document. It did not, in principle, sanction the institution. In fact the framers of 1787 provided political means that could be used for emancipationist purposes, and expressed moral disapproval of slavery by refusing to include the word "slavery" in the text of the fundamental law.[4]

The meaning of equality in the Reconstruction amendments must be understood against the background of the status and rights of blacks in the antebellum period. Although Negroes were citizens in some states at the time the Constitution was adopted, black civil

---

[4] Don E. Fehrenbacher, *The Dred Scott Case: Its Significance in American Law and Politics* (New York: Oxford University Press, 1978), pp. 21–27; John Alvis, "The Slavery Provisions of the U.S. Constitution: Means for Emancipation," *Political Science Reviewer*, 17 (1987), 241–65; Robert A. Goldwin, *Why Blacks, Women, and Jews Are Not Mentioned in the Constitution, and Other Unorthodox Views* (Washington, D.C.: American Enterprise Institute Press, 1990), pp. 9–20.

rights were steadily restricted in the first half of the nineteenth century. While some civil rights advances were made in Massachusetts
and Ohio in the 1850s, these gains were offset by heightened restrictions on black immigration in Illinois, Indiana, and Iowa. No clear
trend toward recognition of Negro civil rights emerged that can be
interpreted as the first stage of an egalitarian movement culminating
in the Reconstruction amendments.[5] In a general sense it is true
that despite a variety of motives, the formation of the Republican
party on a platform of slavery restriction expressed some regard for
blacks' rights. When Republicans ventured beyond the slavery issue,
however, differences of opinion on race relations and civil rights appeared. The persistence of strong racist attitudes in the northern
public thus imposed political limits on Republican civil rights proposals and the meaning of equality as a constitutional concept.

With secession and civil war, questions concerning slavery assumed a secondary and instrumental importance in relation to the
paramount issue of preserving the Union and the Constitution. If
liberalization of racial attitudes was a prominent feature of Republican ideology, as the radical interpretation of the Reconstruction
amendments contends, it might be expected to manifest itself in
emancipation measures that were adopted for military purposes. Yet
in wartime actions against slavery, Congress and the administration
failed to provide legal guarantees of personal liberty for the emancipated slaves. As military emancipation became settled government
policy after the Emancipation Proclamation of January 1, 1863, concern for protecting blacks' liberty emerged. In the last year of the
war a proposal for a constitutional amendment prohibiting slavery
provided the occasion for more deliberate consideration of incipient
civil rights policy.

Congressional debate and public discussion make it unequivocally
clear that the framers and supporters of the Thirteenth Amendment
viewed it as a completion of the Constitution which brought the
nation's organic law into agreement with the principles of the Declaration of Independence. The notion that the Constitution did not
survive the Civil War, and that the Reconstruction amendments
were a new constitution, is simply not supported in the historical
record. Republicans in the Thirty–Eighth Congress consistently de-

---

[5] Earl M. Maltz, "Fourteenth Amendment Concepts in the Antebellum Era,"
American Journal of Legal History, 32 (1988), 306–307.

scribed the Thirteenth Amendment as an outgrowth or expression of existing constitutional principles. The amendment extended the right of personal liberty, due to all individuals in consequence of the principle of equality, to all persons held as slaves. Moreover, the amendment presumed the continued existence of federalism and divided sovereignty; it did not transform regulation of personal liberty and civil rights into an object or end of the national government, as in a unitary government. A Republican editorial writer aptly expressed the limited concept of civil rights behind the Thirteenth Amendment in observing that while Negroes in the South must be protected, this "did not require the overthrow of the whole theory of the Government."[6]

Although the Thirteenth Amendment has recently been interpreted as a comprehensive civil rights guarantee for blacks, in fact it was designed for the narrow purpose of completing and constitutionalizing military emancipation. By long-established constitutional rule, Congress had no power over slavery in the states where it existed. Although under the war power the President could order military emancipation, he could not abrogate state constitutions and laws recognizing or establishing slavery. When Congress in the Wade–Davis reconstruction bill of 1864 tried to abolish slavery and provide a legal guarantee of personal liberty, President Lincoln pocket-vetoed the measure. Thereafter, Congress relied only on constitutional amendment to abolish slavery, the more conservative approach to ending the institution.

The purpose of the Thirteenth Amendment in the most specific and immediate sense was to remove any legal doubt or constitutional uncertainty from the Emancipation Proclamation and other wartime emancipation measures.[7] A second and broader purpose was to complete the American system of liberty and constitutionalize the Dec-

---

[6] *Toledo Blade*, March 28, 1866.

[7] Purpose and intent are related but distinguishable terms that it is necessary to define in analyzing the original understanding of constitutional provisions. The purpose of an amendment is the main relevant reason why the amendment appears in the Constitution. It may be thought of as external to construction of the text, in contrast to intent which is internal to the document, and as providing a standard of choice between two competing interpretations of meaning. Purpose refers to the political and institutional context in which an amendment is proposed. See Robert C. Palmer, "Liberties as Constitutional Provisions, 1776–1791," in *Liberty and Community: Constitution and Rights in the Early American Republic*, ed. Robert C. Palmer and William E. Nelson (Dobbs Ferry, N.Y.: Oceana, 1987), pp. 142–45.

laration of Independence. This purpose was variously expressed, for example, in assertions that the abolition of slavery would remove "the last moral stain from our national escutcheon"; that it would make the republic "thoroughly democratic—resting on human rights as its basis"; that, as a result of the amendment, "we no longer have classes or castes among us. We are made one people and one nation."[8] These statements also convey the idea of completing the Constitution.

In employing the concept of completing the Constitution, we refer to the fact that the authors of the Thirteenth Amendment emulated the original framers by imposing restrictions on the states that affected the ordering of internal affairs. In the words of a Republican congressman, the amendment took from the states "one single subject more in addition to those which were withdrawn by the original Constitution." It did not, however, interfere with or undermine states' rights.[9] The Thirteenth Amendment was in effect a constitutional assertion that the end or object of government in the states was liberty, justice, and the security of rights. Before this time the Constitution contained no such expression, permitting the states to claim that the essential principle of the constitutional system was absolute state autonomy over internal affairs. Preserving divided sovereignty, the antislavery amendment expressed the idea that personal liberty and the security of rights were an object of both national and state governments.[10]

Opponents of the Thirteenth Amendment perceived and vigorously objected to this purpose. In their view the amendment was an unconstitutional and illegitimate exercise of the amending power, intruding upon an area of internal polity permanently reserved to the states. If Congress could amend the Constitution to regulate personal liberty, it could use the amending power to interfere with marital rights, property laws, and other local matters. "If you begin upon this domain," asked a Democratic member of Congress, "where is the limit to the exercise of this plenary amendatory power in domestic affairs?" It is worth noting that opponents did not fear that the Thirteenth Amendment, of its force or through interpreta-

---

[8] Herman Belz, *A New Birth of Freedom: The Republican Party and Freedmen's Rights, 1861–1866* (Westport, Conn.: Greenwood, 1976), p. 116.

[9] Ibid., p. 123.

[10] Michael P. Zuckert, "Completing the Constitution: The Thirteenth Amendment," *Constitutional Commentary*, 4 (1987), 261.

tion, would result in national regulation of Negroes' rights with respect to the judicial process, domestic affairs, education, and other matters. In the area of personal liberty, however, the area the amendment dealt with, Democratic critics said it illustrated the principle of consolidation and was subversive of constitutional government.[11]

Republicans did not claim, as some abolitionists did, that the Thirteenth Amendment was a declaratory provision which did not change the meaning of the Constitution. On the contrary, the amendment was a significant constitutional change. Yet it did not alter the essential nature of the constitutional system. In this way Republicans argued for the consistency of the Thirteenth Amendment with the framers' Constitution. They believed that by prohibiting slavery, the amendment would eliminate the power and interest that had long caused the Constitution to be violated both in letter and in spirit, as when southerners deprived citizens of the rights of freedom of speech and assembly in order to protect slavery. The framers and ratifiers of the Thirteenth Amendment thus believed it would result in the recovery and exercise of constitutional rights. This result would not follow, however, from the exercise of direct national power to secure such rights in an absolute sense, as in a unitary or consolidated system. Federal power would be augmented as freedom of the person became a matter of national concern. Yet the Republican framers of the Thirteenth Amendment understood it as giving Congress no more authority to regulate local affairs than was necessary to secure an individual right not to be held in slavery or involuntary servitude.[12]

As a matter of textual interpretation, the intent of the Thirteenth Amendment, as distinguished from its purpose, was to prevent the existence of slavery in the United States and its territories.[13] In prohibiting slavery, the amendment was logically understood to be a guarantee of liberty. Its libertarian sweep, however, and the scope of authority it conferred on Congress, depended on the meaning of

---

[11] Belz, *New Birth of Freedom*, pp. 122–23.

[12] Zuckert, "Completing the Constitution," 271–76; Belz, *New Birth of Freedom*, p. 124.

[13] Amendment XIII, Section 1: "Neither slavery nor involuntary servitude, except as a punishment for crime whereof the party shall have been duly convicted, shall exist within the United States or any place subject to their jurisdiction." Section 2: "Congress shall have power to enforce this article by appropriate legislation."

slavery. This raises the question of where, on the spectrum running from freedom to unfreedom or the complete dependency of slavery, the line is to be drawn defining the condition prohibited by the Thirteenth Amendment. Although the text was not indicative, the framers of the amendment took a narrow view of slavery as an institution that denied personal liberty.

The text of the Thirteenth Amendment was virtually identical to that of Article 6 of the Northwest Ordinance.[14] The latter was chosen as a model not only because of its historic significance in the antislavery political tradition, but also because it had a long legal history that yielded a clearly understood meaning. The Ordinance was used to keep slavery out of an area where it had never existed, not to abolish slavery. It had been interpreted to prohibit only the master–slave relationship, not to confer civil or political rights on free Negroes. Indeed, the antislavery language of the Ordinance did not preclude indentured service contracts, peonage, or restrictions on the civil rights of blacks. The framers of the Thirteenth Amendment did not distinguish the preventive function of the Northwest Ordinance from the abolition function of the constitutional provision. The latter was evidently regarded as a discrete or finite event in the nature of an act of manumission, rather than as a complex and continuing social and institutional process marked by the presence of long-lasting badges and incidents of slavery. The language of the amendment was not as specific as it might have been. While it did not confer civil rights in a positive or explicit sense, neither did it expressly state that an individual could not hold another as chattel. Since this was the accepted view of slavery at the time, however, the Thirteenth Amendment should be seen as incorporating this meaning, and hence as fixing the line between freedom and slave dependency closer to this narrow definition than to the broader view that defines slavery in terms of its badges and incidents.[15]

That the Thirteenth Amendment was intended to have a narrow civil rights scope is supported by the fact that Congress rejected proposals employing broad egalitarian language. For example, in December 1863 Representative Owen Lovejoy introduced a bill "to

---

[14] Article 6: "There shall be neither slavery nor involuntary servitude in the said territory, otherwise than in the punishment of crimes whereof the party shall have been duly convicted. . . ."

[15] Note. "The 'New' Thirteenth Amendment: A Preliminary Analysis," *Harvard Law Review*, 82 (1969), 1294, 1299–1303; Belz, *New Birth of Freedom*, pp. 125–26.

give effect to the Declaration of Independence and also to certain provisions of the Constitution." Lovejoy's bill stated: "Whereas all men are created equal and endowed by their creator with the inalienable right to life, liberty, and the fruits of an honest toil, . . . all persons held in slavery in any of the States and territories of the United States are declared freedmen and for ever released from slavery."[16] The measure protected freed slaves from unreasonable searches and seizures and conferred the right to sue and be sued and to testify in U.S. courts. In similar manner, Senator Charles Sumner proposed a constitutional amendment stating: "All persons are equal before the law, so that no person can hold another as a slave; and the Congress shall have power to make all laws necessary and proper to carry this declaration into effect everywhere within the United States. . . ." Republican Senators Lyman Trumbull and Jacob Howard, managers of civil rights legislation in 1866, objected that the term "equality before the law" had been used in France to eliminate political and civil ranks and privileges and was not relevant to abolishing slavery. Howard said the language in question was insignificant and meaningless as a clause of the Constitution.[17]

The concept of equality in the Thirteenth Amendment was a limited one. It consisted of the proposition that all persons, including blacks, were entitled to the right of personal liberty. In debate, supporters of the amendment expressed the idea that the right not to be held as a slave carried in its train libertarian consequences of a broader nature, such as protection of person and property.[18] Republican lawmakers made no attempt to enumerate such rights in the Constitution. Analysis of Section 1 of the amendment suggests that while it may be considered to have rendered the property rights of slaveholders invalid, it did not necessarily have any effect on state laws recognizing property in human beings. Section 2 gave Congress power to declare those laws invalid. It also appeared to authorize legislation conferring the essential elements of freedom on emancipated slaves. The nature of slavery was to impose categorical disabilities on individuals, who in a legal sense possessed no personal or

---

[16] 38 Cong., 1 sess., H.R. 21, December 14, 1863, RG 233, 38A–BI, National Archives.

[17] Belz, *New Birth of Freedom*, p. 126.

[18] Ibid., pp. 119–20.

civil rights. Under Section 2 of the amendment, therefore, legislation removing the disabilities of slavery was "appropriate."[19]

The Republican authors of the Thirteenth Amendment did not explicitly resolve the question of the nature of slavery or the quintessential elements of freedom.[20] Black history in the antebellum period suggests that a status between citizenship and slavery might have been defined and rationalized. In the *Dred Scott* case, for example, Chief Justice Taney in effect described free blacks as a class of dependent or subject nationals who were neither citizens nor aliens.[21] American law, however, recognized only two conditions or classifications concerning status in the political community: citizenship and alienage. And although there was disagreement over the definition of citizenship and the rights it entailed, the authors of the Thirteenth Amendment clearly tended to regard emancipated slaves as citizens entitled to protection in the basic rights of person and property.

If the question of citizenship rights was not ready to be conclusively resolved in the framing of the abolition amendment, neither was the issue of federal and state powers in relation to civil rights. Yet a tendency was evident which reflected the Republican party's commitment to divided sovereignty. This tendency was to define American citizenship as consisting of complementary national and state aspects or components. In the Republican view national citizenship, the existence of which was called into question by state sovereignty doctrines before the Civil War, was considered primary and state citizenship secondary and derivative. In accordance with the federal principle, national citizenship consisted mainly in equality before the law as a state citizen. The abolitionist Wendell Phillips said in 1865, for example, that liberty would be secure "When we have given the negro the ballot in his right hand, the land under his feet, and a State Constitution above him, that guarantees him his

---

[19] Robert L. Kohl, "The Civil Rights Act of 1866, Its Hour Come Round at Last: *Jones v. Alfred H. Mayer Co.*," *Virginia Law Review*, 55 (1969), 272, 274–75.

[20] The question continues to be controversial. Cf: *U.S.* v. *Kozminski*, 487 U.S. 931 (1988), in which the Supreme Court says the intent of the Thirteenth Amendment was to prohibit compulsion through physical or legal coercion. The Court rejected a definition of involuntary servitude that includes psychological coercion. 56 LW 4913–14.

[21] Dudley O. McGovney, "American Citizenship," *Columbia Law Review*, 11 (1911), 245–48; Belz, *New Birth of Freedom*, p. 20.

citizenship." Radical Republican Congressman William D. Kelley wrote: "We need not fear that even the existing generation of freedmen will not prove themselves abundantly able to take care of themselves, and maintain the power and dignity of the States of which we shall make them citizens."[22] These ideas of shared power and responsibility over civil rights were crystallized and given clearer expression when Congress dealt with post-emancipation race relations in 1866.

II

Throughout 1865, under President Johnson's direction, the former Confederate states organized loyal governments and determined the status and rights of their former slave population. Although the laws that ensued, known as the Black Codes, conferred rights previously withheld, they also imposed racially conditioned legal disabilities and restrictions on the freedmen. States also administered racially neutral laws in a discriminatory manner. Outside the sphere of public policy or state action, moreover, violence and discrimination against blacks by private individuals were widespread.

Under the circumstances, when Congress met in December 1865 Republican lawmakers' views of national legislative power to protect the civil rights of United States citizens were more expansive than during the framing of the Thirteenth Amendment. Given the turbulent conditions and with the Union army occupying parts of the South, the war power was one source of authority for legislation protecting blacks and white Unionists. Accordingly, military means were employed in the Freedmen's Bureau Act of 1866 to protect the black population in their civil rights and provide temporary economic and educational assistance. The Thirteenth Amendment, which was ratified in December 1865, in the opinion of many Republicans, provided further authority to legislate to protect civil rights. On this basis Congress passed the Civil Rights Act of 1866, a nonmilitary or peacetime plan for securing the fundamental rights of all citizens.

The purpose of the Civil Rights Act was to establish the citizenship of blacks and confer equality before the law in respect of basic

---

[22] Belz, *New Birth of Freedom*, p. 132.

rights for the protection of person and property. Section 1 of the act declared that all persons born in the United States and not subject to any foreign power, excluding Indians not taxed, were citizens of the United States. U.S. citizens "of every race and color . . . shall have the same right, in every State and Territory in the United States, to make and enforce contracts, to sue, be parties, and give evidence, to inherit, purchase, lease, sell, hold, and convey real and personal property, and to full and equal benefit of all laws and proceedings for the security of person and property, as is enjoyed by white citizens. . . ."

The concept of equality embodied in the act was that of limited absolute equality for American citizens under state constitutions and laws.[23] The Civil Rights Act was not intended to confer political rights, or to create total racial equality by prohibiting all forms of discrimination, whether at the hands of state governments or private individuals. That the act was not intended to ban all racial discrimination is seen in the rejection by the House of Representatives of a provision stating "That there shall be no discrimination in civil rights or immunities among the inhabitants of any State or Territory of the United States on account of race, color, or previous condition of slavery."[24] Had this provision become law, Congress would have become involved in protecting civil rights in an abstract and general sense. It would have been forced to provide a detailed federal code regulating ordinary civil rights in all spheres of local community life, including guarantees against private discrimination.[25] Because this comprehensive ban on racial discrimination would have led to the displacement of the states and revolutionized the federal system, it was deleted.

Thus, the Civil Rights Act provided equality in basic economic and legal rights under state law. However the right to make contracts and purchase property might be defined, and whatever procedures for implementing these rights were provided at state law, they were to be enjoyed by individuals without distinction of race. In

---

[23] Earl M. Maltz, "The Concept of Equal Protection of the Laws," *San Diego Law Review*, 22 (1985), 499.

[24] Charles Fairman, *Reconstruction and Reunion, 1865–88, Part I* (New York: Macmillan, 1971), p. 1172.

[25] Earl M. Maltz, "Reconstruction Without Revolution: Republican Civil Rights Theory in the Era of the Fourteenth Amendment," *Houston Law Review*, 24 (1987), 256–57.

other words, the Civil Rights Act conferred rights in the sense of legal capacity or qualification under state law to engage in the activities referred to by the enumerated rights. Republicans believed that when protected by a national guarantee, black citizens would be able to combat private injury and discrimination.[26]

The enforcement provisions of the Civil Rights Act expressed the limiting concept of state action, derived from federalist principles, that formed the constitutional framework for this novel federal legislative policy. Section 2 of the act imposed misdemeanor sanctions on "any person who, under color of any law, statute, ordinance, regulation, or custom, shall subject . . . any inhabitant of any State or Territory to the deprivation of any right secured or protected by this act. . . ." The word "custom" has been interpreted by the Supreme Court since *Jones* v. *Mayer* (1969) as evidence of congressional intent to prohibit private discrimination. In statutory context, however, where it completes a series of terms describing forms of government action, the term "custom" is more reasonably understood as closing a potential loophole than as identifying a new and entirely different category of private discrimination as the object of the act. Section 2 was intended to clarify the fact that the rights conferred in Section 1 created duties on the part of state officials. Only insofar as private individuals might act under color of law were they governed by the Civil Rights Act.[27]

The original understanding of equality in the Civil Rights Act thus consisted of a colorblind federal guarantee of fundamental rights under state laws. Congress intended to establish legal equality and equality of opportunity, defined in a procedural sense with respect to matters such as contract and property rights that were essential to participation in a free labor economy.[28]

Analysis of the Fourteenth Amendment confirms the fact that it was not the meaning of equality, but the respective roles and authority of federal and state governments in regulating civil rights that

---

[26] Belz, *New Birth of Freedom*, p. 168.

[27] Fairman, *Reconstruction and Reunion*, pp. 1238–46. In *Jones* v. *Mayer*, the Supreme Court interpreted Section 1 of the Civil Rights Act of 1866 as guaranteeing rights against both public and private action, but it said Section 2 singled out only state officers for punishment. This means that some other form of legal process and enforcement was intended to protect persons against private discrimination. The Court did not explain what this alternative enforcement process was or why Congress did not provide a civil remedy for private discrimination (ibid., p. 1247).

[28] Maltz, "Reconstruction Without Revolution," 250.

was the more controversial issue in Reconstruction constitutional-ism. The particular problem facing Republican lawmakers in 1866 was to determine an effective method of federal intervention to pro-tect civil rights in the states, and to identify a clear source of consti-tutional authority for doing so by federal legislation. Some lawmakers suggested the naturalization power of Congress and the comity clause as sources of authority for this purpose, but most members of Congress were not persuaded by this argument. In the event, Congress passed the Civil Rights Act with only the Thir-teenth Amendment as a constitutional basis. This does not mean, however, that the antislavery amendment actually was a sufficient source of constitutional power for the legislation, the revisionist his-toriography of *Jones* v. *Mayer* to the contrary notwithstanding. At the time, many Republican civil rights strategists and theoreticians doubted that the Thirteenth Amendment was a sufficient source of authority. It is important to recall the indisputable fact, too often overlooked in radical accounts, that the Fourteenth Amendment was primarily a Reconstruction plan, and that a civil rights component was added to it in order to constitutionalize the Civil Rights Act.

In the framing of Section 1 of the Fourteenth Amendment the problematic issue was the allocation of authority to protect a concept of equality—namely, limited absolute equality—that had been ex-pressed in legislative detail in the Civil Rights Act and that was accepted by the vast majority of Republicans. This can be seen in the series of proposals introduced by Representative John A. Bing-ham of Ohio, who doubted the adequacy of the Thirteenth Amend-ment, for a constitutional amendment guaranteeing basic civil rights.

In December 1865, Bingham proposed an amendment stating that Congress shall have power to pass "all necessary and proper laws to secure to all persons in every State equal protection in their rights of life, liberty, and property." Several Republicans objected to the measure as consolidationist in tendency. In February 1866, Bingham offered another version of a civil rights amendment. This one gave Congress power "to make all laws which shall be necessary and proper to secure to the citizens of each State all privileges and im-munities of citizens in the several States and to all persons in the several States equal protection in the rights of life, liberty, and prop-erty."[29] Although Bingham denied that this measure would lead to

---

[29] Ibid., 267–70.

centralized federal administration of local affairs, saying it was aimed only at state action, several Republicans protested that it did not deal with the problem of state deprivation of civil rights in a clear and direct way.[30] The Joint Committee on Reconstruction then submitted a civil rights constitutional amendment. It stated that "[No] discrimination shall be made by any State or the United States as to the civil rights of persons because of race, color, or previous condition of servitude."[31] Finally, in May 1866, Bingham secured Joint Committee approval of Section 1 as ratified: "No State shall make or enforce any law which shall abridge the privileges or immunities of citizens of the United States; nor shall any State deprive any person of life, liberty, or property without due process of law; nor deny to any person within its jurisdiction the equal protection of the laws." This expressed the congressional intention to prevent improper state action, rather than to regulate private discriminatory conduct.

III

The original understanding of equality in the Fourteenth Amendment is obviously very different from that which prevails in contemporary constitutional law. By way of contrast with some recent definitions of the equal protection concept, the framers of the Fourteenth Amendment did not intend to introduce into the Constitution an open-ended principle for the attainment of total racial equality; or for the prohibition of all unfair classifications, racial as well as nonracial; or the prohibition of racial classifications that stigmatize a group.[32] The amendment was designed to confer limited absolute equality, or a guarantee of fundamental rights of person and property under state authority without distinction of color. Equality in basic rights was justified on the ground that all individuals have

---

[30] Michael P. Zuckert, "Congressional Power Under the Fourteenth Amendment—The Original Understanding of Section Five," *Constitutional Commentary*, 3 (1986), 123–56.

[31] Maltz, "Concept of Equal Protection," 520.

[32] Robert F. Nagel, "Forgetting the Constitution," *Constitutional Commentary*, 6 (1989), 291; Paul P. Dimond, "Strict Construction and Judicial Review of Racial Discrimination Under the Equal Protection Clause: Meeting Raoul Berger on Interpretivist Grounds," *Michigan Law Review*, 80 (1982), 475–76.

natural rights. The Fourteenth Amendment did not embody the general principle that racial discrimination is categorically wrong.

In the late twentieth century, when racial consciousness has become all-absorbing and pervasive, this point of view is hard to understand. Modern theories of equal protection, influenced by the extraordinary importance attached to equality on the one hand and to race on the other hand, have led historians to exaggerate the significance of race for Americans in the Civil War era. To put the matter plainly, it was not racial prejudice and discrimination in general that the framers of the Reconstruction amendments intended to eradicate. Racial distinctions were a part of the historic social order, if not of the natural order, and could hardly be categorically eliminated. The framers and supporters of the Fourteenth Amendment acted to protect civil rights not because they believed in racial equality; they did so despite a belief in racial *inequality*. "Human rights do not depend on the equality of Man or Races, but are wholly independent of them," declared the Republican New York *Tribune*. A Republican congressman asserted in 1866: "Because I am an American citizen, I choose to give [Negroes] what God has given men and every man," namely, the natural rights of civil liberty.[33] Racial classification and discrimination were to be restricted and declared wrong insofar as they led to the denial of fundamental rights to which all persons were entitled by natural law.

The concepts of liberty and equality in the Reconstruction amendments were essentially the same as those that guided the framers in the writing of the Constitution in 1787. Liberty was defined in both community and individual terms, with an emphasis on limitations on government as the essential feature of civil liberty. Equality was conceived of in relation to basic rights of person, property, and access to the legal system that enabled individuals to pursue their interests within the framework of ordered liberty. The question dealt with by the framers of the Reconstruction amendments was whether blacks as a class would be denied the benefit of these principles. The theory of the amendments was that because they were human beings, blacks were not to be categorically denied the benefits of liberty and equality, or excluded from the political community. As individuals they were to be given equality before

---

[33] H. Belz, *Emancipation and Equal Rights: Politics and Constitutionalism in the Civil War Era* (New York: W. W. Norton, 1978), p. 149.

the law in respect of fundamental civil rights. This was the original understanding of equality in the Fourteenth Amendment.

Affirmative action programs, the most prominent feature of contemporary civil rights policy, rest on a concept of equality defined by group rights and equality of result. This concept is antithetical to that on which the Reconstruction amendments are based. In order to justify affirmative action preferences, logical contradictions that deny common sense experience are propounded as syllogistic truths. Thus, a Supreme Court Justice states in support of racial quotas in the *Bakke* case: "In order to get beyond racism, we must first take account of race."[34] Perhaps sensing that such arguments are ultimately contrary to fact and unpersuasive, affirmative action defenders invoke the original intent of the Reconstruction amendments as a justification of race-conscious preference. Yet this history is as distorted and misleading as the logic that proposes to end racism by maintaining racial thinking and consciousness.

The facts of history, though relevant, will not determine the outcome of the affirmative action controversy or the direction of civil rights policy in the future. The Supreme Court conceded as much in its decision in *Patterson* v. *McLean Credit Union* (1989). After requesting reargument on matters of statutory purpose and intent raised in *Runyon* v. *McCrary* (1976), the Court concluded that the historical evidence on whether the Civil Rights Act of 1866 was intended to prohibit private discrimination was not decisive. What was important, said the Court, was that application of the act to private discrimination "is not inconsistent with the prevailing sense of justice in this country."[35] Perhaps this judgment is accurate. Moreover, if it is true, as one commentator has written, that "the Supreme Court as a whole cannot indulge in historical fabrication without thereby appearing to approve the deterioration of truth as a criterion for communication in public affairs," then the Court's decision to avoid affirming the historical interpretation of *Runyon* is also prudent.[36]

The nature of the Constitution as a written instrument of fundamental law implicates history in the practice and maintenance of constitutional government. The historical record has intrinsic value whether it shows continuity between the past and the present, or, as in the interpretation of the Fourteenth Amendment, a fundamental change in the meaning of equality.

---

[34] 438 U.S. 407 (1978).
[35] 109 S. Ct. 2370–71 (1989).
[36] Miller, *Supreme Court and the Uses of History*, p. 195.

9

The Constitution and Reconstruction

DURING THE CONSTITUTIONAL BICENTENNIAL, in a widely noted speech cautioning against making "a blind pilgrimage to the shrine of the original document," Supreme Court Justice Thurgood Marshall posed the issue that is central to the study of the Constitution and Reconstruction. Accepting as historical authority Chief Justice Roger Taney's assertion in the *Dred Scott* case that Negroes had no rights under the Constitution, Justice Marshall stated that "while the Union survived the Civil War, the Constitution did not." "In its place," he said, "arose a new, more promising basis for justice and equality"—the Fourteenth Amendment. In essence, the Fourteenth Amendment was a new Constitution. It was made by men who "refused to acquiesce in outdated notions of 'liberty,' 'justice,' and 'equality'" contained in the original Constitution. The framers of the Reconstruction amendments conceived of "new constitutional principles" guaranteeing "respect for the individual freedoms and human rights . . . we hold as fundamental today." Marshall argued, in effect, that historical knowledge about the constitutional significance of Reconstruction would enable Americans to understand the nature of constitutional government in our own time and liberate us from the error and injustice of the nation's Founding.[1]

Justice Marshall's historical reflections attracted attention because they were not, of course, merely historical. The Constitution to which he referred, whether it be regarded as the framers' document or a new instrument produced in the upheaval of civil war, is the same one that governs our political order today. Since historical analysis continues to be one of the basic approaches to interpreting

---

An earlier version of this chapter appeared in *The Facts of Reconstruction: Essays in Honor of John Hope Franklin*, ed. Eric Anderson and Alfred A. Moss, Jr. (Baton Rouge and London: Louisiana State University Press, 1991), pp. 189–217.
[1] Thurgood Marshall, "Reflections on the Bicentennial of the United States Constitution," *Harvard Law Review*, 101 (1987), 2–4.

the Constitution, historical knowledge about the document may be pertinent to resolving constitutional controversies and public policy disputes.[2] The relevance of constitutional history usually has been discussed in relation to the problem of ascertaining the original intent of the framers. This problem presents itself with even greater clarity and urgency in relation to the Reconstruction amendments, which provide the basis for national civil rights policy. Thus, there has been a constant impetus for studies of the constitutional impact of the Civil War by a long line of jurists, lawyers, and constitutional scholars. Analysis of this body of writing may afford a deeper understanding of the constitutional significance of Reconstruction.

The importance of the Constitution and Reconstruction as a subject of historical study needs little demonstration. The object of postwar policy was to bring the former Confederate states back into the system of republican state governments provided by the Constitution. This process required asking whether the states of the defeated Confederacy were still states in the sense of the Constitution and, if so, what status they occupied and powers they possessed. To answer these questions, it was necessary to consult constitutional principle, theory, law, and history, and there were corollary issues to untangle concerning the status and rights of the freed people and former rebels. Reconstruction, in the sense that is most pertinent to us today, consisted in the civil rights settlement embodied in the Thirteenth, Fourteenth, and Fifteenth Amendments, which together nationalized civil liberty in the United States. Reconstruction was a constitutional problem in the further sense that alternative courses of action were encouraged and reinforced by the separation of powers between the President and Congress, which eventually helped to precipitate the only presidential impeachment in American history. The final phase of Reconstruction concerned the conduct of government and politics in the former rebellious states after their return to Congress. Here, too, a significant constitutional question was raised: namely, whether free republican institutions existed in the Reconstruction South or whether southern politics was so thoroughly based on force and violence as to undermine the assumption of peaceful resolution of conflict on which constitutionalism depends.

---

[2] Walter E. Murphy, James E. Fleming, and William F. Harris II, *American Constitutional Interpretation* (Mineola, N.Y.: Foundation Press, 1986), p. 292.

As a first step toward addressing these issues, a brief consideration of the basic approaches to the Constitution that have shaped historical writing in this field will be useful. Naturally, what lawyers, jurists, and historians have said about Reconstruction and the Constitution has depended in part on their conception of the Constitution and its relationship to political life.

In many accounts the Constitution is regarded as an instrument of power that, although apparently having a fixed and objective form, is in its essential features protean, plastic, and capable of assuming any meaning that those in control of the government decide it should have in order to justify expedient political action. According to this point of view, which one may refer to as the *instrumental* approach, the Constitution does not really limit or control government, but rather functions as a form of rationalization required by the people's quasi-religious attachment to the constitutional text as a symbol of governmental legitimacy. Thus, the Constitution may be said to function in the proper manner when it is rhetorically deployed and manipulated to achieve political ends. A second approach to the Constitution emphasizes its *intrinsic*, rather than its instrumental, value. In this view the Constitution is the forms, procedures, and principles expressed or implied in the documentary text for the conduct of government in accordance with the nature, character, and purposes of the people as constituent power. Without denying that the Constitution was created to accomplish political ends and that it is a useful instrument of power, the argument of intrinsic constitutionalism holds that in order to have force and effect, the document must be regarded as having inherent value. The Constitution must be seen as something good in itself, worthy of being followed for its own sake or for the wisdom, justice, and sound principles it embodies, quite apart from the outcome of specific controversies.[3]

Informed by both the instrumental and the intrinsic perspectives, writing on the Constitution and Reconstruction has been concerned with two general issues: the effect of the Constitution on the events of Reconstruction, and the impact of Reconstruction on the Constitution. Although it is impossible to maintain a fixed distinction between these two analytical concerns, historians and other academic

---

[3] For further discussion of the distinction between instrumental and intrinsic constitutionalism, see Martin Spencer, "Rhetorics and Politics," *Social Research*, 37 (1970), 597–623, and Shirley Letwin, "Law Without Law," *Policy Review*, 26 (1983), 7–16.

scholars have tended to be more interested in the former question, whereas lawyers and jurists, reflecting the practitioner's greater interest in the pragmatic value of history, have dwelt more on the latter issue.

The earliest historical statements that command attention here appeared in Supreme Court opinions interpreting the Reconstruction amendments and the civil rights laws enacted to enforce them. In a series of decisions from the *Slaughter House Cases* through the *Civil Rights Cases*, the Court stated that protection of Negro freedom was the "one pervading purpose" of the Reconstruction amendments.[4] This purpose did not require revolution or fundamental alteration in the constitutional system. Although temporarily deprived of their rights as governmental entities, the former rebellious states were not out of the Union as a result of secession and civil war.[5] The amendments guaranteed personal liberty and civil and political rights for freed blacks and other citizens of the United States. Yet these measures did not essentially alter the division of sovereignty and federal equilibrium that the Constitution provided for between the national government and the states.

The impact of Reconstruction on the Constitution, according to Supreme Court decisions of the postwar period, can be described in a series of general propositions. The Fourteenth Amendment, the principal enumeration of civil rights requirements and other conditions on which the southern states could be readmitted to Congress, prohibited state action denying civil rights. It did not ban private discrimination. Although state failure to protect civil rights might be considered a form of state action, congressional legislation based on this assumption was required to stipulate that the private discrimination in question was racially motivated. The Thirteenth Amendment was a guarantee of personal liberty against both state and private action depriving persons of liberty, and Congress could define and legislate against "badges and incidents" of slavery. (The refusal to admit blacks to a privately owned theater, however, was not a badge of slavery according to the Supreme Court's decision in cases in which this claim was raised.) The rights of United States citizenship were relatively few in number compared with the rights derived from state citizenship, which continued to provide the sub-

---

[4] *Slaughter House Cases*, 16 Wallace 36 (1873).
[5] *Texas v. White*, 7 Wallace 700 (1869).

stance of civil liberty in the American republic. Accordingly, the Fourteenth Amendment did not significantly alter the structure of the federal–state relationship with respect to ordinary civil rights. Finally, blacks were not a separate class, and state laws that were explicitly racially exclusionary, such as laws barring Negroes from jury service, were unconstitutional.

From the perspective of the late twentieth century, the Supreme Court's assertion of Negro freedom as the principal meaning of the Reconstruction amendments may seem disingenuous, if not patently insincere, since the Court's decisions did not prevent wholesale denial of blacks' civil rights. Considered in historical context, however, the Court's holdings on civil rights protected the liberty of the freed people while maintaining the essential principles of the constitutional order. The Court helped prevent the total exclusion and denial of rights for blacks, the alternative desired by the more racist elements in southern society. And the justices rejected the conservative argument that the national government lacked effective power in civil rights matters and must defer to the states.[6]

During the segregation era, roughly from the 1890s to World War II, the Supreme Court's interpretation of the Fourteenth Amendment formed a central theme in the development of constitutional law. In the line of cases delineating substantive due process, the Court protected the civil rights of United States citizens and persons against state interference, in accordance with the broad intent of the authors of the Reconstruction amendments. The rights that received protection, however, were those of economic entrepreneurs and corporations. A new historical interpretation of the purpose of the Fourteenth Amendment—the "conspiracy theory" advanced by Charles A. Beard and other progressive historians—served to explain this development. According to the conspiracy theory, the framers of the Fourteenth Amendment included "persons" along with citizens in the due process clause with a view toward protecting corporations against state regulation. Meanwhile, black Americans, the intended beneficiaries of the Fourteenth Amendment under the earlier Negro-freedom theory, were disfranchised and denied civil

---

[6] Michael Les Benedict, "Preserving Federalism: Reconstruction and the Waite Court," *Supreme Court Review* (1978), 39–79; Robert C. Palmer, "The Parameters of Constitutional Reconstruction: *Slaughter-House*, *Cruikshank*, and the Fourteenth Amendment," *University of Illinois Law Review* (1984), 739–70.

rights as federal officials acquiesced in the imposition of legal segregation in the southern states.

Virtually throughout the segregation era, historical scholarship on the Constitution and Reconstruction was sympathetic to the South and critical of postwar Republican policy. The best scientific historians of the age, including those of the progressive school, described Reconstruction as a tragic time of political error, opportunism, and corruption, precipitated especially by the partisan and irresponsible decision to reorganize southern state governments on the basis of black suffrage. The name of William Archibald Dunning, more than that of any other scholar, is associated with the tragic view of Reconstruction. Dunning's analysis of the postwar period focused on the Constitution and set a scholarly standard for many years to come.

In Dunning's view, the purpose of Reconstruction was to give freedmen and white Unionists power to organize governments and control the former Confederate states indefinitely. This was the political expression of a general effort "to stand the social pyramid on its apex" and impose on southern whites "permanent subjection to another race." Concerned especially with the impact of political events on the Constitution, Dunning treated congressional Reconstruction measures as a virtual overthrow of the fundamental law. "Only in a very narrow sense," he wrote, "was it true that the Union had been preserved." The territorial integrity of the nation had been maintained, but the outcome of Reconstruction revealed that "a new Union had been created."[7]

A student of political thought, Dunning was attentive to theoretical considerations, and into his narrative he wove analyses of theories of Reconstruction and the status of the former Confederate states. Regarding the guarantee clause of the Constitution (Article IV, Section 4) as the principal basis of congressional policy, he showed how Republicans had redefined republican government in order to include blacks as voters, positing a new national power to regulate the suffrage, in deliberate disregard of history and constitutional law. As a progressive intellectual, Dunning admired the energy and capacity for discipline evident both in Republican party rule and in the "just and efficient" rule of military commanders in the occupied South.

---

[7] William A. Dunning, *Essays on the Civil War and Reconstruction* (New York: Macmillan, 1897; repr. New York: Harper & Row, 1965), p. 250; William A. Dunning, *Reconstruction, Political and Economic, 1865–1877* (New York: Harper, 1907), pp. 1, 5.

Nevertheless, the outcome of Reconstruction—"a huge social and political revolution under the forms of law"—placed it outside the constitutional tradition. "The process of reconstruction," Dunning concluded, "presented many situations which could be explained as readily by assuming a revolution to have occurred as by strained interpretation of the constitution."[8]

John W. Burgess, Dunning's Columbia University colleague, offered a more complex analysis of the Constitution and Reconstruction, combining approval of the end—national protection of black civil rights—with disapproval of the means by which it was approached. Strongly Unionist in sympathy, Burgess held that the Constitution permitted—and Congress should have provided—territorial civil government for the former rebellious states until white southerners could be entrusted with local self-government. Meanwhile, a constitutional amendment should have been adopted nationalizing civil liberty. Burgess appreciated the threat to the freedmen's liberty posed by the Black Codes, and he thought Congress morally and legally justified in rejecting President Johnson's Reconstruction policy. Yet he severely criticized congressional Republicans, motivated by partisanship and passion, for the colossal error of creating a new electorate of the freed slaves. Expressing the almost universal judgment of his day, Burgess wrote: "It was a great wrong to civilization to put the white race of the South under the domination of the Negro race."[9]

In Burgess's view, Congress used its power not only unwisely, but also unconstitutionally in enacting military Reconstruction. "There was hardly a line in the entire bill," he said of the Reconstruction Act of 1867, "that would stand the test of the Constitution."[10] Congress further contradicted the organic law in requiring the southern states, as a condition of readmission to the national legislature, to accept terms and provisions that were not yet part of the Constitution. As a political realist, Burgess held that the Johnson governments should have accepted the Fourteenth Amendment, its

---

[8] Dunning, *Essays*, pp. 132–34, 174–75, 250, 135.

[9] John W. Burgess, *Reconstruction and the Constitution* (New York: Scribner's, 1902), pp. viii, 134–35, 53–54, 111, 133.

[10] Ibid., p. 113. Burgess pointed out that Congress wrongly resorted to martial law where the circumstances did not warrant it, deprived the President of the power to act as commander in chief of the army, and denied civil liberties guaranteed by the Bill of Rights.

constitutional irregularity notwithstanding.[11] As a constitutionalist, however, he concluded that imposing on the southern states things not obligatory on the states already in the Union "was tantamount to the creation of a new sort of union with another kind of constitution by an Act of Congress."[12] More so than Dunning, Burgess saw Republican attachment to constitutional ideas as a shaping influence on events. He lamented, for example, Republican lawmakers' regard for the "phantom of the 'indestructible State,'" their willingness to be "haunted by that spectre of an abstract, unorganized 'State' . . . which is nothing more than a Platonic idea."[13]

If they did not stand the test of time, the interpretations of Dunning and Burgess nonetheless served the purposes of historians and the educated public in the early twentieth century. Integrating detailed constitutional analysis into political narrative, their works were not soon superseded. Part of the reason was that historians in these years were turning away from constitutional history, preferring instead to study the social and economic forces that to the progressive mind formed the basis of government, politics, and law.[14] Those persuaded by the basic political argument of the Dunning–Burgess interpretation were therefore little inclined to reexamine its constitutional dimension. Progressive historians also expressed impatience with the constitutionalist assumption apparent in the work of Burgess and Dunning: that the Constitution possessed intrinsic and not merely instrumental value. Commenting on theories of Reconstruction, Walter Lynwood Fleming wrote in 1919: "Unfortunately, American political life, with its controversies over colonial government, its conflicting interpretations of written constitutions, and its legally trained statesmen, had by the middle of the nineteenth century produced a habit of political thought which demanded the settlement of most governmental matters upon a theoretical basis." A decade later, Howard K. Beale summed up the progressive com-

---

[11] Ibid., pp. 80–81, 110. Burgess wrote "Logically and Constitutionally the whole thing was irregular. But it was as it was, and all understood that the way to cut the knot was for the legislatures of the reconstructed 'states' to adopt the proposed Fourteenth Amendment."

[12] Ibid., p. 116. At another point (p. 81), Burgess described the conditions required of the South as "the exaction of . . . an unlawful promise, imposing . . . a degrading discrimination."

[13] Ibid., p. 85.

[14] Cf. James G. Randall, "The Interrelation of Social and Constitutional History," *American Historical Review*, 35 (1929), 1–13.

plaint against intrinsic constitutionalism. Analyzing the critical election of 1866, Beale observed that lawyers and politicians "made lengthy speeches on constitutionality, for this gave them an air of erudition, and satisfied the legalistic conscience of their constituents." Beale added, however, that "constitutional discussions of the rights of the negro, the status of Southern states, the legal position of ex-rebels, and the power of Congress and president determined nothing. They were pure shams." Constitutional arguments were "mere justifications of practical ends."[15]

Yet not all constitutional argument was bombast and rationalization. In spite of themselves, progressives like Beale betrayed a residual belief that valid constitutional principles did exist, possessing intrinsic value and worthy of being defended for their own sake. "Out of a maze of constitutional argument that was mere embroidery for more practical desires," Beale asserted, "there stands out one fundamental constitutional issue that in importance outranks the whole reconstruction question." This was the radical attempt "to remodel the very form of our government into a parliamentary system" and to make "Congress paramount not only to the president, but to the Constitution." Fortunately, Andrew Johnson tenaciously resisted the Radicals, defending the separation of powers, the concept of limited government, and politics based on reason and compromise rather than hatred and distrust. In short, Andrew Johnson was seeking "to preserve the principle of constitutional government."[16]

As forces of social and economic change began to penetrate the South in the 1930s, the received view of Reconstruction as a tragic era came under criticism. A few scholars presented a more favorable view of the postwar period as a time of constructive social and economic reform when the South began to catch up with the rest of the country in matters such as public education and industrial development. If the early revisionists judged political and social results dif-

---

[15] Walter Lynwood Fleming, *The Sequel of Appomattox: A Chronicle of the Reunion of the States* (New Haven, Conn.: Yale University Press, 1919; repr. Toronto: Glasgow, Brook, 1970), p. 54; Howard K. Beale, *The Critical Year: A Study of Andrew Johnson and Reconstruction* (New York: Harcourt, Brace, 1930; repr. New York: Ungar, 1958), pp. 147, 150.

[16] Beale, *Critical Year*, pp. 211, 214; Robert Selph Henry, *The Story of Reconstruction* (Indianapolis and New York: Bobbs-Merrill, 1938; repr. Gloucester, Mass.: P. Smith, 1963), p. 184.

ferently from the orthodox view, however, they were little disposed toward a different constitutional perspective.

W. E. B. Du Bois, for example, one of the first and most forceful of the revisionist writers, regarded constitutional discussion of Reconstruction legislation as "of the same metaphysical stripe characterizing all fetich-worship [*sic*] of the Constitution." At some level, however, Du Bois, like Beale, was forced to acknowledge the objective reality of the Constitution. As the South unconstitutionally made the Constitution a proslavery document, he reasoned, so the North unconstitutionally prevented the destruction of the Union. After the Civil War "revolutionary measures rebuilt what revolution had disrupted, and formed a new United States on a broader basis than the old Constitution and different from its original conception." Du Bois approved this result, for it was "idiotic" for a people "to follow a written rule of government 90 years old" that definitely had been broken. Thaddeus Stevens and the Radicals, understanding that "rule-following, legal precedence, and political consistency are not more important than right, justice, and plain common sense," broke through "the cobwebs of such political subtlety" and imposed military rule on the South until democracy was established. Du Bois thus saw revolutionary constitutionalism sweeping away the Constitution of the framers.[17]

Although mainly interested in social and economic history, Du Bois as an early revisionist was perhaps uncharacteristic in treating the constitutional dimension of Reconstruction. Revisionists who in the 1940s and 1950s elaborated a new view of the postwar period generally ignored the constitutional issues that had concerned earlier writers. John Hope Franklin's *Reconstruction: After the Civil War* illustrates the point. Describing the constitutions in the reconstructed states as satisfactory instruments of state government, Franklin dealt only briefly with the national Constitution. Ignoring the significance that theories of Reconstruction had for contemporaries, he referred to the former Confederate states, without qualification, as "out of the Union, awaiting readmission at the pleasure and mercy of the North." Insofar as Reconstruction warranted consideration as a constitutional conflict, it amounted to a contest between Andrew Johnson's adherence to the southern dogma of states'

---

[17] W. E. Burghardt Du Bois, *Black Reconstruction in America, 1860–1880* (New York: Simon & Schuster, 1935; repr. Cleveland: World, 1962), p. 336.

rights, and Charles Sumner's belief that "anything for human rights is constitutional." Franklin noted the conflict between the executive and legislative branches that culminated in impeachment, but he viewed it as merely a political struggle rather than a confrontation arising out of the structure of the government and involving essential constitutional principles.[18]

Surveying two decades of Reconstruction historiography, Bernard A. Weisberger in 1959 identified inadequate understanding of the constitutional aspect of postwar events as one of the reasons why the revisionist interpretation had failed to win general acceptance. Weisberger asserted that Reconstruction had been treated as an almost isolated episode in federal–state relations. Recalling Du Bois, he attributed this narrow outlook partly to the "national fetish of Constitution-worship." Implying that historians of Reconstruction thought otherwise, Weisberger declared that "constitutional history is not valid as a study of inviolable principles." Therefore, "to talk of Reconstruction's 'constitutionality,' he advised, "is not very useful except as a theoretical exercise." Instead, historians should ask "how the Constitution itself was reconstructed." Weisberger thus identified himself with the instrumental approach to the Constitution. Yet, with a degree of puzzlement, he also noted in the Reconstruction era evidence of intrinsic constitutionalism, that is, a conviction that certain constitutional principles *were* valid and inviolable. President Johnson and other conservatives, for example, believed that the victorious North, out of respect for the Constitution, would promptly restore the southern states to their place in the federal system. "This is a high order of abstraction!" Weisberger exclaimed. "Yet it was fundamentally American." The Radical Republicans too, he observed, "showed a surprising concern for maintaining the forms of the federal system, whatever the realities, and for the appearances of constitutionalism." In Weisberger's view constitutional forms and constitutionalism were perhaps not full-fledged realities. Yet how else to explain why the Radicals did not simply resort to military force and rule the South indefinitely as conquered territory?[19]

A second stage of revisionist writing about Reconstruction began in the 1960s, the era of the civil rights movement. Perhaps per-

---

[18] John Hope Franklin, *Reconstruction: After the Civil War* (Chicago: The University of Chicago Press, 1961), pp. 3, 27, 69–79, 118.

[19] Bernard A. Weisberger, "The Dark and Bloody Ground of Reconstruction Historiography," *Journal of Southern History*, 25 (1959), 427–47.

suaded by contemporary events that principled political action was genuinely possible, historians more readily acknowledged the existence in the Civil War decade of intrinsic constitutionalism. Consider, for example, Kenneth Stampp's synthesis of the revisionist interpretation of Reconstruction. Stampp described how the Radicals and President Johnson engaged in a political dialogue for two years after the end of the war. Although conceding that some of the talk was shrill and irresponsible, Stampp said that much of it was an intensely serious discussion of fundamental problems, such as "the proper relationship of the legislative and executive branches [and] the legitimate areas of federal and state responsibility." Certainly the place of blacks in American society was the central problem, but Stampp believed that "vaguely defined constitutional issues," including "the abstract question of whether the southern states had or had not ever been out of the federal Union," also were relevant to the political conversation over Reconstruction.[20]

To speculate on why history is rewritten would take this essay far beyond its intended scope. In relation to the Constitution and Reconstruction, however, it appears that political and legal efforts to end segregation and secure black civil rights—efforts that in part involved historical arguments about the original intent of the Civil War amendments—helped stimulate further revisionist historical writing.

The constitutional revolution of 1937, which swept away substantive due process and the economic interpretation of the Fourteenth Amendment, had the long-range effect of introducing into constitutional law a distinction between property rights and human or civil rights. Approving federal and state economic legislation, the courts in effect served notice that they would no longer protect property rights against government regulation. A parallel development, also beginning in the 1930s, was judicial support of Negro civil rights claims in a few cases involving criminal procedure, voting rights, and segregation in higher education. These judicial trends were not unrelated, for rejection of the economic interpretation of the Fourteenth Amendment implied a revival of the Negro-freedom theory of the nature and purpose of the Reconstruction amendments. The

---

[20] Kenneth M. Stampp, *The Era of Reconstruction, 1865–1877* (New York: Alfred A. Knopf, 1965), p. 86.

Court's race-relations decisions signaled a new phase in judicial construction and historical interpretation of national civil rights policy based on the Reconstruction amendments.

As civil rights issues began to emerge in constitutional law, two reform-minded legal scholars, Howard Jay Graham and Jacobus Ten Broek, carried on pioneering researches that laid the basis for a new view of the Constitution and Reconstruction. Actively seeking to promote racial equality, Graham and Ten Broek traced the origin of the Thirteenth and Fourteenth Amendments to the antebellum abolitionist movement. They held generally that the framers of the amendments wrote the natural-rights principles of the Declaration of Independence into the Constitution in order to establish civil and political equality for blacks as citizens of the United States. Graham and Ten Broek further contended that the Reconstruction amendments revolutionized the federal system by giving the national government plenary power to legislate directly to protect black civil rights against state and private discrimination. The lawyers John P. Frank and Robert F. Munro advanced a similar original-intent argument concerning the liberal, humanitarian nature of the equal protection clause of the Fourteenth Amendment, a clause Frank and Munro believed was intended to prohibit segregation in public accommodations.[21]

The new, egalitarian view of the Constitution and Reconstruction, based on "law-office history" as its proponents candidly acknowledged, was reinforced by the use of history in civil rights litigation aimed at overthrowing the Jim Crow system. *Brown v. Board of Education*, the school desegregation case, was the principal focus of the attempt to provide an historical jurisprudence to support civil rights. The Supreme Court itself encouraged historical revisionism when it requested the parties to the school desegregation case to submit arguments concerning the intent of the framers of the Fourteenth Amendment on the question of segregated public

[21] Howard Jay Graham, "The 'Conspiracy Theory' of the Fourteenth Amendment (Pt. 1)," *Yale Law Journal*, 47 (1938), 371–403 and "The 'Conspiracy Theory' of the Fourteenth Amendment (Pt. 2)," ibid., 48 (1938), 171–94; Howard Jay Graham, "The Early Antislavery Backgrounds of the Fourteenth Amendment," *Wisconsin Law Review* (1950), 479–507, 610–61; Jacobus Ten Broek, *The Antislavery Origins of the Fourteenth Amendment* (Berkeley: University of California Press, 1951; rev. ed. *Equal Under Law* [New York: Collier, 1965]); John P. Frank and Robert F. Munro, "The Original Understanding of 'Equal Protection of the Laws,'" *Columbia Law Review*, 50 (1950), 131–69.

education.[22] In striking down segregation, the Court ultimately based its decision on contemporary cultural-psychological reasoning, rather than on original intent. Nevertheless, the historical research stimulated by the case became part of the literature of Reconstruction. A number of constitutional lawyers and historians, some of whom were involved in the school desegregation case, wrote accounts emphasizing the far-reaching egalitarian purposes of the Thirteenth and Fourteenth Amendments and their impact on the federal system. Moreover, civil-rights–inspired accounts described the framers of the Reconstruction amendments as humanitarian idealists dedicated to the principle of equal rights. By the mid-1960s, a substantial body of legal-historical writing existed that formed the basis for a constitutional interpretation of Reconstruction and provided historical continuity between the framers' original intent and present-day use of the amendments in the civil rights struggle.[23]

Political histories of Reconstruction written in the 1960s offered a positive assessment of Republican constitutional motives, at the same time calling attention to issues that had been largely ignored since the days of Dunning and Burgess. Less presentist than the legal–historical activists, the revisionist historians in their concern for the impact of the Constitution on Reconstruction reflected the outlook of intrinsic constitutionalism more than instrumentalism. In his study of Andrew Johnson, for example, Eric L. McKitrick did much to restore the seriousness of constitutional theory as an aspect of political action. McKitrick analyzed theories of Reconstruction and the status of the seceded states as an expression of constitu-

---

[22] Howard Jay Graham, *Everyman's Constitution: Historical Essays on the Fourteenth Amendment, the "Conspiracy Theory," and American Constitutionalism* (Madison: State Historical Society of Wisconsin, 1968), pp. 21, 268, 337; Richard Kluger, *Simple Justice: The History of "Brown v. Board of Education" and Black America's Struggle for Equality* (New York: Alfred A. Knopf, 1976), pp. 617–56.

[23] Howard Jay Graham, "The Fourteenth Amendment and School Segregation," *Buffalo Law Review*, 111 (1953), 1–24; Howard Jay Graham, "Our 'Declaratory Fourteenth Amendment," *Stanford Law Review*, 7 (1954), 3–39; Alexander M. Bickel, "The Original Understanding and the Segregation Decision," *Harvard Law Review*, 69 (1955), 1–65; Alfred H. Kelly, "The Fourteenth Amendment Reconsidered: The Segregation Decision," *Michigan Law Review*, 54 (1956), 1049–86; Laurent B. Frantz, "Congressional Power to Enforce the Fourteenth Amendment Against Private Acts," *Yale Law Journal*, 73 (1964), 1352–84. C. Vann Woodward, a consultant to the NAACP in the Brown case, also wrote *The Strange Career of Jim Crow* (New York: Oxford University Press,, 1955), showing segregation to be a late nineteenth-century development and thus not part of the original civil rights settlement of the Reconstruction period.

tional principle and conviction that both accommodated and restricted political passions and policy choices. Without ingrained constitutional scruples to mark the boundaries of dispute, he suggested, it might have taken much longer to achieve a postwar settlement.[24]

LaWanda Cox and John H. Cox described Republicans as principled supporters of equal rights rather than as expedient politicians seeking to ruin or revolutionize the constitutional order. In the Coxes' view, Andrew Johnson was constitutionally inconsistent in opposing any modification of states' rights even for the sake of protecting black civil rights, and primarily responsible for the Reconstruction controversy. Indeed, according to the Coxes, the nationalization of civil rights, asserted as a moral and constitutional principle, was the central fact of Reconstruction. Writing from an English point of view, W. R. Brock explored tensions within Republican constitutionalism and claimed that in asserting national power over the states and congressional authority over the executive, Republicans verged on a constitutional revolution. The revolution was incomplete, however, because despite a tendency to believe in the unlimited power of the majority to do right, Republicans were unwilling to give up the idea of constitutional checks on the popular will. Evaluating the effects of the Constitution on Reconstruction, Brock observed critically that it magnified unwise actions and encouraged deadlock between opposed interests. Yet it remained the one symbol of nationality on which Americans could unite.[25]

More specialized studies by constitutional historians extended the revisionist analysis of the Constitution and Reconstruction as an intellectual foundation for civil rights advances. Cognizant of the contemporary relevance of his subject, Harold M. Hyman did much to constitutionalize revisionism.[26] Hyman disposed of the lingering

---

[24] Eric L. McKitrick, *Andrew Johnson and Reconstruction* (Chicago: The University of Chicago Press, 1960), pp. 93–119.

[25] LaWanda Cox and John H. Cox , *Politics, Principle, and Prejudice, 1865–1867: Dilemma of Reconstruction America* (New York: Free Press, 1963), pp. viii–ix, 136–38; W. R. Brock, *An American Crisis: Congress and Reconstruction, 1865–1867* (New York: St. Martin's, 1963), pp. 250–73.

[26] Hyman wrote in 1966: "Constitutional concepts and political attitudes analogous to those of the Civil War and Reconstruction scene are again current. One can hope that when a century hence historians come to evaluate our time, they will give it as good a report as the young French journalist Georges Clemenceau felt able to send from Washington in 1865: 'The events of the last four years have taught me never to give up hope for this country' " (Harold M. Hyman, "Reconstruction and

notion that Republicans were constitutional radicals or revolutionists by presenting Reconstruction as a positive expression of American constitutionalism. Drawing on a wide array of popular as well as professional legal writings, Hyman introduced the idea of "constitutional adequacy" as an organizing principle of Civil War and Reconstruction politics. He told how northerners, having come within a hair's breadth of losing their Union and Constitution in the secession crisis, discovered in the actions of Abraham Lincoln that they had a real government and a real constitution that provided all necessary power. Far from repudiating the nation's organic law, Unionists based the war effort on "the concept of constitutional adequacy for any ends that political institutions demanded." Americans' insistence on quarreling over constitutionalism, Hyman reasoned, showed renewed reverence for the Constitution. It indicated their "addiction to constitutional bases for political positions."[27] If this characterization superficially recalled Beale's description of constitutional arguments as claptrap, the difference lay in Hyman's belief that constitutional forms and principles had a real impact on events. Constitutional debate was evidence of principled political action and of the intrinsic value of constitutionalism.

To those less certain of the blessings of liberal nationalism, the muscular constitutionalism of Hyman's revisionist account might appear to contradict the idea of limited government.[28] Yet Hyman contended that wartime and postwar policies also reflected the belief that whether at the state or federal level, "coping had to be done constitutionally." He added that "constitutional permissiveness" was "never absolute." In his account of emancipation in particular, Hyman described tensions between constitutional doctrines of national power and the "felt limitations on the allowable functions of government."[29]

Political–Constitutional Institutions: The Popular Expression," in *New Frontiers of the American Reconstruction*, ed. Harold M. Hyman [Urbana: University of Illinois Press, 1966]), p. 39).

[27] Ibid., pp. 38, 285.

[28] See Alfred H. Kelly, "Comment on Harold M. Hyman's Paper," in *New Frontiers of the American Reconstruction*, ed. Hyman, pp. 40–58. Kelly viewed Hyman's "adequacy constitutionalism" as the assertion of a new constitution based on the revolutionary doctrine of the popular will, along the lines of the Dunning–Beale point of view.

[29] Harold M. Hyman, *A More Perfect Union: The Impact of the Civil War and Reconstruction on the Constitution* (New York: Alfred A. Knopf, 1973), pp. 414–15.

A number of studies in the 1960s and 1970s focused on specific constitutional problems of Reconstruction. These included accounts of wartime reconstruction efforts, with emphasis on the constitutional status of the rebellious states; of the civil rights settlement and federal–state relations as defined by the Reconstruction amendments and civil rights laws; of executive–legislative relations and the impeachment of Andrew Johnson; and of the Reconstruction Acts of 1867 and 1868.[30] The general argument of constitutional revisionism was that Republican Reconstruction aimed at extending the principles of liberty, equality, and consent in the original Constitution to all persons or citizens of the United States, doing so within the framework of a modified but still essentially state-centered federal system. The "grasp-of-war" theory of federal power and the guarantee-of-republican-government clause of the Constitution were identified as sources of authority that could be used to reorganize state governments without the need for a radical restructuring of the Union. Even the most far-reaching national intervention under the Military Reconstruction Act refrained from outright and unilateral coercion, allowing southerners public space within which voluntarily to participate in and consent to state reorganization. Similarly, the Thirteenth Amendment, although authorizing federal intervention against both state and private action, was adopted under a narrow theory of the slavery/freedom dichotomy. When the prohibition of slavery was found to be insufficient protection for the freed people, the Civil Rights Act of 1866 and the Fourteenth Amendment were adopted to provide more effective safeguards for civil rights. These

---

[30] Herman Belz, *Reconstructing the Union: Theory and Policy During the Civil War* (Ithaca, N.Y.: Cornell University Press, 1969); Charles Fairman, *Reconstruction and Reunion, 1864-88, Part I* (New York: Macmillan, 1971); William M. Wiecek, *The Guarantee Clause of the U.S. Constitution* (Ithaca, N.Y.: Cornell University Press, 1972); Michael Les Benedict, *A Compromise of Principle: Congressional Republicans and Reconstruction, 1863–1869* (New York: W. W. Norton, 1974); Michael Les Benedict, "Preserving the Constitution: The Conservative Basis of Radical Reconstruction," *Journal of American History*, 61 (1974), 65–90; Phillip S. Paludan, *A Covenant with Death: The Constitution, Law, and Equality in the Civil War Era* (Urbana: University of Illinois Press, 1975); Herman Belz, *A New Birth of Freedom: The Republican Party and Freedmen's Rights, 1861–1866* (Westport, Conn.: Greenwood, 1976); Raoul Berger, *Government by Judiciary: The Transformation of the Fourteenth Amendment* (Cambridge, Mass.: Harvard University Press, 1977); Donald G. Nieman, *To Set the Law in Motion: The Freedmen's Bureau and the Legal Rights of Blacks, 1865–1868* (Millwood, N.Y.: KTO Press, 1979); Earl Maltz, "Reconstruction Without Revolution: Republican Civil Rights Theory in the Era of the Fourteenth Amendment," *Houston Law Review*, 24 (1987), 221–79.

measures confined their effects to state actions, however, and did not reach private discrimination. The states continued to have primary or initial responsibility to regulate civil liberty, albeit under federal constitutional guarantees of equality before the law within local jurisdictions. The federal–state balance was altered, but no revolution in federalism occurred. Finally, the revisionist constitutional interpretation, emphasizing the legitimacy of the civil rights issue, regarded presidential impeachment as a politically and constitutionally justified response to Andrew Johnson's obstruction of congressional legislation.

Establishing the historical basis on which modern civil rights policy rested, constitutional revisionism reopened the question of the failure of Reconstruction. In the Dunning–Burgess interpretation, Reconstruction failed because Republicans reorganized southern governments on the basis of black suffrage, preventing sectional reconciliation and dividing American politics along the color line. In the 1960s, as the civil rights movement gave rise to black-power politics, the failure of Reconstruction appeared to some scholars to lie in the fact that blacks were denied real equality, notwithstanding the civil rights constitutional amendments and statutes.[31] Without denying that full equality lay in the future, revisionists offered a more positive assessment that emphasized the achievements and partial success of Reconstruction. Harold Hyman, for example, although acknowledging pervasive racism in American society, nevertheless concluded that "in the face of . . . enormous impediments, further complicated by the politics and constitutionalism of federalism, there was considerable advance." Neither the nation nor the states, Hyman said, "ever abandoned the constitutional law or the sense of social responsibility implicit in policies and institutions created during the . . . Reconstruction decade. Even constrained constitutionalism allowed maintenance of the war's great advances." LaWanda Cox, answering the argument that Reconstruction failed because Republicans were unwilling to use maximum force to uphold blacks' civil rights, explained that "the amount of force necessary to realize equal civil and political rights in the South was impossible to sustain in a nation whose democratic tradition and constitutional structure

---

[31] Cf. C. Vann Woodward, "Seeds of Failure in Radical Race Policy," in *New Frontiers of the American Reconstruction*, ed. Hyman, pp. 125–47.

limited the use of power, exalted the rule of law, and embodied the concept of government by the consent of the governed."[32]

In the constitutional revisionist view, the crux of the Reconstruction problem was the tension between Republicans' desire to protect the liberty of the freed blacks and their commitment to preserving the essential principles of the constitutional order. Constitutional limitations restricted the range of options open to Reconstruction policy-makers. Yet considerable progress was made in securing the results of emancipation by establishing a foundation for national civil rights policy; moreover, the preservation of constitutional limitations was an achievement of great importance. Even if adherence to constitutional principle restrained the humanitarian impulse to secure more complete justice for the freedmen, the nation in the long run benefited from the revival of intrinsic constitutionalism that shaped Reconstruction.

The revisionist interpretation of the Constitution and Reconstruction confirmed the principle of equal rights without distinction as to color as the historic basis of the civil rights movement. As that movement took a more radical turn in the late 1960s, asserting the idea of "affirmative action" to overcome the effects of past discrimination, further historical revisionism occurred. Historians reflecting a neo-abolitionist perspective, for example, contended that Reconstruction failed because it neglected to address the problem of economic democracy. Without confiscation and redistribution of property to the freed blacks, they argued, measures for securing civil and political rights were bound to be ineffectual. Republicans thus were seen not only as immobilized by constitutional restrictions, but also as concentrating on the wrong area of public policy. Permitted to retain its economic and social power, the southern planter class was able to overthrow the Reconstruction governments, deprive blacks of their civil and political rights, and rule them as a servile labor force.[33]

---

[32] Hyman, *More Perfect Union*, pp. 416, 544; LaWanda Cox, *Lincoln and Black Freedom: A Study in Presidential Leadership* (Columbia: University of South Carolina Press, 1981), p. 169.

[33] Cf. Eric L. McKitrick, "Reconstruction: Ultraconservative Revolution," in *The Comparative Approach to American History*, ed. C. Vann Woodward (New York: Basic Books, 1968), pp. 146–59; Louis S. Gerteis, *From Contraband to Freedman: Federal Policy Toward Southern Blacks, 1861–1865* (Westport, Conn.: Greenwood, 1973); C. Peter Ripley, *Slaves and Freedmen in Civil War Louisiana* (Baton Rouge: Louisiana

The view that Reconstruction could have succeeded had it been more radical with respect to economic redistribution or political and military coercion was expressed in the writings of a number of legal scholars in the post-civil rights period.[34] Concerned to provide a historical justification for affirmative action, neo-abolitionist legal writers argued that the Civil War amendments and civil rights laws were the kinds of genuinely radical measures needed to make Reconstruction successful. If blacks did not achieve real equality after the war, the fault lay in a failure of political will rather than a lack of constitutional authority. In fact, contended neo-abolitionist legal historians, Reconstruction revolutionized the constitutional system, giving the national government all necessary power to fulfill the promise of equality contained in the Civil War amendments.

As noted earlier, the attempt to ground the 1954 school desegregation decision in the original intent of the Fourteenth Amendment was unsuccessful. Partly as a result of criticism of the sociological and psychological bases of *Brown* v. *Board of Education*, and partly because of the need to establish historical continuity between the Reconstruction amendments and modern civil rights policy, the quest for original intent persisted.[35] An original-intent argument justifying Fourteenth Amendment equal protection claims was incorporated in concurring opinions in *Bell* v. *Maryland* (1964), dealing with the sit-in controversy and the right of private property owners to discriminate [36] In 1968 the Supreme Court adopted a neo-abolition-

---

State University Press, 1976); William Cohen, "Negro Involuntary Servitude in the South, 1865–1940: A Preliminary Analysis," *Journal of Southern History*, 42 (1976), 31–60; George C. Rable, *But There Was No Peace: The Role of Violence in the Politics of Reconstruction* (Athens: University of Georgia Press, 1984). For discussion of the relevant writings, see "The New Orthodoxy in Reconstruction Historiography," *Reviews in American History* (March 1973), 106–13 (a revised version is reprinted above as Chapter 7), and Eric Foner, "Reconstruction Revisited," ibid., 10 (December 1982), 82–100.

[34] Cf. Michael Perman, *Reunion Without Compromise: The South and Reconstruction, 1865–1868* (Cambridge: Cambridge University Press, 1973), for a political history emphasizing the theme of political coercion.

[35] Cf. Charles L. Black, Jr., "The Lawfulness of the Segregation Decision," *Yale Law Journal*, 69 (1960), 421–30.

[36] 378 U.S. 226 (1964). In this sit-in case, Justices Douglas and Goldberg said a right to equal public accommodations was an attribute of United States citizenship and was inherent in the historic purpose and original intent of the framers of the Fourteenth Amendment. Cf. Charles A. Miller, *The Supreme Court and the Uses of History* (Cambridge, Mass.: The Belknap Press of Harvard University Press, 1969), pp. 100–18.

ist historical interpretation in deciding an open-housing case on the basis of an original-intent argument concerning the Thirteenth Amendment. The Court declared in *Jones* v. *Alfred H. Mayer Co.* that a right to be protected against private discrimination in the purchase of property under the Civil Rights Act of 1866 was constitutionally justified by the power of Congress under the Thirteenth Amendment to prohibit the "badges and incidents" of slavery.[37] In response to this decision, as well as to the general redirection of civil rights policy signified by affirmative action, neo-abolitionist scholars elaborated an interpretation of Reconstruction and the Constitution aimed at justifying the egalitarian vision of contemporary civil rights policy-makers.

The general conclusion of neo-abolitionist revisionism was that the Reconstruction amendments were intended to give Congress primary, plenary, and ultimate authority to protect the civil rights of United States citizens and other persons.[38] Despite the apparent focus of the Fourteenth Amendment on state action, the neo-abolitionists denied any limitation on national sovereignty in the field of civil rights. If Congress chose, according to Robert Kaczorowski, "it could legislate criminal and civil codes that displaced those of the states." Indeed, it could even destroy the states as separate and autonomous political entities. More important than the identification of specific civil rights was the transfer of sovereignty to the national government in order to implement the egalitarian vision of the authors of the Thirteenth and Fourteenth Amendments.[39] Although neo-abolitionist scholars deny that Reconstruction abol-

---

[37] 392 U.S. 409 (1968).

[38] Cf. Arthur Kinoy, "The Constitutional Right of Negro Freedom," *Rutgers Law Review*, 21 (1967), 387–441; Robert L. Kohl, "The Civil Rights Act of 1866, Its Hour Come Round at Last: *Jones v. Alfred H. Mayer Co.*," *Virginia Law Review*, 55 (1969), 272–300; G. Sidney Buchanan, *The Quest for Freedom: A Legal History of the Thirteenth Amendment* (Houston: Houston Law Review, 1976), Robert J. Kaczorowski, *The Politics of Judicial Interpretation: The Federal Courts, Department of Justice, and Civil Rights, 1866–1876* (Dobbs Ferry, N.Y., Oceana, 1985); Robert J. Kaczorowski, "To Begin the Nation Anew: Congress, Citizenship, and Civil Rights After the Civil War," *American Historical Review*, 92 (1987) 45–68. Robert J. Kaczorowski "Revolutionary Constitutionalism in the Era of the Civil War and Reconstruction," *New York University Law Review*, 61 (1986), 863–940.

[39] Kaczorowski, *Politics of Judicial Interpretation*, pp. 1–3, 8; Robert J. Cottrol, "The Thirteenth Amendment and the North's Overlooked Egalitarian Heritage" (paper presented to the American Society of Legal History, October, 1987), pp. 18–19 and passim; Paul Finkelman, "Prelude to the Fourteenth Amendment: Black Legal Rights in the Antebellum North," *Rutgers Law Journal*, 17 (1986), 415–82.

ished federalism and created a unitary government, the denial appears insignificant. For although the states continued to exist, they possessed only the power to protect civil rights—and only as that power was defined and regulated by the national government. Old constitutional forms continued, but in reality a new Constitution came into existence.

Neo-abolitionist legal historians further found in Reconstruction an egalitarian vision of "an undefined and indefinitely broad body of natural rights" that expands in accordance with the changing demands of national civil rights policy. According to one scholar, the Reconstruction amendments created a substantive and absolute right of black freedom that was intended to make blacks equal participants in the American political community. The amendments did not confer ordinary civil rights on the freed people, but rather a special body of rights—separate, distinct, and exclusively national in nature—that was enforceable by the federal government through direct and affirmative legislation. In a general sense, this argument supports race-conscious policies intended to eliminate the effects of historic societal discrimination. Neo-abolitionist legal historians also seek, in freedmen's legislation enacted after the Civil War, more specific justification for affirmative action.[40]

The litigation-driven neo-abolitionist interpretation finds expression in recent general accounts of Reconstruction. Harold Hyman and William Wiecek emphasize the Thirteenth Amendment as an institutionalization of abolitionist ideas that provided protection in "the full and equal rights of freedom, some of which history had identified and a multitude of which remained for the inscrutable future to reveal." Indeed, the nature and purpose of the Fourteenth Amendment, they reason, can best be understood not by examining the debates on the amendment, but by considering the intentions of the framers of the Thirteenth Amendment. Eric Foner reflects neo-abolitionist, affirmative action ideas in stating that blacks claimed a right to the land as compensation for their unrequited toil as slaves and viewed the accumulated property of the planters as illegitimately acquired. He argues that the freedmen forged from the American and black experience a coherent political response to

---

[40] Kaczorowski, *Politics of Judicial Interpretation*, p. 8; Kinoy, "Constitutional Right of Negro Freedom"; Eric Schnapper, "Affirmative Action and the Legislative History of the Fourteenth Amendment," *Virginia Law Review*, 71 (1985), 753–98.

emancipation, the distinctive feature of which was a black interpretation of the concept of full incorporation as citizens of the republic.[41]

In adopting the Constitution, Publius observed in *The Federalist*, Americans had the opportunity to decide "whether societies of men are really capable or not of establishing good government from reflection and choice, or whether they are forever destined to depend for their political constitutions on accident and force."[42] This question was raised anew at the end of the Civil War as Americans faced the problem of resuming a common political life. Were the Reconstruction amendments principally the result of accident and force, despite the forms that marked their adoption? And did they establish a new Constitution?

Historians of the tragic interpretation of Reconstruction saw the Civil War amendments as a new Constitution imposed by force. They believed the Fourteenth Amendment was invalid and unconstitutional because of the methods used to secure its adoption. Revisionist historians in the civil rights era disagreed, contending that Reconstruction extended and completed the original Constitution by applying the principles of liberty and equality of the Declaration of Independence to the entire nation. Neo-abolitionist writers have revived the thesis of revolutionary constitutionalism, but from a perspective of racial equality opposite that of the white-supremacist Dunning–Burgess school. In the neo-abolitionist view, the Reconstruction Constitution, despite formal continuity, differed from the framers' Constitution in two fundamental respects. First, the original Constitution, recognizing and protecting slavery, contained no principle of equality and excluded blacks from membership in the national political community. Second, the idea of liberty embodied in the Constitution was in fact a fundamentally flawed concept of possessive individualism that permitted property in man. The Thirteenth and Fourteenth Amendments, containing a more valid conception of liberty and introducing the principle of equality, replaced

---

[41] Harold M. Hyman and William M. Wiecek, *Equal Justice Under Law: Constitutional Development, 1835–1875* (New York: Harper & Row, 1982), p. 390; Eric Foner, *Nothing but Freedom: Emancipation and Its Legacy* (Baton Rouge: Louisiana State University Press, 1983), pp. 55–56; Foner, "Reconstruction Revisited," 90.

[42] James Madison, Alexander Hamilton, and John Jay, *The Federalist*, ed. Edward Mead Earle (Washington: D.C.: National Home Library Foundation, 1938), p. 3.

the framers' outdated ideas and established a new Constitution. In neo-abolitionist legal history one thus can see the provenance of Justice Thurgood Marshall's argument rejecting the Constitution of the framers.[43]

Whether the framers' Constitution was destroyed in the Civil War and replaced by a new organic law adopted in Reconstruction is an historical question. It has political and philosophical implications, however, that make it difficult to resolve on strictly empirical historical grounds. It might seem realistic, for example, to argue that whether the nation retained its original Constitution or made a new one is merely a theoretical question. Yet however the framing and ratification of the Fourteenth Amendment be conceptualized—as a valid exercise of the amending power or as a revolutionary congressional act—the fact is that this key measure, the real substance of the Reconstruction Constitution, became an accepted rule of action. As a result of history alone, if nothing else, it acquired legitimacy.[44]

From another standpoint, however, the theoretical question of whether the Reconstruction amendments extended the principles of the Founding or made a revolutionary new beginning is a realistic and historically legitimate one to ask insofar as there is an obligation to understand the amendments as their authors intended them to be understood. Then as now, the question of constitutional theory—in particular the issue of the authority of the Founding—formed a real part of the political situation.

The theory of the American Constitution posits a fixed, binding, and permanent supreme law, superior to the government and alter-

---

[43] Justice Marshall developed his historical argument more fully in his dissenting opinion in *University of California Regents* v. *Bakke*, 438 U.S. 265 (1978), at 369–97.

[44] An important issue in the discussion of Reconstruction until well into the twentieth century was whether the Fourteenth Amendment was illegitimate and unconstitutional because it was ratified by the former Confederate states under compulsion of national authority. The matter apparently was laid to rest by the Supreme Court in *Coleman* v. *Miller* (1939), holding that the question was a political one resolved by the action of Congress declaring the amendment ratified, and confirmed by history and usage. In the civil rights era, however, the issue arose once again and provoked scholarly comment. See Walter J. Suthron, Jr., "The Dubious Origins of the Fourteenth Amendment," *Tulane Law Review*, 28 (1953), 22–44; Pinckney G. McElwee, "The Fourteenth Amendment to the Constitution of the United States and the Threat That It Poses to Our Democratic Government," *South Carolina Law Quarterly*, 11 (1959), 484–519; Joseph L. Call, "The Fourteenth Amendment and Its Skeptical Background," *Baylor Law Review*, 13 (1961), 1–20; Ferdinand F. Fernandez, "The Constitutionality of the Fourteenth Amendment," *Southern California Law Review*, 39 (1966), 378–407.

able by the people only in the manner prescribed in the document. The high public status accorded the document as the source and symbol of governmental legitimacy expresses and is a consequence of this theory. The theory is the key to understanding the intrinsic value of the Constitution as the foundation for the rule of law in the United States. If history shows the theory to be false, if during the Civil War and Reconstruction Americans revolutionized their government and made a new constitutional beginning, that would be a precedent of great importance. It would make it easier in future political crises further to abandon the constitutionalism of the Founding. Much is at stake, therefore, in the historical controversy over the Constitution and Reconstruction.

Of the three interpretations of Reconstruction examined in this essay, the revisionist view is the most historically accurate. Republicans in the 1860s sought to implement more fully and effectively the principles of liberty, equality, and consent set forth in the Declaration of Independence. Anchored in the Founding, the Reconstruction amendments were intended to complete the Constitution and make permanent the expansion of liberty and civil rights resulting from the abolition of slavery.

This purpose was evident in the first Republican abolition proposal introduced into Congress in December 1863: "A bill to give effect to the Declaration of Independence and also to certain provisions of the Constitution of the United States." [45] Numerous statements in support of the Thirteenth and Fourteenth Amendments in the next several years expressed the same intention. Congressman Godlove Orth of Indiana explained in January 1865 that the prohibition of slavery would result in a practical application of the principle that life, liberty, and the pursuit of happiness were inalienable rights of all men. According to the Republican Congressman John A. Kasson of Iowa, the Thirteenth Amendment would carry into effect the clause of the Constitution entitling citizens of each state to "all Privileges and Immunities of Citizens in the several States." During the debate on the Thirteenth Amendment, Senator Charles Sumner of Massachusetts said: "It is only necessary to carry the Republic back to its baptismal vows, and the declared sentiments of its origins. There is the Declaration of Independence: let its solemn prom-

---

[45] H.R. 21, 38 Cong., 1 sess., introduced by Owen Lovejoy, in Record Group 233 (38A–B1), National Archives.

ises be redeemed. There is the Constitution: let it speak, according to the promises of the Declaration." Defending the civil rights section of the Fourteenth Amendment in 1866, Congressman George F. Miller of Pennsylvania argued that it was "so clearly within the spirit of the Declaration of Independence . . . that no member of this House can seriously object to it."[46]

In a philosophical sense, moreover, the authors of the Reconstruction amendments appealed to the same conception of liberty that guided the making of the Constitution. This was not a narrowly self-seeking, strictly economic conception of freedom, as progressive historiography has assumed. Property was a natural right and interest protected by the Constitution, yet it received no special sanction; nor was it elevated to a position of political dominance.[47] Replacing classical virtue as the end or purpose of government, self-interest properly considered—enlightened self-interest—assumed positive moral meaning in a balanced system of republican freedom. Comprising political, religious, social, and economic aspirations, the liberty of the Founding began in individuality and ended in common choice, under constitutional forms and procedures agreed upon by the people.[48] The liberty defended by the Republican party in the Civil War and Reconstruction was similarly grounded in the natural rights of individuals and the principles of equality and consent.

Reflection on the nature of liberty in the American regime requires comment on the place of slavery in the original Constitution. Since slavery was part of the social environment in which the Constitution was adopted, it is possible to argue that the document was intended in principle as well as practical effect to sanction and preserve the South's peculiar institution. Provisions concerning fugitive slaves, the three-fifths ratio for federal representation, and the im-

---

[46] *Congressional Globe*, 38 Cong., 2 sess., 142, 153; ibid., 38 Cong., 1st sess., 1202; ibid., 39 Cong., 1 sess., 726.

[47] Henry Steele Commager, "The Constitution: Was It an Economic Document?" *American Heritage*, 10 (1958), 58–61; James H. Hutson, "The Constitution: An Economic Document?" in *The Framing and Ratification of the Constitution*, ed. Leonard W. Levy and Dennis J. Mahoney (New York: Macmillan, 1987), pp. 259–70.

[48] Glen E. Thurow, " 'The Form Most Eligible': Liberty in the Constitutional Convention" (paper presented to the Liberty Fund Conference on Liberty and the Constitution, Philadelphia, November, 1987), p. 13. See also Richard Vetterli and Gary Bryner, *In Search of the Republic: Public Virtue and the Roots of American Government* (Totowa, N.J.: Rowman & Littlefield, 1987); Thomas L. Pangle, *The Spirit of the Modern Republicanism: The Moral Vision of the American Founders and the Philosophy of Locke* (Chicago: The University of Chicago Press, 1988).

portation and migration of slaves are seen as expressing the framers' proslavery original intent.[49] This argument has the effect of discrediting the Constitution as "fundamentally imperfect" and unworthy of surviving the Civil War[50]

More historically sound is the view that although the Constitution recognized the existence of slavery, it did not in principle sanction the institution, but rather placed upon it marks of disapprobation that were the source of antislavery aspiration. This argument was advanced by Frederick Douglass and Abraham Lincoln before the Civil War. Douglass, after philosophical reflection, concluded that slavery lacked authority and was not established under the Constitution. Reasoning that not a word in the document authorized slavery, Douglass elevated constitutional principle above the practice of the government in rejecting the Garrisonian view that the Constitution was a proslavery document. Lincoln, noting that slavery was mentioned in the Constitution only in "covert language," stated that the founders "marked" the institution "as an evil not to be extended, but to be tolerated and protected" only insofar as was necessary to form the Union.[51]

At issue in the controversy over slavery and the Constitution is the problem of ascertaining the meaning of the Constitution. Ultimately, as Don E. Fehrenbacher has written, "the law inheres most essentially in the text of the document."[52] And the undeniable fact

---

[49] Denying that the Constitution was essentially open-ended or noncommittal on the question, Paul Finkelman states that "slavery was given both explicit and implicit sanction throughout the Constitution" ("Slavery and the Constitutional Convention: Making a Covenant with Death," in *Beyond Confederation: Origins of the Constitution and American National Identity*, ed. Richard Beeman et al. [Chapel Hill: University of North Carolina Press, 1987], pp. 190–93); William Wiecek, although using somewhat less forceful language describing how the Constitution "acknowledged," "accommodated," and "protected" the institution, concludes that slavery was "ensconced" and "established" in the Constitution (*The Sources of Antislavery Constitutionalism in America, 1760–1848* [Ithaca, N.Y.: Cornell University Press, 1977], pp. 62–74).

[50] Finkelman, "Slavery and the Constitutional Convention," p. 190.

[51] Waldo E. Martin, Jr., *The Mind of Frederick Douglass* (Chapel Hill: University of North Carolina, 1984), p. 37; Roy P. Basler et al., eds., *The Collected Works of Abraham Lincoln*, 9 vols. (New Brunswick, N.J.: Rutgers University Press, 1953), 3:307, 535; 4:22.

[52] Don E. Fehrenbacher, *The Dred Scott Case: Its Significance in American Law and Politics* (New York: Oxford University Press, 1978), p. 27. See also Robert C. Palmer, "Liberties as Constitutional Provisions, 1776–1791," in *Liberty and Community: Constitution and Rights in the Early American Republic*, ed. William E. Nelson and Robert C. Palmer (Dobbs Ferry, N.Y.: Oceana, 1987), pp. 142–43.

is that the text of the Constitution did not contain the word "slavery." Although neo-abolitionist historians discount the significance of this fact, it seems accurate to say that the framers' choice of language conveys the idea of moral disapproval of slavery.[53] The conclusion follows that the founders gave slavery as little political protection as possible in an instrument of government that contained emancipationist potential. James Madison put the matter aptly in stating at the constitutional convention that it would be "wrong to admit in the Constitution the idea that there could be property in man."[54]

The Reconstruction amendments were intended to remove the exceptions to liberty and equality signified by the slavery provisions and complete the Constitution by bringing it into conformity with the Declaration of Independence. Republicans did not regard the Thirteenth Amendment as a declaratory measure that merely expressed the true meaning of the Constitution. They viewed it rather as a change in the organic law, a change consistent with the principles of liberty that were embodied in the Constitution but had been imperfectly realized because of the existence of slavery. The purpose of the amendment was to remove impediments to the exercise of constitutional rights and to complete the American system of lib-

---

[53] See John Alvis, "The Slavery Provisions of the U.S. Constitution: Means for Emancipation," *Political Science Reviewer*, 17 (1987), 241–65. Alvis writes: "The one thing evidently agreed upon between delegates from slaveholding states and their opponents at Philadelphia was the propriety of excising any direct mention of slavery from the clauses that would regulate the institution. . . . Consequences attach to the Framers' verbal fastidiousness. Disinfecting the document of any direct acknowledgement of slavery imparts to the concessions regarding census and the return of fugitive slaves a shamed character. . . . Lincoln said that the draftsmen of the Constitution 'left [slavery] with many clear marks of disapprobation upon it.' Conspicuous omission is one such mark of disapprobation. More substantial for antislavery constitutionalism, the avoidance of any explicit acknowledgement of slavery suggests that one cannot look to the supreme law of the land for authorization in owning human beings" (247). See also Fehrenbacher, *Dred Scott Case*, pp. 20–27. Even neo-abolitionist scholars acknowledge the significance of the language of the Constitution on this point. Referring to the omission of the word "legally" to describe persons "held to Service of Labor in one state, under the Laws thereof" (Art. IV, sec. 2), Finkelman concedes that "in the most technical linguistic sense" it was true that "the Constitution did not recognize the legality of slavery" ("Slavery and the Constitutional Convention," 224).

[54] Robert Goldwin, "Why Blacks, Women, and Jews Are Not Mentioned in the Constitution," *Commentary*, 83 (1987), 28–33; Walter Berns, "Comment: Equality as a Constitutional Concept," *Maryland Law Review*, 44 (1987), 22–27. Madison quotation in Fehrenbacher, *Dred Scott Case*, p. 21.

erty. When the Thirteenth Amendment proved inadequate for the task of protecting civil liberty, Republicans proposed the Fourteenth Amendment to secure the civil rights of United States citizens against denial by the states. The framers of the Reconstruction amendments intended neither a revolution in federalism nor a radical transformation in the meaning of liberty and equal rights. Their aim was to extend to the freed people the protection of person and property that delineated the condition of civil liberty under United States citizenship.[55]

The Reconstruction amendments embodied a racially impartial conception of equality before the law. Their purpose was to remove the racial qualification that had impaired the implementation of the principles of equality and consent contained in the Constitution. Reconstruction policy-makers conferred on the emancipated slaves citizenship and ordinary civil rights, not a special right of Negro freedom and equality. In a practical sense, of course, any post-emancipation measures reasonably related to the end of integrating the freed people into the political order were bound to operate mainly for the benefit of blacks, and hence might be regarded as compensatory or preferential. The question is whether the nature and meaning of the constitutional principles that provide the foundation of civil rights policy are to be defined with reference to this historical circumstance, or to the universal principles of liberty and equality expressed in the language and legislative history of the Reconstruction amendments. Although context and circumstance are necessary considerations in policy-making and political action, common sense suggests that changing historical circumstances and relative social conditions can never be the source of the fixed principles and standards on which constitutional government and the rule of law depend. In basing the Reconstruction amendments on the natural rights principles of the Declaration of Independence, the constitution makers of the 1860s recognized this fact.

Historical study of the Constitution has practical consequences because the document is directly pertinent to the conduct of government. Accounts of constitutional changes during Reconstruction have had a bearing on race relations and civil rights policy, and will

---

[55] Belz, *New Birth of Freedom*, pp. 113–34; Michael P. Zuckert, "Completing the Constitutional Power Under the Fourteenth Amendment: The Original Understanding of Section Five," *Constitutional Commentary*, 2 (1986), 123–56.

probably continue to be relevant if the present controversy over affirmative action is to be resolved conclusively. What the historical record shows is that the framers of the Reconstruction amendments neither intended nor effected a revolutionary destruction of the states, as the tragic interpretation held; nor did they posit black freedom and equality as salient features of a new constitution, as the neo-abolitionist view argued. The intent of the Reconstruction framers was to protect the civil rights of United States citizens, including most importantly the freed slaves, under the Constitution of the Founding Fathers. This is the principal conclusion to be drawn from historical reflection on the Constitution and Reconstruction.

Conclusion: Legitimacy, Consent, and Equality in the Reconstruction Settlement

AMERICANS WENT TO WAR in 1861 to resolve fundamental ambiguities in the nature of the Union and the status of slavery as an institution in republican society. In the 1840s, in the context of territorial expansion that was bound to alter the relative political power of South and North as constituent sections of the country, slavery and the nature of the Union became inextricably related. Animated by mutual apprehension at the revolutionary threat which each section believed the other posed to its social order, a pattern of politics took shape that by the late 1850s demanded resolution of these issues. The question was whether the ambiguities at the root of the conflict would be resolved through political means, including constitutional amendment, legislative policy, and judicial decision, or the alternative of war.

The Civil War initiated the process of clarifying the nature of republican liberty in the United States. Reconstruction completed it—at least to the satisfaction of the generation of Americans who fought the war. Reconstruction was intended to resolve the substantive issues over which the war was fought. First, was the Union a political association of sovereign states in the nature of a compact, or a union of individuals in the aggregate constituting a sovereign nation? A second issue, arising out of the policy of slave emancipation made necessary by the war, concerned the status and rights of the country's black population. Were blacks to be recognized as citizens and integrated into society on an equal basis with the white population, or would they be assigned a separate classification on the basis of racial identity? A third issue was the relationship between the federal government and the states with respect to the regulation of personal liberty and civil rights. Before the war a subject almost exclusively within the state police power, wartime emancipation interjected the federal government into this sphere of public policy. Would reconstruction policy recognize the authority of the states with respect to civil rights, or would it revolutionize the federal system by giving the federal government plenary authority in this area?

The political process of Reconstruction resolved these questions with varying degrees of clarity. To the extent that it did so, accomplishing its basic purpose of providing a political settlement of the military conflict, it might logically be considered successful. If there is one conclusion that stands out in historical accounts of the postwar era, however, it is that Reconstruction was a failure, if not an unmitigated disaster. One reason for this view, evident in writing about Reconstruction since the events in question, is the fact of continuing sectional hostility. More than a century later controversy over flying the Confederate flag, to mention a merely symbolic issue, suggests that the hostility persists. In the historiography of the past generation, in contrast, the failure of Reconstruction is seen as lying elsewhere: in the inability of Americans of the Civil War generation to solve the problem of race relations by guaranteeing the civil rights of the emancipated slaves. If nonresumption of war as the criterion of successful Reconstruction is so minimal as to be meaningless, however, to make resolution of the race question the criterion may be to adopt a utopian standard of judgment.

Reconstruction was controversial in part because of the inherently difficult theoretical and practical issues it involved. Controversy was intensified in the context of political party competition that was the medium of Reconstruction policy-making. Republicans, resuming their partisan identity after translating themselves into the Union party during the Civil War, were challenged by resilient Democrats hopeful of reestablishing their party on a national basis. Within each party factional conflict complicated the problem of achieving the consensus needed for policy-making coherence. Referring to the pursuit of partisan advantage and local interest, the Reconstruction has been characterized as "politics as usual," in contrast to a higher, more noble politics of vision and purpose that ought to have been practiced—and would have been had statesmen of principle been listened to. The identity of such putative statesmen varies in different accounts, but the point is that fundamental issues were at stake which narrow partisanship prevented from being addressed in their proper light.

Although the distinction between low and high politics may be questionable, reconstruction concerned fundamental issues in the American political tradition. Broadly conceived, they were the nature of political legitimacy, the requirements of government by consent, and the meaning of equality. Because the meaning of these concepts does not fully emerge from the historical context, it is necessary briefly to discuss them from the standpoint of political theory.

Political legitimacy refers to the intrinsic value or validity that an act or measure possesses by virtue of its conformity with fundamental law or standards of justice and right. In practical terms legitimacy is indicated by acquiescence to or compliance with the act or measure as justified, binding, or worthy of obligation. In contrast to the rule-based procedural and formal concerns that define the concept of legalism, political legitimacy involves substantive matters of moral principle and philosophy.[1]

In the American political tradition, arguments and judgments about political legitimacy involve, preeminently, the principles of consent and equality. The uncoerced, voluntary assent that individuals give to acts of legitimate political authority derives from and is a continuing expression of the unanimous consent given by individuals which in social contract theory is assumed to be the basis on which government is created. The consent of the governed is more than a practical and convenient arrangement for the conduct of politics. It is grounded on and required by the equality principle. In the words of the Declaration of Independence, governments are instituted to secure the natural rights of individuals, and derive their just powers from the consent of the governed.

In any political system, obligation or obedience is secured at the margin by force or the threat of force. When law enforcement ceases to be marginal and becomes the principal activity of the state, it is a sign that authority has failed and legitimacy has disappeared.[2] Under the Union theory of secession as a rebellion of individuals against their government, the Civil War was a demonstration of this principle on a massive scale. Although to nothing like the same extent as in wartime, the problem of legitimacy also existed during Reconstruction, as a result of claimed violations of the principles of equality and consent in the southern states. Across the political spectrum, the legitimacy of government authority was questioned in conditions of political and social unrest that in the view of many rendered poli-

---

[1] I rely here on Bertrand DeJouvenel, *Sovereignty: An Inquiry into the Political Good* (Chicago: The University of Chicago Press, 1957), pp. 26–33, and John Finnis, *Natural Law and Natural Rights* (Oxford: Oxford University Press, 1980), pp. 245–52.

[2] DeJouvenel, *Sovereignty*, p. 33.

tics as usual irrelevant and raised the specter of revolutionary upheaval.

The significance for Reconstruction of the problem of legitimacy,
arising from conflicting claims of equality and consent, is the subject
of this chapter. I shall explore this theme in relation to specific issues which implicated it, including the revolutionary or conservative
character of Reconstruction, the question of its success or failure,
and its meaning for contemporary race relations. This approach will
also involve commentary on the manner in which recent studies of
Reconstruction treat these questions.

I

The inherent theoretical and practical difficulty of Reconstruction
was complicated by the question—procedural in form though substantive in effect—of where authority lay to decide the specific issues in which it consisted. To the extent that the Civil War was a
genuine war under the law of nations, this question ought not to
have arisen. The rules of war gave the victor the right to settle matters. In American Reconstruction, however, the question of authority
was raised by the legal theory under which the Union government
justified the use of military force.

From the moment Fort Sumter was attacked, the Lincoln administration insisted that the conflict was a rebellion of lawless individuals against their government, not a war between sovereign nations or
confederations of states. Secession was said to be a legal nullity; the
rebellious states were not out of the Union, merely out of their
proper practical relation to it. Yet if the ex-Confederate states and
their citizens were in a real sense still members of the Union, they
presumably had a right to have their views represented and taken
into account in the disposition of the basic questions of postwar
policy. If the war was fought to keep the Confederate states in the
Union, and if the Union was a political association based on the
consent of equal member-states, as a substantial body of constitutional law argued, then Reconstruction ought not to be simply an
imposed settlement.

The importance given to practical reason in the study of politics
makes it difficult at times to appreciate the significance of theoretical questions. Lincoln illustrated this tendency when he said, in a

discussion of Reconstruction, that the question of whether the seceded states were in or out of the Union was "a merely pernicious abstraction."[3] Nevertheless, the logical dilemma that the Union theory of the war posed for planners of Reconstruction policy had practical consequences. To some extent it created a moral and political dilemma that, in combination with other issues, made Reconstruction an almost insoluble problem.

If, consistent with the purpose of the war, the basic goal of Reconstruction was to restore the former Confederate states to the Union, success would be measured by the extent to which the states were reintegrated into the federal system. Since the civil rights revolution of the 1960s, this has become an unacceptably narrow criterion for evaluating Reconstruction because it disregards the problem of race relations and civil rights equality for blacks. If inherent limitations in the structure of Reconstruction politics made successful civil rights integration impossible, however, it would be unreasonable to conclude simply and categorically that Reconstruction failed. Failure to accomplish what is impossible to be performed may suggest a lack of practical wisdom, but not necessarily moral deficiency.

Northern ambivalence about the justice and constitutional propriety of a dictated peace after the Civil War complicated a situation fraught with contradictory elements. Even the most earnest Republicans, desiring a radical transformation of southern society, were prepared at some point to restore the ex-Confederate states to the Union. Moderate Republicans, more ambivalent, were inclined to give former Confederates greater scope for consenting to the terms of the settlement offered. Yet this settlement fundamentally served the interests of the Republican party, and the party was bound to impose it by the nature of the war. The fact that no Confederate government official—not even President Jefferson Davis—was brought to trial for treason and rebellion indicates that the war was not really a rebellion of lawless individuals.

Southerners were denied seats in the Thirty-Ninth Congress, which met in December 1865 to formulate a reconstruction policy. Congress enacted Freedmen's Bureau legislation, the Civil Rights Act of 1866, the Fourteenth Amendment, and the Military Reconstruction Act of 1867, providing for the reorganization of govern-

---

[3] Roy P. Basler et al., eds., *The Collected Works of Abraham Lincoln*, 9 vols. (New Brunswick, N.J.: Rutgers University Press, 1953–1955), 8:403.

ments in the former Confederate states on the basis of new state constitutions. Excluded from shaping this basic Reconstruction statute, southerners were nevertheless given a decisive role in its implementation. Under the Military Reconstruction Act southerners could vote on whether to hold conventions to rewrite their state constitutions, to elect convention delegates, and to ratify the new constitutions. At first, Congress required ratification by a majority of registered voters in each state. When the white citizens of Alabama, refusing to vote, used this rule to prevent the new state constitution from going into effect, Congress changed the law. It required ratification of new state constitutions by a majority of actual voters. With whites abstaining, the state constitutions were approved by majorities composed almost exclusively of black voters.[4]

The point is, not that it would have been better to impose a Reconstruction settlement denying republican consent, but that the theory of an unbroken Union and the war as a rebellion was problematic. Notwithstanding the political necessity of categorically denying the validity of secession as a form of state action, the theory introduced a major obstacle to the implementation of Reconstruction policy. Ultimately, the question arises whether it was not illogical, paradoxical, and self-defeating to force lawmakers and executives in republican state governments to accept measures, the legitimacy of which depends on the giving of voluntary consent.

In this light it can be argued that the constitutional changes of Reconstruction resulted from "accident and force," rather than the "reflection and choice" intended by the framers of the Constitution as the basis of republican constitutions.[5] The changes might thus be viewed as unconstitutional.[6] This is not to deny that the Reconstruc-

---

[4] Michael Les Benedict, "The Problem of Constitutionalism and Constitutional Liberty in the Reconstruction South," in *An Uncertain Tradition: Constitutionalism and the History of the South*, ed. Kermit L. Hall and James W. Ely, Jr. (Athens: University of Georgia Press, 1989), pp. 230–32.

[5] *The Federalist Papers*, ed. Clinton Rossiter (New York: New American Library, 1961), p. 33.

[6] Southerners of course advanced this argument at the time. It is noteworthy that Bruce Ackerman, a prominent liberal scholar, views the political circumstances surrounding the ratification of the Fourteenth Amendment as reason for concluding that it was not in conformity with Article V requirements for amending the Constitution (*We the People: Foundations* [Cambridge, Mass.: The Belknap Press of Harvard University Press, 1991], p. 45). Only by using a theory of constitutional amendment by congressional legislation, outside the Article V amendment process, does Ackerman find the Reconstruction amendments constitutional.

tion settlement can be seen as legitimate, considered as the conclusion of a war between belligerent states. Nor is it to hold that southerners, having withdrawn their consent from the constitutional compact in the revolutionary act of secession, were morally justified in claiming that Reconstruction measures violated their right of consent. The authors of Reconstruction measures, however, did not appeal to this authority. In conservative fashion they insisted on the unbroken legal continuity of the Union and the Constitution, in effect inviting the former Confederates to claim rights as members of the Union. Although the Constitution anticipated war, it did not contemplate a genuine war between belligerent American governments. At the same time, the constitutionalist belief persisted that limited government required a written constitution, making it practically impossible to suspend the Constitution as the framework of political legitimacy.[7]

The emphasis in modern scholarship on the failure of Reconstruction as a civil rights–race relations project implies that a realistic possibility of success existed in the postwar situation. This is an understandable response to the hopes and expectations generated by the civil rights movement. In the 1960s many historians studied the Civil War and Reconstruction conscious of the contribution they might make to the success of the second Reconstruction.[8] Two decades later, following the affirmative action revolution, the success of the second Reconstruction seemed unclear. Under the circumstances the history of the first Reconstruction became even more

---

[7] William Whatley Pierson, Jr., "Texas *Versus* White," *Southwestern Historical Quarterly*, 18 (1915), 17.

[8] Merton L. Dillon has noted the belief of many historians that the issue of racial justice, which the civil rights movement presented, was directly connected to events in the Civil War era. Referring to the participation of Civil War scholars in civil rights protest marches, Dillon wrote: "In this manner men whose careers focused on the study of past crises concerning race announced their intention to plunge into what many then regarded as the very eye of the twentieth century's racial storm" (*The Abolitionists: The Growth of a Dissenting Minority* [New York: W. W. Norton, 1979], p. vii). Harry V. Jaffa, reviewing Kenneth M. Stampp's revisionist history of Reconstruction, viewed the book as, "quite deliberately, a contribution to the consummation of the *new* Reconstruction, quite as much as it is an attempt to correct misunderstanding of the old" (*The Conditions of Freedom: Essays in Political Philosophy* [Baltimore: The Johns Hopkins University Press, 1975], p. 260). Stampp, it should be noted, said his purpose was to counteract the legend of Reconstruction as a tragic period of federal tyranny and Negro rule, by giving more currency to the findings of new scholarship (*The Era of Reconstruction, 1865–1877* [New York: Alfred A. Knopf, 1965], pp. vii–viii).

relevant. Revisionist historians assumed that Reconstruction was an enlightened civil rights policy which should have succeeded. If it could be shown, historically, that it *could* have succeeded, there was all the more reason to believe the open-ended goals of the second Reconstruction could be achieved. If, on the other hand, Reconstruction was doomed from the outset, if its failure was the inevitable result of the historical situation—including the theory on which the North fought the war—then pessimistic implications might be drawn about contemporary race relations.

The relevance of the past in shaping perceptions of present-day issues cannot be denied. Ultimately, however, the value of historical knowledge and understanding is not narrowly instrumental. Like knowledge in general, historical knowledge is an intrinsic good that provides the basis for practical reason. It is broadly practical—in the way that having a purchase on reality is practical.

The point of these observations is to suggest that there is a limit to the utilitarian value of Reconstruction history in relation to contemporary race relations. The story of Reconstruction politics and the civil rights settlement should be told for what it is worth as an account of the past, not as a precedent, model, or justification for any particular policy in the twentieth century. Nineteenth-century Reconstruction should not be overlaid on or confused with contemporary civil rights issues. When the differences between the affirmative action civil rights agenda and the assumptions and goals of the post–Civil War settlement are understood, Reconstruction can be viewed with greater detachment and objectivity. Without discounting the post-emancipation aspirations of the freed slaves, it becomes possible to see Reconstruction as a compromise settlement, shaped both by contingent factors and by essential features in the American political tradition, that marked significant though nonrevolutionary changes in politics, society, and the constitutional order.

II

Of the many aspects in which the problem of reconstruction presented itself, the political-constitutional was primary. Regardless of the extent of social and economic change, if the seceded states were not restored to the Union, Reconstruction would not have occurred. As a political and constitutional matter Reconstruction consisted of two main issues. The first was the status and rights of former officials and citizens of the Confederate states on the one hand, and the status and rights of the emancipated slaves on the other. The second issue was the nature and extent of governmental authority in the former seceded states. If the states were members of the Union, the resolution of these issues implicated and in some sense depended on the application of basic principles and rules defining the Union as a federal system. In a practical sense it was necessary to decide in what sense the members of the former Confederate states were states in the Union, as the theory of the war held.

From the point of view of those responsible for dealing with these issues, basic questions arose about which choices were required.[9] Could the Union of states be transformed into a sovereign nation-state, in the nature of a unitary or consolidated government of individuals? If it was not already, might it become, less radically, a federal state with new authority to regulate the personal liberty and rights of citizens and inhabitants of the states? The Civil War was not a revolution; the Union government fought the war for conservative ends. Nevertheless, in the opinion of many contemporaries as well as scholars, a revolutionary situation existed at the end of the war. Eric Foner, author of an acclaimed recent work on Reconstruction, writes: "like the [American] Revolution, Reconstruction was an era when the foundations of public life were thrown open for discussion."[10]

Although it is possible to determine retrospectively whether a rev-

---

[9] One can argue that the Civil War answered these questions. Harry V. Jaffa, for example, comparing the character of the Civil War as a political experience with that of Reconstruction, states: " . . . the Civil War was a period of nobility and heroism, not because human nature changed, and not because there wasn't just as much political corruption, but because great and fundamental decisions concerning the future of the American Republic were being made then: the indissolubility of the American Union, the end of chattel slavery, and the nationalization of American citizenship. Nothing so fundamental was being decided during Reconstruction, and probably nothing so fundamental could have been decided then" (*Conditions of Freedom*, p. 261). It seems to me that this view exaggerates the clarity of the military decision resulting from the Civil War, as a constitutional decision about the nature of the Union. The record of political controversy reflects awareness that although the war settled the question whether there would be one American nation or two, in the framing of Reconstruction amendments and measures there was opportunity, if not necessity, to make specific determinations about the nature of the constitutional order.

[10] Eric Foner, *Reconstruction: America's Unfinished Revolution, 1863–1877* (New York: Harper & Row, 1988), p. 278.

olutionary situation existed at a particular point in history, no agreed-upon measure exists to answer this question. In a phenomenological sense, revolution is the eruption or intrusion of violence into political and civil relations. Analytically, the decisive element defining a revolution is the withdrawal, disintegration, or loss of legitimate authority.[11] To the extent that political and governmental institutions are perceived as lacking legitimacy, or legitimate political authority is believed not to exist, a situation can be described as revolutionary. Although not simply political, it is a question that involves political judgment and is thus inherently controversial.

Among individuals, groups, and political parties of varying points of view in the postwar South the perception was widespread that political and governmental institutions were not legitimate. The Confederate state governments in place at the end of the war lacked legitimacy in the eyes of the victorious Unionists.[12] The state governments organized under President Andrew Johnson in 1865 were considered illegitimate by most Republicans. The authority of federal military and civilian officials in the South was not accepted as legitimate by many white southerners. And when governments in ten states of the former Confederacy were organized under the Military Reconstruction Act of 1867, by a new political party consisting almost exclusively of blacks and white northerners, the first task of these governments was to gain legitimacy in the eyes of the citizens of those states. More than at any time since the establishment of the federal government in 1789, circumstances made a revolutionary transformation of the constitutional order a practical possibility.

For most Americans in the nineteenth century the concept of revolution did not hold the appeal it does for many twentieth-century historians. Surveying postwar conditions, they tend to see a revolutionary situation offering the hope of democracy, social justice, and racial equality. Contemporaries were more impressed by the danger of disrupting traditional constitutional structures, forms, and relationships. In the view of nineteenth-century Americans, a revolution

---

[11] Chalmers Johnson, *Revolutionary Change* (Boston: Little, Brown, 1966), pp. 1, 114–15, 136.

[12] It was therefore remarkable that President Lincoln in April 1865, until his cabinet persuaded him otherwise, considered the possibility of using the Confederate government in Virginia, and presumably other states, to make peace terms and begin the process of reconstruction (Basler et al., eds., *Collected Works of Abraham Lincoln*, 8:389).

had already occurred when South Carolina and six other seceding states threw off the Union before Lincoln was inaugurated in 1861. When the Union government used military force to resist this change in the government of those states, four additional southern states seceded. This was revolution enough for most Americans. What was required after the war, as many in both sections understood the moment South Carolina seceded, was reorganization and reform of the constituent elements of American government, not a radical transformation of social values and institutions in the manner of twentieth-century revolutionary movements. Reconstruction was the issue facing Americans at the end of the Civil War, and most of them conceived of it in nonrevolutionary terms.

Considered abstractly, reconstruction is an ambiguous concept in that it is unclear whether the thing in question is to be reconstructed or rebuilt according to the plan and specifications of the original design. The concept is not ambiguous, however, insofar as it implies that destruction of a thing has occurred. In this sense reconstruction connotes loss, and raises the question whether the thing destroyed should be rebuilt. After secession began, the word 'reconstruction' was initially used by those who proposed to restructure political relationships between the American states. Southern secessionists and border-state accommodationists, anticipating reconstruction of the Union on revised constitutional terms, employed the concept.[13] Those who opposed constitutional revision objected to the language of reconstruction because it implied that the Union was dissolved.[14]

Perhaps because of its practical implications, Lincoln was averse to the language of reconstruction. He disliked especially the theoretical yet politically controversial question which discussion of reconstruction inevitably raised: namely, whether the seceded states were in or out of the Union. As noted, Lincoln viewed it "a merely pernicious abstraction" that was "practically immaterial" and "could have no effect other than the mischievous one of dividing our friends."[15]

---

[13] John Pendleton Kennedy, *The Border States: Their Power and Duty in the Present Disordered Condition of the Country* (N.p., 1860), pp. 34–35; David N. Potter, *Lincoln and His Party in the Secession Crisis* (New Haven, Conn.: Yale University Press, 1967), pp. 219–48.

[14] *Congressional Globe*, 36 Congress, 2 session, February 14, 1861, p. 909, remarks of Representative James H. Campbell.

[15] Basler et al., eds., *Collected Works of Abraham Lincoln*, 8:403.

Since everyone used the term, Lincoln had to also. Nevertheless, in referring to reconstruction he conveyed his dissatisfaction with the idea. Thus he spoke of "what is called reconstruction," referred to "*a* plan of re-construction (as the phrase goes)," and did not use the word in the text of his Proclamation of Amnesty and Reconstruction in December 1863.[16]

If the language of reconstruction was unavoidable, Lincoln nevertheless gave it the connotation of restoring the preexisting federal system. He spoke of "the re-inauguration of the national authority" and the need "to reinaugurate loyal State governments."[17] Language that might have implied revolutionary change, such as "framing a new State government," acquired a conservative cast when linked with the intention of "maintaining the political framework of the States," "the name of the State, the boundary, the subdivisions, the constitution, and the general code of laws" that existed before the war.[18] Restoration of previous political and constitutional arrangements was subject only to conditions stipulated in the Reconstruction Proclamation of December 1863. The most important of those conditions required reorganized state governments to recognize and declare the "permanent freedom" of emancipated slaves.[19]

III

In retrospect it is easy to see that the establishment of permanent freedom for millions of emancipated slaves was incompatible with the reinauguration of national and state authority according to the rules and practices of prewar federalism. The extent of this incompatibility was not clear at the time, and has been debatable ever since. The central constitutional issue in the postwar settlement, it can be taken as a measure of the revolutionary character of Reconstruction, either in the nineteenth-century sense of throwing off an existing government or in the modern sense of a radical transformation of social institutions and values intended to create a new order of liberty and equality.

As a principle of political organization, federalism depended on

---

[16] Ibid., 7:52–56, 8:401.
[17] Ibid., 8:400, 7:55.
[18] Ibid., 7:52.
[19] Ibid., 7:55–56.

the distinction between the objects and powers of the federal government and those of the state governments. This distinction was defensible more in practical than in theoretic terms. The authority of the federal government was limited to such general objects as diplomacy, war, and the regulation of commerce among the states and between the United States and other nations. The state governments had jurisdiction over the range of subjects falling within the sphere of municipal or local affairs. Although clear as an abstract principle, in practice this distinction was hard to maintain because both the federal and the state governments, according to liberal political theory, were genuine governments deriving their authority from the people as constituent power. Both governments therefore had authority to protect the natural rights of individuals, administer justice for the security of person and property, and promote the common good. Thus, while the federal and state governments were differentiated by the assignment of general and local objects respectively, from the standpoint of liberal political theory both governments shared the end of protecting natural rights and securing justice. If the dualistic structure of American government offered a double security for the rights of the people, it also encouraged conflict between the federal government and the states.

If it was hard to maintain a principled distinction between the objects and authority of the federal government and the states before the Civil War, it was all the more difficult in the postwar period. It is not too much to say that in the unsettled state of affairs, before the national authority was "reinaugurated" and state governments reorganized in the former Confederacy, the rule of generality and locality did not really exist.[20] Exacerbating the situation, and virtually guaranteeing conflict between the federal and the state governments, was the introduction of racial attitudes into political party competition after the abolition of slavery.

Although it is now generally agreed that race has always been a factor in American politics, the forms and effects of racial thinking have varied. If slavery was protected by a racist consensus, its abolition destroyed that consensus and made racism openly debatable.

---

[20] This is what the concept of "the grasp of war" was intended to convey. Asserting that the federal government held the seceded states in the "grasp of war," Republicans claimed this as a source of authority for intervening in the reconstruction of state governments (Benedict, "Problem of Constitutionalism and Constitutional Liberty in the Reconstruction South," p. 230).

Racial attitudes became a more clearly recognized and controversial element in partisan politics. This effect was enhanced or exaggerated by the problem of pretext and motive in the politics of federalism.

As noted, federalism depended on the distinction between generality and locality with respect to the objects and powers of the general and the state governments. Although this distinction was procedural insofar as it indicated the level of government that should decide a particular matter, it was substantive in the sense that failure to maintain the distinction could have consequences for the federal system. If the federal government gained too much power, consolidation would result. If the power of the states expanded too much, dissolution of the Union would occur. A concern to maintain the rule of generality and locality, upholding either federal or state power depending upon circumstances, was, therefore, a principled concern. It supplied a legitimate motive of political action in the federal system. However, since both federal and state governments were entitled to protect natural rights and secure the ends of justice and the common good, a claim to uphold the rule of generality and locality, expressed in the defense of either federal or state power, could be used as a pretext for political action to promote the substantive ends of liberty, justice, and the common good.

Historians have generally concluded that a consequence of the abolition of slavery was the interjection into politics of modern racism and racial ideology.[21] At the same time, an attempt was made, to some extent at least, to declare racial motive and purpose unlawful and illegitimate as the basis of public policy. Under the Fourteenth Amendment and the Civil Rights Acts of 1866 and 1870–71, for example, it was unlawful for states to make a distinction because of race in legislation respecting fundamental civil rights, and in the administration of justice concerning the security of persons and property. Litigation to enforce civil rights laws and constitutional amendments subsequently showed that it was difficult to prevent unlawful racial discrimination because, among other things, it was hard to determine whether a particular measure of government or act of a private individual was motivated by unlawful intent to discriminate on account of race. This practical difficulty was compli-

---

[21] Herbert G. Gutman, *The Black Family in Slavery and Freedom, 1750–1925* (New York: Pantheon, 1976), pp. 531–44.

cated by the problem of pretextual motive in the politics of federalism. Intent to maintain the rule of generality and locality was a legitimate motive in conflicts between the federal and the state governments. Logically and by rights, one might argue, it should not have been legitimate to use the federalism argument as a pretext for discrimination because of race. Yet in political competition and debate it was impossible to prevent such arguments from being made.

In the context of partisan competition, these factors influenced Reconstruction policy-making. If not perceived as having the same constitutional value as preserving the federal–state balance or protecting the natural rights of citizens, partisan activity—what is often pejoratively described as "politics as usual"—was unquestionably legitimate. Moreover, it was lawful, if not noble and high-minded, to assert a claim to uphold the federal principle as a pretext for gaining partisan advantage, or to appeal to partisanship as a pretext for maintaining the federal–state balance. When racial motives began to serve a politically expressive purpose after the abolition of slavery, the possibilities for mixing and confusing constitutional principle, natural rights and justice, and partisanship as grounds for political action increased exponentially.[22] For these reasons, to say nothing of the demands imposed by social and economic disruption, Reconstruction policy was formulated in a volatile and unstable environment in which legitimate authority was questionable or did not clearly exist.

IV

Postwar conditions can be seen as offering either the promise of a revolutionary transformation of political, constitutional, and social values and institutions, or the conservative alternative of reconstruction of the polity on the basis of existing political and constitutional principles. In either of these perspectives, the task of guaranteeing the permanent freedom of the emancipated slaves appeared daunt-

---

[22] The idea of political action having an expressive purpose refers to the attempt of a partisan organization to win support by affirming the core values and principles of its constituent groups. It is contrasted to a competitive strategy which seeks support by appealing to the interests of uncommitted or nonaligned groups (Michael Perman, *The Road to Redemption: Southern Politics, 1869–1879* [Chapel Hill: University of North Carolina Press, 1984], pp. 23–24).

ing in view of widespread, though not universal, hostility or indiffer-
ence toward blacks arising from prevailing racial attitudes.

Viewed from the perspective of the affirmative action revolution
in contemporary civil rights policy, the guarantee of permanent freedom for black Americans was fundamentally incompatible with preservation of the federal–state balance. Even if the federal government
did not categorically displace the state governments with respect to
the regulation of personal liberty and civil rights, the constitutional
meaning of Reconstruction was that it had authority to do so whenever it was necessary to guarantee the permanent freedom of black
citizens. In the conservative view of reconstruction as a reform of
the federal system, the guarantee of civil rights for blacks was consistent with, if not required by, original constitutional principles.
Grounded in natural rights philosophy, those principles, as understood by Republicans in the Civil War era, applied as a matter of
right throughout the United States, although the existence of slavery limited the scope of their application in practical terms. Completing the extension of liberty as a fundamental right that was
implied in wartime emancipation, reconstruction was intended to
affirm the "new birth of freedom" proclaimed by Lincoln in the
Gettysburg Address. This meant realizing or making operational, in
relation to a class of people to whom it had practically been denied,
the principle of the natural equality of individuals. Lincoln's words
at Gettysburg did not refer to a new concept of freedom hitherto
unknown in the world.[23]

As seen in previous chapters, the revolutionary and conservative
perspectives provide the theoretical framework for traditional and
revisionist interpretations of Reconstruction in the twentieth century. Recent historiography continues to reflect these perspectives.
What distinguishes much recent scholarship, perhaps even more
than earlier accounts, is its ideologically committed, presentist character.

It is easy to see in retrospect that writing about Reconstruction in
the early twentieth century, notwithstanding prevailing assumptions
about scientific history, was influenced by contemporary social concerns. The same can be said of revisionist history written in the era

---

[23] It was in the progressive era of the early twentieth century that reformers
introduced the language of a "new freedom," implying something fundamentally
different from the old freedom of the Founding.

of the civil rights movement. A generation later, when the idea of historical objectivity is disavowed by professional scholars,[24] there is all the more reason why Reconstruction history should reflect presentist concerns. When historians in principle deny the ideal of objectivity and detachment, it becomes all the more difficult to establish the relevant context in which past events are to be considered.

As the concerns of the civil rights movement have been absorbed in multiculturalism, events in the past are studied with heightened emphasis on the social context of racism, sexism, and class relations. Racism, most pertinent for the present discussion, tends to be viewed as a pervasive social and cultural force that has no real limits. The effect is to transform race as a contextual factor into an essential principle of social organization. Racism becomes foundational and transcendent, assuming different forms in changing historical circumstances.[25] From this perspective, the events of Reconstruction can be studied both in historical context and with a view toward influencing contemporary civil rights policy. While recognizing that in a formal sense slavery was abolished at the end of the Civil War, it can be argued that as long as racism exists, slavery in effect still exists, and the permanent freedom of black Americans is denied. Beyond a professional concern to provide a contextually grounded account, this perception imparts into historical scholarship a desire to provide a right moral understanding of Reconstruction applicable to present-day race relations.

This approach can be seen in the revolutionary interpretation of Reconstruction advanced by David A. J. Richards. Richards argues that because the Constitution tolerated slavery, it became decadent and in need of purification and regeneration. In his view, abolitionist moral philosophy was the regenerative force that, in the form of the Reconstruction amendments, revolutionized the Constitution. The Fourteenth Amendment in particular introduced a new political theory of human rights into the fundamental law. Directed at the courts, it expressed a constitutional imperative requiring that the Reconstruction amendments be given the broadest possible interpretation to provide maximum protection for human rights. According to Richards, the revolutionary constitutionalism of the

---

[24] Peter Novick, *That Noble Dream: The "Objectivity Question" and the American Historical Profession* (Cambridge and New York: Cambridge University Press, 1988).

[25] Paul M. Sniderman and Thomas Piazza, *The Scar of Race* (Cambridge: Harvard University Press, 1993), pp. 56–63.

Reconstruction amendments embodies a theory of redistributive justice, conferring economic rights of provision as constitutional guarantees of minimum welfare entitlements.[26]

A recent statement of the liberal revisionist view of Reconstruction is William E. Nelson's study of the Fourteenth Amendment. Writing in the tradition of Howard Jay Graham and Jacobus Ten Broek, Nelson emphasizes the origins of the amendment in the egalitarian ideology of the abolitionists. The embodiment of the equality principle in Section 1 of the Fourteenth Amendment, however, was ambiguous. Written in vague and imprecise language, the amendment was in essence a Republican campaign platform intended to express in rhetorical form the political value that the idea of equality had for all Americans. Because Americans disagreed on how the equality principle should be applied in specific circumstances, its framers and supporters were unwilling to say what the equality principle required with respect to legal guarantees of rights, or what precise limits the amendment imposed on state authority to regulate civil rights. Nelson concludes that in the immediate historical context, the Fourteenth Amendment, a model of ambiguity, was not meant to be applied by courts as a determinative legal text to resolve conflicts over civil rights. Judicial application of the amendment, in effect construing it as a new charter of liberty and equality, would come in the twentieth century in the form of judicial policy-making, which Congress must be presumed to have anticipated and approved by inserting into the text the open-ended language of the due process and equal protection clauses.[27]

Nelson objects that historical research into constitutional original intent is used to support preconceived judicial decisions based on contemporary policy choices. To counteract this distortion of history, Nelson proposes a more genuinely historical analysis. Yet his principal conclusion—that the Fourteenth Amendment was not intended to limit or provide guidance for judges in deciding cases—conflicts with the historical fact that the Constitution was a normative text, intended to have a prescriptive and configurative effect on political life and the conduct of government. Nelson offers his account for

---

[26] David A. J. Richards, *Conscience and the Constitution: History, Theory, and Law of the Reconstruction Amendments* (Princeton, N.J.: Princeton University Press, 1993), pp. 108–48, 233–51.

[27] William E. Nelson, *The Fourteenth Amendment: From Political Principle to Judicial Doctrine* (Cambridge, Mass.: Harvard University Press, 1988), pp. 3–11.

its purely historical value in resolving scholarly controversy over the revolutionary or conservative nature of the Fourteenth Amendment. His ultimate purpose, however, is to bridge the gap between the constitutional world of the nineteenth century and that of the twentieth century so "the intentions of the framers can control contemporary adjudication."[28]

The conservative perspective in recent scholarship is represented by Earl M. Maltz's *Civil Rights, the Constitution, and Congress, 1863–1869* (1990). Maltz sees Reconstruction as a process of reallocation of constitutional authority that projected federal authority into areas hitherto reserved exclusively to the states. After the Thirteenth Amendment abolished slavery, the Fourteenth Amendment revised federal–state relations by defining United States citizenship and guaranteeing protection of fundamental civil rights without regard to race. The broad language of Section 1 of the amendment provided constitutional authority for the protection of specific rights enumerated in the Civil Rights Act of 1866. Viewing racism as the most important factor in the political context of Reconstruction, Maltz emphasizes the extent to which racial attitudes limited the scope of the Reconstruction settlement. Civil rights policy was not based on a utopian aspiration to eliminate all racial distinctions in the society. Its purpose was to establish racially impartial protection of fundamental rights, referred to by Maltz as limited absolute equality. Far from having an open-ended revolutionary intent, the Fourteenth Amendment was conceived of as an extension of original constitutional principles. Maltz, too, as a constitutional lawyer, presents his findings with a view toward validating original intent jurisprudence as a method of constitutional decision-making.[29]

Whether reflecting a revolutionary or conservative perspective, these accounts agree that Reconstruction included a major civil rights component. Although none views Reconstruction civil rights policy as completely successful, they recognize that the postwar settlement marked substantial improvement in the condition of the country's black population. Confirming this conclusion is Eric Fon-

---

[28] Ibid., pp. 11–12.

[29] Earl M. Maltz, *Civil Rights, the Constitution, and Congress, 1863–1869* (Lawrence: University Press of Kansas, 1990), pp. ix–xii. The conservative view of Reconstruction is also illustrated in Michael W. McConnell, "The Fourteenth Amendment: A Second American Revolution or the Logical Culmination of the Tradition?" *Loyola of Los Angeles Law Review*, 25 (1992), 1159–76.

er's *Reconstruction: America's Unfinished Revolution, 1863–1877* (1988), a synthesis of modern revisionist scholarship that underscores the positive aspects of Reconstruction as the seminal political experience in the history of American blacks.

Foner views Reconstruction as a liberal republican revolution rooted in the American political tradition. While appreciating the concern of radical "new orthodoxy" scholars for economic redistribution, Foner argues that politics, at least in the historical situation facing the freedmen in 1865, was more important than economics. Acting as a new social class in southern society, the freed people mobilized themselves for political action within the ideological framework of small-producer republicanism. They made significant social gains by utilizing church, school, and fraternal and civic organizations available to them for the first time. By exercising the rights of citizens, blacks "Americanized" themselves. Foner concludes that Reconstruction transformed the lives of southern blacks, reducing the gap between the conditions of African-American life and the white society into which they were integrated.[30]

V

Inquiry into the black political experience in the Civil War era focuses on three basic questions: What was the nature of Reconstruction politics in the South? What, if anything, was accomplished by and for the emancipated black population? How and why did Reconstruction come to an end in 1877?

To revisionist historians of the 1960s no explanation was needed to show that Reconstruction had failed. The conclusion was self-evident in the system of racial segregation and discrimination that was established in the late nineteenth and early twentieth centuries. Nevertheless, emphasis on the failure of Reconstruction implied that a contrary result might have obtained, logically requiring a definition of successful reconstruction and how it might have occurred. Foner, probably expressing the view of most historians, defined successful reconstruction in relation to the goals of securing

---

[30] Foner, *Reconstruction, 1863–1877*, pp. 346–411, 602–12; Foner, "Reconstruction Revisited," in *The Promise of American History: Progress and Prospects*, ed. S. Kutler and S. Katz (Baltimore: The Johns Hopkins University Press, 1982), pp. 82–112.

blacks' rights as citizens and free laborers and establishing an enduring Republican party presence in the South.[31] Presumably this
meant a revival of normal democratic politics in a competitive two-
party system, in a social atmosphere purged of racism, under state
governments restored to their proper practical relations to the
Union.

Considering the use of states' rights to impose second-class citizenship on blacks after the end of Reconstruction, it may seem historically counterintuitive to say that successful civil rights
enforcement could ever depend on the resumption of normal political competition in the South. It is nevertheless true that partisan
competition at the national level was critical to the success of the
civil rights movement in the 1960s. Furthermore, although it took
far longer to establish than anyone at the time imagined, a competitive two-party system in the South has been beneficial to black social
progress since then. Belief in the value of political competition for
civil rights enforcement was, therefore, a sound assumption of Reconstruction policy. Yet it is hard to resist the conclusion that social
and cultural attitudes in the nineteenth century made it impossible
to combine or reconcile partisan competition, or politics as usual,
with the protection of civil rights.

The history of government and politics in the Reconstruction
South divides into three phases: the presidentially created governments of 1865–66, the state governments organized under the Reconstruction Acts of 1867–68, and the political process known as
"Redemption," whereby white conservatives, acting through the
Democratic party, gained control of the reconstructed state governments. In the second of these phases, the reorganized state governments under Republican control sought to protect the civil rights of
black citizens and win acceptance for the party as a legitimate political association. The Reconstruction governments faced overwhelm-
ing obstacles, however, which made accomplishment of these goals
practically impossible.

The most problematic element was the character of the Republican party as an organization of "outsiders." Consisting of blacks and
northern whites, with only a small proportion of southern whites, the
party did not receive the presumptive legitimacy accorded political
groups indigenous to the community. This circumstance resulted

---

[31] Foner, *Reconstruction, 1863–1877*, p. 602.

from the fact that the Republican party did not develop spontane-ously in response to local conditions, but was in effect created by federal legislation.[32] The party advocated suffrage for blacks not only as an act of justice, but also as an expedient measure on which its existence depended. The Republican organization proposed to abandon—or to prevent from being established—the color line that emerged as a basic feature of southern politics following the aboli-tion of slavery.

After state governments were formed under the Military Recon-struction Act of 1867, the Democratic and Republican parties, de-spite their different racial constituencies, initially competed on the basis of rational interest-group appeals. Before long, however, as the social reality of changing race relations had its effect, the appeal to race became irresistible. From 1872 to 1876, openly and aggressively, the Democrats became a white supremacist party and the Republi-cans a pro-black party.

The central issue in southern Reconstruction politics was whether the restoration of conservative white political control was politically and constitutionally legitimate, or illegitimate because based on force and violence. This question forms part of the larger interpre-tive problem of the failure of Reconstruction: Was Republican post-war policy a sound program for reuniting the nation and modernizing southern society, which failed because it was overcome by superior force? Or did Reconstruction end when the North lost interest in the task of reforming southern society, withdrawing support for a program that was morally questionable and constitutionally un-sound?

To consider the former interpretation, the legitimacy of the Re-deemer governments of the 1870s can be questioned on the ground that white conservative political action depended on violence—either acts of pure and simple terrorism such as were perpetrated by the Ku Klux Klan and other groups, or more refined methods of physical and psychological intimidation and coercion.[33] According to this interpretation, conservative white politicians believed that "power *did* flow from the barrel of a gun," and peace was war carried on by other means.[34] To say that Reconstruction politics was a form

---

[32] Perman, *Road to Redemption*, p. 23.

[33] George C. Rable, *But There Was No Peace: The Role of Violence in the Politics of Reconstruction* (Athens: University of Georgia Press, 1984).

[34] James M. McPherson, "Redemption or Counterrevolution? The South in the 1870s," *Reviews in American History*, 13 (1985), 549.

of guerrilla warfare, however, may imply more than proponents of this interpretation intend. It suggests that laying down arms in 1865 was only a formality; in reality the war continued. If so, it is reasonable to assume not only that both sides in the political battles of Reconstruction employed violent means appropriate to war, but also that it was legitimate to do so.[35]

A more balanced view of Reconstruction politics, taking into account the ambiguities in the historical situation, recognizes politicians' concern for the legality and legitimacy characteristic of normal politics. In this regard it is pertinent to observe that Klan terrorism—if it can accurately be described as having a rational political purpose—was ineffective as a means of restoring conservative white elites to political control.[36] After the experience of the Ku Klux Klan, the Democratic party, using an expressive electoral strategy, sought to regain political control by making an overt appeal to constituents on racial grounds. The party also adopted techniques for winning elections more in conformity with accepted standards of legality governing electoral competition. According to Michael Perman, whose account captures the ambiguity in the situation, Democrats were "desperate yet traditional politicians" whose aim, in part, was to use violent and illegal means in order to win power legitimately, through the electoral process.[37] The restoration of "home rule" by white southerners was at least to be given the appearance of legitimacy.

A leading motive of southern Democrats was to regulate the civil rights of the black population as an inferior class in society. On this basis alone the political process known as Redemption, or counter reconstruction as it is referred to in some accounts, can be considered morally illegitimate. At some point, however, for individuals living under a government of questionable authority as well as in the view of an outside observer, the appearance of legitimacy may become the fact or reality of legitimacy.

The nature of legitimacy and how it comes into existence resists

---

[35] Michael Les Benedict, *The Fruits of Victory: Alternatives in Restoring the Union, 1865–1877*, rev. ed. (Lanham, Md.: University Press of America, 1986), p. 63.

[36] Michael Perman, "Counter Reconstruction," in *The Facts of Reconstruction: Essays in Honor of John Hope Franklin*, ed. Eric Anderson and Alfred A. Moss (Baton Rouge: Louisiana State University Press, 1991), p. 129. Concerning the aims of the Klan, Foner says its "purposes were political, but political in the broadest sense" of affecting power relations throughout the South, both in the public and in the private spheres (*Reconstruction, 1863-1877*, p. 425).

[37] Perman, "Counter Reconstruction," p. 132.

the method of historical explanation, limited as it is to empirical observation and required, to some extent at least, to understand historical actors as they understood themselves. This helps explain why most historians have viewed the end of Reconstruction, not-withstanding elements of coercion and intimidation in the situation, as the outcome of legitimate political competition. This conclusion probably reflects the understanding most historians have of political legitimacy, which Eric Foner expresses when he writes: "Like beauty, political legitimacy resides in the eyes of the beholder."[38] Legitimacy, in other words, is a subjective, personal experience not susceptible to judgment by objective standards. Whether or not this is true, in the American political tradition judgments about legiti-macy are political and inescapably controversial, revolving as they do around the contested principles of equality and consent.

The nature and legitimacy of Reconstruction politics, to return to our point of departure, is fundamentally related to the perspective one assumes on the Civil War. If the war was really a war between belligerent states, then the central issue in Reconstruction politics can be viewed as the restoration of "home rule" or local self-govern-ment by the defeated Confederates. In a somewhat different sense, this is also true if the war is viewed as a conflict over the terms, conditions, and forms of association in a reorganized American state system. Under either aspect, Reconstruction concerned the south-ern white attempt, beginning in the antebellum period and pursued in a revolutionary manner in the secession movement, to achieve political autonomy.[39]

Democrats viewed the Republican Reconstruction governments as alien impositions, and blacks as a social class not entitled to a permanent role in the political community.[40] Republicans, seeking to create a political order in the South in conformity with the na-tion's founding principles, had reason to regard the Democratic party in equivalent terms as illegitimate. To the extent that they did not view Democrats—in something close to belligerent terms—as an enemy, their political strategy may have been unwise.[41] Without pre-

---

[38] Foner, *Reconstruction, 1863–1877*, p. 346.

[39] Perman, "Counter Reconstruction," p. 139.

[40] Foner, *Reconstruction, 1863–1877*, p. 346.

[41] Seeking to account for the failure of blacks to respond to the terrorist attacks of the Ku Klux Klan, Foner writes: "Perhaps the problem was that Republicans, black and white, took democratic processes more seriously than their opponents." Observing that the legacy of slavery did not produce a broad tradition of violent

suming to judge the moral equivalency of the contending factions in the half-war of Reconstruction politics, it is enough to observe historically the operation of a political system in which legality and legitimacy were complicated with tendencies toward force and violence, more so than is usually the case in American politics.

VI

Americans' continuing effort to understand the Civil War transcends the question of blame or responsibility for causing the war. The more basic issue, more than tangentially related to contemporary race relations, is whether significant good came of the war—or at least enough to justify the cost, including the political methods of Reconstruction.

The war established that southern republican liberty, based on slavery, was not legitimate republican liberty in the sense of the Constitution. This was an intrinsic good, but its practical significance depended on the guarantee of the permanent freedom of the country's black population. Although a policy aiming at this end could be considered a long-range implication of the policy of wartime emancipation, it was not the principal purpose of the war. Public opinion was therefore not prepared to accept a comprehensive radical program of constitutionally prescribed racial equality simply as a matter of course. Republican civil rights policy attempted far less than this. Yet it encountered social, economic and cultural obstacles that blocked its implementation. This circumstance has led proponents of the "new orthodoxy" interpretation, discussed in a previous chapter, to conclude that no really significant changes occurred in southern politics and society as a result of Reconstruction. But this view is mistaken. The policy of extending the original constitutional principle of national limitation of states' rights, in order to protect citizens' natural rights, would not have been so passionately contested had it been understood as merely a formal, rhetorical, or symbolic matter, rather than a matter of urgent practical import.

---

retaliation against abuse, he says this may explain why Republicans did not respond in kind to violent attacks. A possible implication of this analysis is that resistance to terrorism would have been reasonable and justifiable. The practical obstacles to armed resistance were so formidable, however, Foner adds, that " the failure of nerve, if such it was, extended up and down the Republican hierarchy, and was not confined to one race" (ibid., p. 436).

The fundamental rights of personal liberty, labor, property, and family were of incalculable practical value. And although the exercise of these rights by blacks was often forcefully impeded, the rights were not extinguished at the end of Reconstruction. It is true that within a generation the right to vote was denied to blacks in the southern states. It was upheld in the rest of the country, however, and in the twentieth century was the main instrument by which social and economic changes, and more enlightened racial attitudes outside the South, were given political expression in national civil rights policy. In broad outline and in essential content, the civil rights movement of the 1960s aimed at the fulfillment of Reconstruction constitutional principles.[42]

The civil rights acts of the 1960s were widely perceived, however, not merely as the completion of nineteenth-century Reconstruction, but also as constituting a second Reconstruction. The affirmative action revolution, calling for racial group preference as a means of enforcing the equality principle, raised the question whether these laws were intended to transform and go beyond the objects of the first Reconstruction. In the dialectical manner of historical scholarship, this question focused attention, again, on the reasons for the failure of the postwar settlement. Historians asked whether Reconstruction was a soundly conceived civil rights policy that was overthrown by racist violence, or a flawed policy that failed because it was inadequate as a guarantee of the permanent freedom of black Americans.

In seeking the overthrow of racial segregation, the civil rights movement and the revisionist historiography that supported it viewed Reconstruction as sound policy that was limited in practice by prescriptive racism and conservative attachment to states' rights. In contrast, new orthodoxy historians held that Reconstruction civil rights policy was flawed because it failed to redistribute property as the basis of genuine liberty for the freed blacks. If economic redistribution and transfer of wealth were still needed in the late twentieth century, then completion of a misconceived first Reconstruction was all the less adequate for securing the permanent freedom of black Americans.

---

[42] Richard P. Young and Jerome S. Burstein, "Federalism and the Demise of Prescriptive Racism in the United States," *Studies in American Political Development*, 9 (1995), 1–54.

Foner's synthesis of modern Reconstruction scholarship reflected the intellectual tensions produced by the civil rights ideology of the second Reconstruction. At one level Foner questioned the new orthodoxy interpretation by stressing the political–constitutional reforms of Reconstruction that permitted an authentic black republicanism to develop. At a deeper level, however, Foner adopted the assumptions of the new orthodoxy in stating that free labor ideology, a key component of the small-producer republicanism created by black political action, was inadequate to the needs of the freed people as a new social class.[43] He argued that free labor ideology, as a theory of political economy, was irrelevant to post-emancipation social realities because it assumed that the interests of the black laboring class and white planter-employers were compatible. In historical context, Foner said, free labor ideology was an unrealistic social theory that in practical terms resulted in a policy of coercion.[44]

Like the new orthodoxy historians, Foner assumes that a realistic alternative to the free market political economy existed after the Civil War. A better policy would have been to make blacks owners of productive property, an outcome for which radical government action was required. Foner critically observes, however, that most Republicans, including Radicals, failed to grasp this alternative because they continued to believe in free labor ideology. Foner concludes that Reconstruction was inherently flawed to the extent that it did not go "beyond equality" and engage the "questions of class relations" that were crucial to securing the permanent freedom of the emancipated slaves.[45] Reconstruction is America's "unfinished revolution," and completing it will require a transformation of the concept of equal opportunity.

In the view of many civil rights strategists, race-conscious affirmative action promised the transformation of equality needed to overcome the limitations of free market ideology that caused the failure of the first Reconstruction. To justify the affirmative action revolution, several legal scholars claimed to discover its roots in the Freedmen's Bureau policies, civil rights laws, and constitutional amendments of the 1860s.[46] The use of Reconstruction history to

---

[43] Foner, *Reconstruction, 1863–1877*, p. 144.

[44] Ibid., pp. 156, 164.

[45] Ibid., pp. 236–37.

[46] Eric Schnapper, "Affirmative Action and the Legislative History of the Fourteenth Amendment," *Virginia Law Review*, 71 (1985), 753–98; James E. Jones, Jr.,

support contemporary civil rights policy was further evident in the submission, in a major racial discrimination case, of historical research claiming to prove that the post–Civil War constitutional settlement prohibited private racial discrimination.[47]

Whatever its merit as a legal strategy, the attempt to justify affirmative action racial preference on the basis of the Reconstruction amendments is historically unconvincing. Intended to guarantee the permanent freedom of the emancipated slaves, the tenor of Reconstruction laws and amendments was to eliminate race as a condition of civil liberty. Sensitive to the racial attitudes of their constituents, the Republican majority did not presume categorically to prohibit racial reference and classification in the organization of society. For that reason, in the debate over how to formulate the party's antidiscrimination purpose, the language of equal protection of the laws was preferred to that of nondiscrimination by race.[48] No Republican affirmed preferential treatment for blacks either as the practical purpose or the essential principle of civil rights policy. The only contemporary evidence linking Reconstruction policy with racial group preference came from Democratic opponents of civil rights legislation.[49]

VII

For many scholars in the 1960s the goal of providing a true account of the past coincided with the ends of racial justice and equality. A

"The Rise and Fall of Affirmative Action," in *Race in America: The Struggle for Equality*, ed. Herbert Hill and James E. Jones, Jr. (Madison: University of Wisconsin Press, 1993), pp. 345–69. Historical argument for the Reconstruction origins of affirmative action was included in the opinion of Justice Thurgood Marshall in *Regents of the University of California v. Bakke*, 438 U.S. 265 (1978), at 398.

[47] See Brief *Amicus Curiae* of Eric Foner, John Hope Franklin, Louis R. Harlan, Stanley N. Katz, Leon F. Litwack, C. Vann Woodward, and Mary Frances Berry in the case of *Brenda Patterson* v. *McLean Credit Union*, Supreme Court of the United States, October term 1987. Tension between the requirements of scholarly accuracy and the demands of legal-historical advocacy, as seen in the writing of Eric Foner in particular, is noted by Randall Kennedy, "Reconstruction and the Politics of Scholarship," *Yale Law Journal*, 98 (1989), 536–38.

[48] Andrew Kull, *The Color-Blind Constitution* (Cambridge, Mass.: Harvard University Press, 1992), pp. 53–87.

[49] Paul Moreno, "Racial Classifications and Reconstruction Legislation," *Journal of Southern History*, 61 (1995), 283–84.

generation later the confidence with which historians presumed to apply insights gained from study of the past in the cause of improved race relations seems misplaced, if understandable. Nevertheless, although the "American dilemma" has not been resolved, changes in American and world politics afford a perspective from which a deeper understanding of the fundamental issues in the Civil War is possible.

More than anyone at the time could appreciate, the revisionist interpretation of Reconstruction in the 1960s reflected the assumptions of the modern liberal nationalist consensus. Basic to this outlook was the aspiration toward egalitarian redistribution of wealth that inspired liberal democratic polities in both Europe and America in the age of the Great Depression and World War II. A generation later, in the light of the failure of socialism in Europe and growing opposition to statist liberalism in the United States, this aspiration is less realistic. It is less likely to be projected back into the past as a way of influencing the present. The result is that historians are able to see more clearly the enduring appeal of the principles of private property, individual rights, the economic market, and limited government in the American political tradition. In the Civil War era this is illustrated in the focus on free labor ideology, natural rights republicanism, the equality of individuals, and federalism as central themes in the Reconstruction settlement. Although evaluation of these issues may differ, recognition of their salience and priority in the accounts of radical as well as conservative scholars shows the continuity of Civil War constitutionalism with the principles of the Founding, far more than it anticipates the political-constitutional world of the twentieth century.

At the end of Reconstruction, as at the Founding, the principles of equality and consent formed the ground of legitimacy in American politics. Compared to the prewar Union, the equality of individuals rather than states was more prominent as the predicate of the consent principle on which legitimacy depended. The equality of states in the Union and states' rights were derived from the natural equality of individuals posited in social contract theory. The abolition of slavery removed the major obstacle in the original Constitution to the extension of the equality principle to the country's black population. In the Reconstruction amendments this recognition of individual equality came at the expense of state equality. It did not, however, transform the Union into a unitary government of individuals. "The Constitution, in all its provisions," declared the Supreme Court in *Texas v. White*, "looks to an indestructible Union, composed of indestructible States."[50] This meant that secession was unconstitutional, on the ground that the Union was a government of equal individuals united by the principle of consent. And it meant that consolidation was unconstitutional in virtue of the fact that the Union was a political association based on state equality and consent.

From the end of Reconstruction until the mid-twentieth century, conflicts over equality and consent, in the Civil War context of federalism, race relations, and civil rights, occurred only on the margins of American politics. By the 1950s the legitimacy of the Reconstruction settlement was questionable, and in the civil rights acts of the 1960s it was repudiated. What appeared to be a new civil rights settlement, however, based on the principle of individual equality, proved fragile and unstable in the face of the affirmative action revolution. This unexpected development destroyed the sense of historical parallelism and continuity between the Reconstruction settlement and modern civil rights policy. However painful this realization has been, it has made it possible to see Reconstruction more clearly as a form of limited-government constitutionalism concerned with the equality and consent of states in federalism, and the equality and consent of individuals in laissez-faire liberty.

---

[50] 7 *Wallace* 725 (1869).

BIBLIOGRAPHY

ARTICLES

Abbott, Richard H. "Massachusetts and the Recruitment of Southern Negroes, 1863–65." *Civil War History*, 14 (September 1968).

Alvis, John. "The Slavery Provisions of the U.S. Constitution: Means for Emancipation." *Political Science Reviewer*, 17 (1987), 241–65.

Belz, Herman. "Abraham Lincoln and American Constitutionalism." *The Review of Politics*, 50 (Spring 1988), 169–97.

———. "The New Orthodoxy in Reconstruction Historiography." *Reviews in American History*, 1 (1973), 103–13.

Benedict, Michael Les. "Preserving Federalism: Reconstruction and the Waite Court." *Supreme Court Review* (1978), 39–79.

———. "Preserving the Constitution: The Conservative Basis of Radical Reconstruction." *Journal of American History*, 61 (1974), 65–90.

Bernard, Kenneth A. "Lincoln and Civil Liberties." *Abraham Lincoln Quarterly*, 6 (September 1951), 374–99.

Berns, Walter. "Comment: Equality as a Constitutional Concept." *Maryland Law Review*, 44 (1987), 22–27.

Bestor, Arthur. "The American Civil War as a Constitutional Crisis." *American Historical Review*, 69 (January 1964), 327–52.

Bickel, Alexander M. "The Original Understanding and the Segregation Decision." *Harvard Law Review*, 69 (1955), 1–65.

Black, Charles L., Jr. "The Lawfulness of the Segregation Decision." *Yale Law Journal*, 69 (1960), 421–30.

Boucher, David. "Language, Politics, and Paradigms: Pocock and the Study of Political Thought." *Polity*, 17 (Summer 1985), 761–76.

Bradford, M. E. "The Lincoln Legacy: A Long View." *Modern Age*, 24 (Fall 1980), 355–63.

Call, Joseph L. "The Fourteenth Amendment and Its Skeptical Background." *Baylor Law Review*, 13 (1961), 1–20.

Cohen, William. "Negro Involuntary Servitude in the South, 1865–1941: A Preliminary Analysis." *Journal of Southern History*, 42 (1976), 31–60.

Cole, A. C. "Lincoln and the American Tradition of Civil Liberty." *Illinois State Historical Society Journal*, 19 (October 1926–January 1927), 102–14.

Commager, Henry Steele. "The Constitution: Was It an Economic Document?" *American Heritage*, 10 (1958), 58–61.

"The Constitution: Written and Unwritten." *The American Review: A Whig Journal of Politics, Literature, Art, and Science*, 6 (July 1847), 1–3.

Corlett, William S., Jr. "The Availability of Lincoln's Political Religion." *Political Theory*, 10 (November 1983), 520–40.

Cox, LaWanda. "The Promise of Land for the Freedmen." *Mississippi Valley Historical Review*, 45 (December 1958), 413–40.

Current, Richard N. "Lincoln After 175 Years: The Myth of the Jealous Son." *Papers of the Abraham Lincoln Association*, 6 (1984), 15–24.

———. "The Lincoln Presidents." *Presidential Studies Quarterly*, 9 (Winter 1979), 25–35.

Davis, James Chowning. "Lincoln: The Saint and the Man." *Presidential Studies Quarterly*, 17 (Winter 1987), 71–94.

Dean, Eric T., Jr. "Rethinking the Civil War: Beyond 'Revolutions,' 'Reconstructions,' and the 'New Social History.'" *Southern Historian*, 15 (1994), 28–50.

Diamond, Raymond T. "No Call to Glory: Thurgood Marshall's Thesis on the Intent of a Pro-Slavery Constitution." *Vanderbilt Law Review*, 42 (1989), 93–131.

Dimond, Paul P. "Strict Construction and Judicial Review of Racial Discrimination Under the Equal Protection Clause: Meeting Raoul Berger on Interpretivist Grounds." *Michigan Law Review*, 80 (1982), 462–511.

Douglass, Frederick. "Reconstruction." *Atlantic Monthly* (December 1866), 761–65.

Dowd, Morgan D. "Lincoln, the Rule of Law, and Crisis Government: A Study of His Constitutional Law Theories." *University of Detroit Law Journal*, 39 (June 1962), 633–49.

Eden, Robert. "Tocqueville on Political Realignment and Constitutional Forms." *The Review of Politics*, 48 (Summer 1986), 349–73.

Engeman, Thomas S. "Assessing Jaffa's Contribution." *The Review of Politics*, 49 (Winter 1987), 127–30.

———. "Presidential Statesmanship and the Constitution: The Limits of Presidential Studies." *The Review of Politics*, 44 (April 1982), 266–81.

Eskridge, William N., and Philip Frickey, "Statutory Interpretation as Practical Reasoning." *Stanford Law Review*, 42 (1990), 321–84.

Fehrenbacher, Don E. "The Anti-Lincoln Tradition." *Papers of the Abraham Lincoln Association*, 4 (1982), 7–28.

———. "Only His Stepchildren: Lincoln and the Negro." *Civil War History*, 20 (December 1974), 293–310.

Fernandez, Ferdinand F. "The Constitutionality of the Fourteenth Amendment." *Southern California Law Review*, 39 (1966), 378–407.

Finkelman, Paul. "Prelude to the Fourteenth Amendment: Black Legal

Rights in the Antebellum North." *Rutgers Law Journal*, 17 (1986), 415–82.

Fisher, Sydney George. "The Suspension of Habeas Corpus During the War of the Rebellion." *Political Science Quarterly*, 3 (September 1888), 454–85.

Foner, Eric. "The Causes of the American Civil War: Recent Interpretations and New Directions." *Civil War History*, 20 (1974), 197–214.

———. "Reconstruction Revisited." *Reviews in American History*, 10 (December 1982), 82–100.

Ford, Henry Jones. "The Growth of Dictatorship." *Atlantic Monthly*, 121 (1918), 632–40.

Frank, John P., and Robert F. Munro. "The Original Understanding of 'Equal Protection of the Laws.'" *Columbia Law Review*, 50 (1950), 131–69.

Frantz, Laurent B. "Congressional Power to Enforce the Fourteenth Amendment Against Private Acts." *Yale Law Journal*, 73 (1964), 1352–84.

Goerner, E. A. "Letter and Spirit: The Political Ethics of the Rule of Law Versus the Political Ethics of the Rule of the Virtuous." *The Review of Politics*, 45 (October 1983), 553–75.

Graham, Howard Jay. "The 'Conspiracy Theory' of the Fourteenth Amendment (Pt. 1)." *Yale Law Journal*, 47 (1938), 371–403.

———. "The 'Conspiracy Theory' of the Fourteenth Amendment (Pt. 2)." *Yale Law Review*, 48 (1938), 171–94.

———. "The Early Antislavery Backgrounds of the Fourteenth Amendment." *Wisconsin Law Review* (1950), 479–507, 610–61.

———. "The Fourteenth Amendment and School Segregation." *Buffalo Law Review*, 111 (1953), 1–24.

———. "Our 'Declaratory' Fourteenth Amendment." *Stanford Law Review*, 7 (1954), 3–39.

Harding, Vincent Gordon. "Wrestling Toward the Dawn: The Afro-American Freedom Movement and the Changing Constitution." *Journal of American History*, 74 (1987), 718–39.

Jacobsohn, Gary J. "Abraham Lincoln 'On This Question of Judicial Authority': The Theory of Constitutional Aspiration." *Western Political Quarterly*, 36 (March 1983), 52–70.

Jaffa, Harry V. "What Were the 'Original Intentions' of the Framers of the Constitution of the United States?" *University of Puget Sound Law Review*, 19 (Spring 1987), 351–95.

Kaczorowski, Robert J. "Revolutionary Constitutionalism in the Era of the Civil War and Reconstruction." *New York University Law Review*, 61 (1968), 863–940.

———. "To Begin the Nation Anew: Congress, Citizenship, and Civil Rights After the Civil War." *American Historical Review*, 92 (1987), 45–68.

Kelly, Alfred H. "The Fourteenth Amendment Reconsidered: The Segregation Decision." *Michigan Law Review*, 54 (1956), 1049–86.

Kennedy, Randall. "Reconstruction and the Politics of Scholarship." *Yale Law Journal*, 98 (1989), 536–38.

King, Willard L., and Allan Nevins."The Constitution and Declaration of Independence as Issues in the Lincoln–Douglas Debates." *Journal of the Illinois State Historical Society*, 52 (Spring 1959), 7–32.

Kinoy, Arthur. "The Constitutional Right of Negro Freedom." *Rutgers Law Review*, 21 (1967), 387–441.

Kohl, Robert L. "The Civil Rights Act of 1866, Its Hour Come Round at Last: *Jones v. Alfred J. Mayer Co.*" *Virginia Law Review*, 55 (1969), 272–300.

Krug, Mark M. "The Republican Party and the Emancipation Proclamation." *Journal of Negro History*, 48 (April 1963), 98–114.

Letwin, Shirley. "Law Without Law." *Policy Review*, 26 (1983). 7–16.

Luraghi, Raimondo. "The Civil War and the Modernization of American Society: Social Structure and Industrial Revolution in the Old South Before and During the Civil War." *Civil War History*, 18 (1972), 230–50.

Maltz, Eric. "The Concept of Equal Protection of the Laws." *San Diego Law Review*, 22 (1985), 499–540.

——— "Fourteenth Amendment Concepts in the Antebellum Era." *American Journal of Legal History*, 21 (1988), 305–46.

——— "Reconstruction Without Revolution: Republican Civil Rights Theory in the Era of the Fourteenth Amendment." *Houston Law Review*, 24 (1987), 221–79.

Mansfield, Harvey C., Jr. "The Forms and Formalities of Liberty." *The Public Interest*, No. 70 (Winter 1983), 121–31.

McConnell, Michael W. "The Fourteenth Amendment: A Second American Revolution or the Logical Culmination of the Tradition?" *Loyola of Los Angeles Law Review*, 25 (1992), 1159–76.

McCrary, Peyton. "The Party of Revolution: Republican Ideas About Politics and Social Change, 1862–1867." *Civil War History*, 30 (1984), 330–50.

McElwee, Pinckney G. "The Fourteenth Amendment to the Constitution of the United States and the Threat That It Poses to Our Democratic Government." *South Carolina Law Quarterly*, 11 (1959), 484–519.

McGovny, Dudley O. "American Citizenship." *Columbia Law Review*, 11 (1911), 231–50.

McLaughlin, Andrew C. "Lincoln, the Constitution, and Democracy." *International Journal of Ethics*, 47 (October 1936), 1–24.

McPherson, James M. "Redemption or Counterrevolution? The South in the 1870s." *Reviews in American History*, 13 (1985), 545–50.

Meier, August. "Negroes in the First and Second Reconstruction." *Civil War History*, 13 (June 1967), 114–30.

Moreno, Paul."Racial Classifications and Reconstruction Legislation." *Journal of Southern History*, 61 (1995), 271–304.

Murphy, Walter F. "Who Shall Interpret? The Quest for the Ultimate Constitutional Interpreter." *The Review of Politics*, 48 (Summer 1986), 401–23.

Nagel, Robert F. "Forgetting the Constitution." *Constitutional Commentary*, 6 (1989), 289–98.

Neely, Mark E., Jr. "Abraham Lincoln's Nationalism Reconsidered." *Lincoln Herald*, 76 (Spring 1974), 12–28.

———. "Andrew C. McLaughlin on Lincoln and the Constitution." *Lincoln Lore*, No. 1761 (November 1984), 1–3.

———. "Lincoln and the Constitution: An Overview." *Lincoln Lore*, No. 1777 (March 1987), 2–4.

———. "The Lincoln Theme Since Randall's Call: The Promises and Perils of Professionalism." *Abraham Lincoln Association Papers*, 1 (1979), 10–70.

Note. "The 'New,' Thirteenth Amendment: A Preliminary Analysis." *Harvard Law Review*, 82 (1969), 1294–1321.

Olson, Otto H. "Abraham Lincoln as Revolutionary." *Civil War History*, 24 (1978), 213–24.

Palmer, Robert C. "The Parameters of Constitutional Reconstruction: *Slaughter-House*, *Cruikshank*, and the Fourteenth Amendment." *University of Illinois Law Review* (1984), 739–70.

Paludan, Phillip S. "Lincoln, the Rule of Law, and the American Revolution." *Journal of the Illinois State Historical Society*, 70 (February 1977), 10–17.

Pargellis, Stanley. "Lincoln's Political Philosophy." *Abraham Lincoln Quarterly*, 3 (June 1945), 275–90.

Pierson, William Whatley, Jr., "Texas *Versus* White." *Southwestern Historical Quarterly*, 18 (1915), 341–67.

Pressly, Thomas J. "Bullets and Ballots: Lincoln and the 'Right of Revolution.'" *American Historical Review*, 67 (April 1962), 647–62.

Randall, James G. "The Interrelation of Social and Constitutional History." *American Historical Review*, 35 (1929), 1–13.

———. "Lincoln in the Role of Dictator." *South Atlantic Quarterly*, 28 (July 1929), 236–52.

Rawley, James A. "The Nationalism of Abraham Lincoln." *Civil War History*, 9 (September 1963), 283–98.

Rogin, Michael Paul. "The King's Two Bodies: Abraham Lincoln, Richard Nixon, and Presidential Self-Sacrifice." *Massachusetts Review*, 20 (Autumn 1979), 553–73.

Rossiter, Clinton. "Constitutional Dictatorship in the Atomic Age." *The Review of Politics*, 11 (October 1949), 395–418.

Schnapper, Eric. "Affirmative Action and the Legislative History of the Fourteenth Amendment," *Virginia Law Review*, 71 (1985), 753–98.

Spector, Robert E. "Lincoln and Taney: A Study in Constitutional Polarization." *American Journal of Legal History*, 14 (July 1971), 199–214.

Spencer, Martin E. "Plato and the Anatomy of Constitutions." *Social Theory and Practice*, 5 (Fall 1978), 95–130.

———."Rhetorics and Politics." *Social Research*, 37 (1970), 597–623.

Stromberg, Joseph A. "The War for Southern Independence; A Radical Libertarian Perspective." *Journal of Libertarian Studies*, 3 (1979), 31–54.

Suthron, Walter J., Jr. "The Dubious Origins of the Fourteenth Amendment." *Tulane Law Review*, 28 (1953), 22–44.

Toews, John E. "Intellectual History After the Linguistic Turn: The Autonomy of Meaning and the Irreducibility of Experience." *American Historical Review*, 92 (October 1987), 879–907.

Thurow, Glen E. "Reply to Corlett." *Political Theory*, 10 (November 1982), 541–46.

Weisberger, Bernard A. "The Dark and Bloody Ground of Reconstruction Historiography." *Journal of Southern History*, 25 (1969), 427–47.

Wiecek, William M. "Clio as Hostage: The United States Supreme Court and the Uses of History." *California Western Law Review*, 24 (1987–1988), 227–68.

———. "The Great Writ and Reconstruction: The Habeas Corpus Act of 1867." *Journal of Southern History*, 36 (November 1970), 530–48.

Williams, T. Harry. "Abraham Lincoln—Principle and Pragmatism in Politics: A Review Article." *Mississippi Valley Historical Review*, 40 (June 1953), 89–106.

Wilson, Major L. "Lincoln and Van Buren in the Steps of the Fathers: Another Look at the Lyceum Address." *Civil War History*, 29 (September 1983), 197–211.

Young, Richard P., and Jerome S. Burstein, "Federalism and the Demise of Prescriptive Racism in the United States." *Studies in American Political Development*, 9 (1995), 1–54.

Zuckert, Michael P. "Completing the Constitution: The Thirteenth Amendment." *Constitutional Commentary*, 4 (1987), 259–83.

———. "Congressional Power Under the Fourteenth Amendment—The Original Understanding of Section Five." *Constitutional Commentary*, 2 (1986), 123–86.

BOOKS

[Abbott, Lyman.] *The American Union Commission: Its Origin, Operations, and Purposes*. New York: Sanford Harroun, 1865.

———. *The Results of Emancipation in the United States of America*. New York: American Freedman's Union Commission, 1867.

Abbott, Lyman. *Reminiscences*. Boston: Houghton Mifflin, 1915.

Ackerman, Bruce. *We the People: Foundations*. Cambridge, Mass.: The Belknap Press of Harvard University Press, 1991.

Aikman, William. *The Future of the Colored Race in America*. New York: A. D. F. Randolph, 1862.

The American Union Commission Speeches of Hon. W. Dennison, J. P. Thompson, N. C. Taylor, J. R. Doolittle, J. A. Garfield . . . Washington, February 12, 1865. New York: Sanford Harroun, 1865.

Anastaplo, George. "Abraham Lincoln's Emancipation Proclamation." In *Constitutional Government in America*. Ed. Ronald L. K. Collins. Durham, N.C.: Carolina Academic Press, 1980. Pp. 421–46.

Anderson, Dwight G. *Abraham Lincoln: The Quest for Immortality*. New York: Alfred A. Knopf, 1982.

Arendt, Hannah. *On Revolution*. New York: Viking Press, 1963.

Barber, Sotirios A. *On What the Constitution Means*. Baltimore: The Johns Hopkins University Press, 1984.

Basler, Roy P. *The Lincoln Legend: A Study in Changing Convictions*. Boston: Houghton Mifflin, 1935.

Basler, Roy P., et al. *The Collected Works of Abraham Lincoln*. 9 vols. New Brunswick, N.J.: Rutgers University Press, 1953–1955.

Beale, Howard K. *The Critical Year: A Study of Andrew Johnson and Reconstruction*. New York: Harcourt, Brace, 1930. Repr. New York: Ungar, 1958.

Beale, Howard K., ed. *The Diary of Edward Bates, 1859–1866*. Washington, D.C.: U.S. Government Printing Office, 1933.

Beard, Charles A. *The Republic*. New York: Viking Press, 1944.

Beard, Charles A., and Mary R. Beard. *The Rise of American Civilization* II. New York: Macmillan, 1930.

Belz, Herman. *Emancipation and Equal Rights: Politics and Constitutionalism in the Civil War Era*. New York: W. W. Norton, 1978.

———. *A New Birth of Freedom: The Republican Party and Freedmen's Rights, 1861–1866*. Westport, Conn.: Greenwood, 1976.

———. *Reconstructing the Union: Theory and Policy During the Civil War*. Ithaca, N.Y.: Cornell University Press, 1969.

———. "The South and the American Constitutional Tradition at the Bicentennial." In *An Uncertain Tradition: Constitutionalism and the History of the South*. Ed. Kermit L. Hall and James W. Ely, Jr. Athens: University of Georgia Press, 1989. Pp. 17–60.

Benedict, Michael Les. *A Compromise of Principle: Congressional Republicans and Reconstruction, 1863–1869*. New York: W. W. Norton, 1974.

———. *The Fruits of Victory: Alternatives in Restoring the Union, 1865–1877*. Rev. ed. Lanham, Md.: University Press of America, 1986.

———. *The Impeachment and Trial of Andrew Johnson*. New York: W. W. Norton, 1973.

————. "The Problem of Constitutionalism and Constitutional Liberty in the Reconstruction South." In *An Uncertain Tradition: Constitutionalism and the History of the South*. Ed. Kermit L. Hall and James W. Ely, Jr. Athens: University of Georgia Press, 1989. Pp. 225–49.

Bentley, George R. *A History of the Freedmen's Bureau*. Philadelphia: University of Pennsylvania Press, 1955.

Berger, Raoul. *Government by Judiciary: The Transformation of the Fourteenth Amendment*. Cambridge, Mass.: Harvard University Press, 1977.

Berlin, Ira, et al. *Slaves No More: Three Essays on Emancipation and the Civil War*. Cambridge: Cambridge University Press, 1992.

Bessette, Joseph M. and Jeffrey Tulis, eds. *The Presidency in the Constitutional Order*. Baton Rouge: Louisiana State University Press, 1981.

Black, Charles L., Jr. *Structure and Relationship in Constitutional Law*. Baton Rouge: Louisiana State University Press, 1969.

Brock, W. R. *An American Crisis: Congress and Reconstruction, 1865–1867*. New York: St. Martin's, 1963.

Brooks, Robert C. *Deliver Us From Dictators!* Philadelphia: University of Pennsylvania Press, 1935.

Buchanan, Sidney. *The Quest for Freedom: A Legal History of the Thirteenth Amendment*. Houston: Houston Law Review, 1976.

Burgess, John W. *The Civil War and the Constitution*. 2 vols. New York: Scribner's, 1901.

————. *Recent Changes in American Constitutional Theory*. New York: Columbia University Press, 1923.

————. *Reconstruction and the Constitution*. New York: Scribner's, 1902.

Cain, Marvin R. *Lincoln's Attorney General: Edward Bates of Missouri*. Columbia: University of Missouri Press, 1965.

Carter, Lief H. *Contemporary Constitutional Lawmaking: The Supreme Court and the Art of Politics*. New York: Pergamon, 1985.

Charnwood, Lord (Godfrey Rathbone Benson). *Abraham Lincoln*. New York: Henry Holt, 1917. Repr. New York: Garden City Publishing, 1938.

Cobban, Alfred. *Dictatorship: Its History and Theory*. New York: Scribner's, 1939.

Cornish, Dudley T. *The Sable Arm: Negro Troops in the Union Army, 1861–65*. New York: W. W. Norton, 1966.

Cornwell, Elmer E., Jr. "The American Constitutional Tradition: Its Impact and Development." In *The Constitutional Convention as an Amending Device*. Ed. Kermit L. Hall, Harold M. Hyman, and Leon V. Sigal. Washington, D.C.: American Historical Association and American Political Science Association, 1981. Pp. 1–36.

Corwin, Edward S. "Constitution v. Constitutional Theory." *American Constitutional History: Essays by Edward S. Corwin*. Ed. A. T. Mason and G. Carvey. New York: Harper & Row, 1964. Pp. 99–108.

————. *The President: Office and Powers.* 4th rev. ed. New York: New York University Press, 1957.

Cox, LaWanda. *Lincoln and Black Freedom: A Study in Presidential Leadership.* Columbia: University of South Carolina Press, 1981.

Cox, LaWanda, and John H. Cox. *Politics, Principle, and Prejudice, 1865–1867: Dilemma of Reconstruction America.* New York: Free Press, 1963.

Croly, Herbert. *The Promise of American Life.* New York: Macmillan, 1909.

Cruden, Robert. *The Negro in Reconstruction.* Englewood Cliffs, N.J.: Prentice-Hall, 1969.

Current, Richard N. *The Lincoln Nobody Knows.* New York: Hill & Wang, 1958.

Current, Richard N., ed. *The Political Thought of Abraham Lincoln.* Indianapolis: Bobbs-Merrill, 1967.

Curry, Leonard P. *Blueprint for Modern America: Nonmilitary Legislation of the First Civil War Congress.* Nashville: Vanderbilt University Press, 1968.

Davis, Henry Winter. *Speeches and Addresses Delivered in the Congress of the United States. . . .* New York: Harper & Brothers, 1867.

Davis, Michael. *The Image of Lincoln in the South.* Knoxville: University of Tennessee Press, 1971.

DeJouvenel, Bertrand. *Sovereignty: An Inquiry into the Political Good.* Chicago: The University of Chicago Press, 1957.

Dietze, Gottfried. *America's Political Dilemma: From Limited to Unlimited Democracy.* Baltimore: The John Hopkins University Press, 1968.

Diggins, John P. *The Lost Soul of American Politics: Virtue, Self-Interest, and the Foundations of Liberalism.* New York: Basic Books, 1984.

Dillon, Merton L. *The Abolitionists: The Growth of a Dissenting Minority.* New York: W. W. Norton, 1979.

Donald, David. "Abraham Lincoln and the American Pragmatic Tradition." In *Lincoln Reconsidered: Essays on the Civil War Era.* New York: Alfred A. Knopf, 1956. Pp. 187–208.

————. *Charles Sumner and the Rights of Man.* New York: Alfred A. Knopf, 1970.

Du Bois, W. E. Burghardt. *Black Reconstruction in America, 1860–1880.* New York: Simon & Schuster, 1935. Repr. Cleveland: World, 1962.

Dunning, William A. *Essays on the Civil War and Reconstruction.* New York: Macmillan, 1897. Repr. New York: Harper & Row, 1965.

————. *Reconstruction, Political and Economic, 1865–1877.* New York: Harper, 1907.

Eaton, John. *Grant, Lincoln, and the Freedmen: Reminiscences of the Civil War.* New York: Longmans, Green, 1907.

Edelstein, Tilden G. *Strange Enthusiasm: A Life of Thomas Wentworth Higginson.* New Haven, Conn.: Yale University Press, 1968.

Ellis, Richard J. *American Political Cultures.* New York: Oxford University Press, 1993.

Ely, John Hart. *Democracy and Distrust: A Theory of Judicial Review.* Cambridge, Mass.: Harvard University Press, 1980.

Engeman, Thomas S. "Utopianism and Preservation: The Rhetorical Dimension of American Statesmanship." In *The American Founding: Politics, Statesmanship, and the Constitution.* Ed. Gary L. McDowell and Ralph A. Rossum. Port Washington, N.Y.: Kennikat, 1981. Pp. 143–56.

Fairman, Charles. *Reconstruction and Reunion, 1865–88, Part I.* New York: Macmillan, 1971.

The Federalist Papers. Ed. Clinton Rossiter. New York: New American Library, 1961.

Fehrenbacher, Don E. *The Dred Scott Case: Its Significance in American Law and Politics.* New York: Oxford University Press, 1978.

———. "Lincoln and the Constitution." In *The Public and the Private Lincoln: Contemporary Perspectives.* Ed. Cullom Davis. Carbondale: Southern Illinois University Press, 1979. Pp. 121–36.

———. *Prelude to Greatness: Lincoln in the 1850s.* Stanford: Stanford University Press, 1962.

———. "The Words of Lincoln." In *Abraham Lincoln and the American Political Tradition.* Ed. John L. Thomas. Amherst: University of Massachusetts Press, 1986. Pp. 31–49.

Finkelman, Paul. "Slavery and the Constitutional Convention: Making a Covenant with Death." In *Beyond Confederation: Origins of the Constitution and American National Identity.* Ed. Richard Beeman et al. Chapel Hill: University of North Carolina Press, 1987. Pp. 188–225.

Finnis, John. *Natural Law and Natural Rights.* Oxford: Oxford University Press, 1980.

Fish, Carl Russell. *The American Civil War.* Ed. William E. Smith. New York: Longmans, Green, 1937.

Fisher, Sidney George. *The Trial of the Constitution.* Philadelphia: J. P. Lippincott, 1862.

Fleming, Walter Lynwood. *The Sequel of Appomattox: A Chronicle of the Reunion of the States.* New Haven, Conn. Yale University Press, 1919.

Flower, Frank A. *Edwin McMasters Stanton: The Autocrat of Rebellion, Emancipation, and Reconstruction.* New York: W. W. Wilson, 1905.

Foner, Eric. *Free Soil, Free Labor, Free Men: The Ideology of the Republican Party Before the Civil War.* New York: Oxford University Press, 1970.

———. *Nothing but Freedom: Emancipation and Its Legacy.* Baton Rouge: Louisiana State University Press, 1983.

———. *Reconstruction: America's Unfinished Revolution, 1863–1877.* New York: Harper & Row, 1988.

Foner, Philip S., ed. *The Life and Writings of Frederick Douglass.* 5 vols. New York: International, 1955.

Forgie, George B. *Patricide in the House Divided: A Psychological Interpretation of Lincoln and His Age.* New York: W. W. Norton, 1979.

Franklin, John Hope. *Reconstruction: After the Civil War*. Chicago: The University of Chicago Press, 1961.

Fredrickson, George. "The Search for Order and Community." In *The Public and Private Lincoln: Contemporary Perspectives*. Ed. Cullum Davis. Carbondale: University of Southern Illinois Press, 1979. Pp. 86–100.

Garnet, Henry Highland. *A Memorial Discourse . . . February 12, 1865*. Philadelphia: J. M. Wilson, 1865.

Gerteis, Louis S. *From Contraband to Freedman: Federal Policy Toward Southern Blacks, 1861–1865*. Westport, Conn.: Greenwood, 1973.

Goldwin, Robert A. *Why Blacks, Women, and Jews Are Not Mentioned in the Constitution, and Other Unorthodox Views*. Washington, D.C.: American Enterprise Institute Press, 1990.

Graebner, Norman A. "Abraham Lincoln: Conservative Statesman." *The Enduring Lincoln*. Ed. Norman A. Graebner. Urbana: University of Illinois Press, 1959. Pp. 67–94.

Graham, Howard Jay. *Everyman's Constitution: Historical Essays on the Fourteenth Amendment, the "Conspiracy Theory," and American Constitutionalism*. Madison: State Historical Society of Wisconsin, 1968.

Grimes, Alan P. *American Political Thought*. New York: Henry Holt, 1955.

Gutman, Herbert G. *The Black Family in Slavery and Freedom, 1750–1925*. New York: Pantheon, 1976.

Hartz, Louis. *The Liberal Tradition in America*. New York: Harcourt, Brace, 1955.

Henry, Robert Selph. *The Story of Reconstruction*. Indianapolis and New York: Bobbs-Merrill, 1938. Repr. Gloucester, Mass.: P. Smith, 1963.

Higginson, Thomas Wentworth. *Army Life in a Black Regiment*. East Lansing: Michigan State University Press, 1960.

Hockett, Homer C. *The Constitutional History of the United States, 1826–1876*. New York: Macmillan, 1939.

Hofstadter, Richard. *The American Political Tradition*. New York: Alfred A. Knopf, 1948.

Howe, Daniel Walker. *The Political Culture of the American Whigs*. Chicago: The University of Chicago Press, 1979.

Hutson, James H. "The Constitution: An Economic Document?" In *The Framing and Ratification of the Constitution*. Ed. Leonard W. Levy and Dennis J. Mahoney. New York: Macmillan, 1987. Pp. 259–70.

Hyman, Harold M. *A More Perfect Union: The Impact of the Civil War and Reconstruction on the Constitution*. New York: Alfred A. Knopf, 1973.

———. "Reconstruction and Political–Constitutional Institutions: The Popular Expression." In *New Frontiers of the American Reconstruction*. Ed. Harold M. Hyman. Urbana: University of Illinois Press, 1966. Pp. 1–39.

Hyman, Harold M., and William M. Wiecek, *Equal Justice Under Law: Constitutional Development, 1835–1875*. New York: Harper & Row, 1982.

Jacobsohn, Gary J. *The Supreme Court and the Decline of Constitutional Aspiration*. Totowa, N.J.: Rowman & Littlefield, 1985.

Jaffa, Harry V. *American Conservatism and the American Founding*. Durham, N.C.: Carolina Academic Press, 1984.

———. *The Conditions of Freedom: Essays in Political Philosophy*. Baltimore: The Johns Hopkins University Press, 1975.

———. *Crisis of the House Divided: An Interpretation of the Issues in the Lincoln–Douglas Debates*. New York: Doubleday, 1959. Repr. Chicago: The University of Chicago Press, 1965.

———. *Equality and Liberty: Theory and Practice in American Politics*. New York: Oxford University Press, 1965.

———. *How to Think About the American Revolution: A Bicentennial Cerebration*. Durham, N.C.: Carolina Academic Press, 1978.

Johannsen, Robert W. "Lincoln, Liberty, and Equality." In *Liberty and Equality Under the Constitution*. Ed. John Agresto. Washington, D.C.: American Historical Association and American Political Science Association, 1983. Pp. 53–62.

Johnson, Chalmers. *Revolutionary Change*. Boston: Little, Brown, 1966.

Jones, James E., Jr. "The Rise and Fall of Affirmative Action." In *Race in America: The Struggle for Equality*. Ed. Herbert Hill and James E. Jones, Jr. Madison: University of Wisconsin Press, 1993. Pp. 345–69.

Kaczorowski, Robert J. *The Politics of Judicial Interpretation: The Federal Courts, Department of Justice, and Civil Rights, 1866–1876*. Dobbs Ferry, N.Y.: Oceana Publications, 1985.

Kelly, Alfred H. "Comment on Harld M. Hyman's Paper." In *New Frontiers of the American Reconstruction*. Ed. Harold M. Hyman. Urbana: University of Illinois Press, 1966. Pp. 40–58.

Kendall, Willmoore, and George W. Carey. *The Basic Symbols of the American Political Tradition*. Baton Rouge: Louisiana State University Press, 1970.

Kennedy, John Pendleton. *The Border States: Their Power and Duty in the Present Disordered Condition of the Country*. N.p., 1860.

Kluger, Richard. *Simple Justice: The History of "Brown v. Board of Education" and Black America's Struggle for Equality*. New York: Alfred A. Knopf, 1976.

Kull, Andrew. *The Color-Blind Constitution*. Cambridge, Mass.: Harvard University Press, 1992.

Kyvig, David E. *Explicit and Authentic Acts: Amending the U.S. Constitution, 1776–1995*. Lawrence: University Press of Kansas, 1996.

Lerner, Ralph. *The Thinking Revolutionary: Principle and Practice in the New Republic*. Ithaca, N.Y.: Cornell University Press, 1987.

Maltz, Earl M. *Civil Rights, the Constitution, and Congress, 1863–1869* Lawrence: University Press of Kansas, 1990.

Mansfield, Harvey C., Jr. *Taming the Prince: The Ambivalence of Modern Executive Power*. New York: Free Press, 1989.

Martin, Waldo E., Jr. *The Mind of Frederick Douglass*. Chapel Hill: University of North Carolina, 1984.

McFeely, William S. *Yankee Stepfather: General O. O. Howard and the Freedmen*. New York: W. W. Norton, 1968.

McDowell, Gary L. *The Constitution and Contemporary Constitutional Theory.*" Cumberland, Va.: Center for Judicial Studies, 1985.

McKitrick, Eric L. *Andrew Johnson and Reconstruction*. Chicago: The University of Chicago Press, 1960.

———. "Reconstruction: Ultraconservative Revolution." In *The Comparative Approach to American History*. Ed. C. Vann Woodward. New York: Basic Books, 1968. Pp. 146–59.

McPherson, James M. "Abraham Lincoln and the Second American Revolution." In *Abraham Lincoln and the American Political Tradition*. Ed. John L. Thomas. Amherst: University of Massachusetts Press, 1986. Pp. 142–60.

———. *Abraham Lincoln and the Second American Revolution*. New York: Oxford University Press, 1991.

———. *The Struggle for Equality: Abolitionists and the Negro in the Civil War and Reconstruction*. Princeton, N.J.: Princeton University Press, 1964.

Merriam, Charles E. *A History of American Political Theories*. New York: Macmillan, 1903.

Miller, Charles A. *The Supreme Court and the Uses of History*. Cambridge, Mass.: The Belknap Press of Harvard University Press, 1969.

Milton, George Fort. *The Use of Presidential Power, 1789–1943*. Boston: Little, Brown, 1944.

Minar, David W. *Ideas and Politics: The American Experience*. Homewood, Ill.: Dorsey, 1964.

Moore, Barrington, Jr. *Social Origins of Dictatorship and Democracy*. Boston: Beacon, 1966.

Morgenthau, Hans J., and David Hein. *Essays on Lincoln's Faith and Politics*. Ed. Kenneth W. Thompson. Lanham, Md.: University Press of America, 1983.

Murphy, Walter E., James E. Fleming, and William F. Harris II. *American Constitutional Interpretation*. Mineola, N.Y.: Foundation Press, 1986.

Nelson, William E. *The Fourteenth Amendment: From Political Principle to Judicial Doctrine*. Cambridge, Mass.: Harvard University Press, 1988.

Nevins, Allan. *The Statesmanship of the Civil War*. 2nd ed. New York: Collier Books, 1962.

Nieman, Donald G. *To Set the Law in Motion: The Freedmen's Bureau and the Legal Rights of Blacks, 1865–1868*. Millwood, N.Y.: KTO Press, 1979.

Oates, Stephen B. "Abraham Lincoln: Republican in the White House." In *Abraham Lincoln and the American Political Tradition*. Ed. John L. Thomas. Amherst: University of Massachusetts Press, 1986. Pp. 98–110.

O'Connor, Thomas H. *The Disunited States: The Era of the Civil War and Reconstruction*. New York: Dodd, Mead, 1972.

Pagden, Anthony, ed. *The Languages of Political Theory in Early-Modern Europe*. Cambridge: Cambridge University Press, 1987.

Palmer, Robert C. "Liberties as Constitutional Provisions, 1776–1791." In *Liberty and Community: Constitution and Rights in the Early American Republic*. Ed. William E. Nelson and Robert C. Palmer. Dobbs Ferry, N.Y.: Oceana, 1987. Pp. 55–148.

Paludan, Phillip S. *A Covenant with Death: The Constitution, Law, and Equality in the Civil War Era*. Urbana: University of Illinois Press, 1975.

———. "A People's Contest": *The Union and Civil War, 1861–1865*. New York: Harper & Row, 1988.

Pangle, Thomas L. *The Spirit of the Modern Republicanism: The Moral Vision of the American Founders and the Philosophy of Locke*. Chicago: The University of Chicago Press, 1988.

Pearson, Henry Greenleaf. *The Life of John A. Andrew, Governor of Massachusetts, 1861–65*. Boston and New York: Houghton Mifflin, 1904.

Perman, Michael. "Counter Reconstruction." In *The Facts of Reconstruction: Essays in Honor of John Hope Franklin*. Ed. Eric Anderson and Alfred A. Moss. Baton Rouge: Louisiana State University Press, 1991. Pp. 121–40.

———. *Reunion Without Compromise: The South and Reconstruction, 1865–1868*. Cambridge: Cambridge University Press, 1973.

———. *The Road to Redemption: Southern Politics, 1869–1879*. Chapel Hill: University of North Carolina Press, 1984.

Pierce, Edward L. *Memoir and Letters of Charles Sumner*. 4 vols. Boston: Roberts, 1877–1894.

Pierce, Paul S. *The Freedmen's Bureau: A Chapter in the History of Reconstruction*. Iowa City: State University of Iowa Press, 1904.

Pious, Richard M. *The American Presidency*. New York: Basic Books, 1979.

Pocock, J. G. A. *Politics, Language, and Time: Essays on Political Thought and History*. New York: Atheneum, 1973.

Potter, David N. *Lincoln and His Party in the Secession Crisis*. New Haven, Conn.: Yale University Press, 1942.

Pressly, Thomas J. *Americans Interpret Their Civil War*. New York: Collier Books, 1962.

Rable, George C. *But There Was No Peace: The Role of Violence in the Politics of Reconstruction*. Athens: University of Georgia Press, 1984.

Randall, James G. *Constitutional Problems Under Lincoln*. Rev ed. Urbana: University of Illinois Press, 1951.

———. *Lincoln the Liberal Statesman*. New York: Dodd, Mead, 1947.

Rawley, James A. *The Politics of Union: Northern Politics During the Civil War*. Hinsdale, Ill.: Dryden, 1974.

Rhodes, James Ford. *History of the United States from the Compromise of 1850 to the Final Restoration of Home Rule at the South in 1877*. 7 vols. New York: Macmillan, 1893–1900.

Richards, David A. J. *Conscience and the Constitution: History, Theory, and the Law of the Reconstruction Amendments*. Princeton, N.J.: Princeton University Press, 1993.

Riker, William H. *The Art of Political Manipulation*. New Haven, Conn.: Yale University Press, 1986.

Ripley, C. Peter. *Slaves and Freedmen in Civil War Louisiana*. Baton Rouge: Louisiana State University Press, 1976.

Rose, Willie Lee. *Rehearsal for Reconstruction: The Port Royal Experiment*. Indianapolis: Bobbs-Merrill, 1964.

Rossiter, Clinton. *Constitutional Dictatorship: Crisis Government in the Modern Democracies*. Princeton, N.J.: Princeton University Press, 1948.

Schlesinger, Arthur M., Jr. *The Imperial Presidency*. Boston: Houghton Mifflin, 1973.

Shannon, Fred A. *The Organization and Administration of the Union Army, 1861–1865*. 2 vols. Cleveland: A. H. Clark, 1928.

Skidmore, Max J. *American Political Thought*. New York: St. Martin's, 1978.

Skrentny, John David. *The Ironies of Affirmative Action: Politics, Culture, and Justice in America*. Chicago: The University of Chicago Press, 1996.

Sniderman, Paul M., and Thomas Piazza, *The Scar of Race*. Cambridge, Mass.: Harvard University Press, 1993.

Stampp, Kenneth M. *The Era of Reconstruction, 1865–1877*. New York: Alfred A. Knopf, 1965.

Stephenson, Nathaniel W. *Abraham Lincoln and the Union*. New Haven, Conn.: Yale University Press, 1918.

———. *Lincoln*. Indianapolis and New York: Bobbs-Merrill, 1922.

Strauss, Leo. *Natural Right and History*. Chicago: The University of Chicago Press, 1953.

Strozier, Charles B. *Lincoln's Quest for Union: Public and Private Meanings*. New York: Basic Books, 1982.

Ten Broek, Jacobus. *The Antislavery Origins of the Fourteenth Amendment*. Berkeley: University of California Press. Rev. ed. *Equal Under Law*. New York: Collier, 1965.

Thomas, Benjamin P., and Harold M. Hyman. *Stanton: The Life and Times of Lincoln's Secretary of War*. New York: Alfred A. Knopf, 1962.

Thomas, John L., ed. *Abraham Lincoln and the American Political Tradition*. Amherst: University of Massachusetts Press, 1986.

Thurow, Glen E. *Abraham Lincoln and American Political Religion*. Albany: State University of New York Press, 1976.

Trefousse, Hans L. *The Radical Republicans: Lincoln's Vanguard for Racial Justice*. New York: Alfred A. Knopf, 1969.

Trelease, Allen W. *Reconstruction: The Great Experiment*. New York: Harper & Row, 1971.

Tulis, Jeffrey. "On Presidential Character." In *The Presidency in the Constitu-*

tional Order. Ed. Joseph M. Bessette and Jeffrey Tulis. Baton Rouge: Louisiana State University Press, 1981. Pp. 283–311.

Voegeli, V. Jacque. *Free But Not Equal: The Midwest and the Negro During the Civil War*. Chicago: The University of Chicago Press, 1967.

Weigley, Russell F. *History of the United States Army*. New York: Macmillan, 1967.

Wheare, K. C. *Abraham Lincoln and the United States*. London: English Universities Press, 1948.

Wheeler, Kenneth W., ed. *For the Union: Ohio Leaders in the Civil War*. Columbus: Ohio State University Press, 1968.

Whiting, William. *War Powers Under the Constitution of the United States*. 43rd ed. Boston: Lee & Shepard, 1871.

Wiecek, William M. *The Guarantee Clause of the U.S. Constitution*. Ithaca, N.Y.: Cornell University Press, 1972.

———. *The Sources of Antislavery Constitutionalism in America, 1760–1848*. Ithaca, N.Y.: Cornell University Press, 1977.

Wilson, Edmund. *Patriotic Gore: Studies in the Literature of the American Civil War*. New York: Oxford University Press, 1962.

Wills, Garry. *Lincoln at Gettysburg: The Words That Remade America*. New York: Simon & Schuster, 1992.

Woodward, C. Vann. "Seeds of Failure in Radical Race Policy." In *New Frontiers of the American Reconstruction*. Ed. Harold M. Hyman. Urbana: University of Illinois Press, 1966. Pp. 125–47.

———. *The Strange Career of Jim Crow*. New York: Oxford University Press, 1955.

INDEX